To John

Christmas 1987.

IN THE
ORCHESTRA

IN THE
ORCHESTRA

JACK BRYMER

HUTCHINSON
London Melbourne Auckland Johannesburg

© Jack Brymer 1987

All rights reserved

This edition first published in 1987 by Hutchinson, an imprint of Century Hutchinson Ltd, Brookmount House, 62–65 Chandos Place, London WC2N 4NW

Century Hutchinson Australia Pty Ltd
PO Box 496, 16–22 Church Street, Hawthorn, Victoria 3122, Australia

Century Hutchinson New Zealand Limited
PO Box 40–086, Glenfield, Auckland 10, New Zealand

Century Hutchinson South Africa (Pty) Ltd
PO Box 337, Berglvei, 2012 South Africa

British Library Cataloguing in Publication Data

Brymer, Jack
    In the orchestra : the life and work of orchestral musicians.
    1. Clarinettists—Great Britain—Biography
    I. Title
    788'.62'0924   ML419.B7/

    ISBN 0–09–168450–1

Photoset by Deltatype Ltd, Ellesmere Port
Printed and bound in Great Britain by Anchor Brendon Limited, Tiptree, Essex

CONTENTS

CONTENTS

QUEEN'S HALL, LANGHAM PLACE, W.

Sole Lessees - Messrs. CHAPPELL & CO., Ltd.

. . THE . .

LONDON SYMPHONY ORCHESTRA

(CONSISTING OF RECENTLY RESIGNED MEMBERS OF THE QUEEN'S HALL ORCHESTRA AND OTHER EMINENT INSTRUMENTALISTS)

FIRST

SYMPHONY CONCERT,

THURSDAY, JUNE 9TH, 1904, AT 3 P.M.

DR. HANS RICHTER

HAS MOST GENEROUSLY CONSENTED TO CONDUCT ON THIS OCCASION.

PRINCIPAL VIOLIN:

MR. ARTHUR W. PAYNE.

ANALYTICAL PROGRAMME, PRICE SIXPENCE.

PREFACE

No book which deals with such a vast and widespread subject as orchestral activity as it exists today can hope to be even reasonably complete. One which attempted to be so would be not only lengthy, but unbearably boring. I have therefore excluded from this rambling discourse any orchestra outside my personal experience. There are, for instance, orchestras in Japan and South America which employ very good friends of mine, and are certainly very much in the musical swim in a global sense; but I know very little of their activities at a personal level and would hesitate merely to reproduce figures supplied by them or others to try to give an impression of their lives. I have tried to describe orchestras I know in some intimate detail. They probably disagree with my impressions, and there may be others who resent their absence. For this I apologise. I have enjoyed browsing over the impressions which follow – impressions gained in over forty years of fascinated involvement.

Jack Brymer
1987

ACKNOWLEDGEMENTS

Although this book is for the most part a series of rambling personal reminiscences, in writing it I have assembled a great deal of *detailed* information which had to be sifted through and assessed. This has most kindly been supplied by many heads of orchestral organizations the world over, and also by many friendly orchestral colleagues in several countries. It is impossible to pay tribute to them all, but I want them to know how grateful I am for their trouble and cooperation. A few of those who have helped are: Clive Gillinson, Managing Director, London Symphony Orchestra; John Willan, Managing Director, London Philharmonic Orchestra; Ian Maclay, Managing Director, Royal Philharmonic Orchestra; Christopher Bishop, Chief Administrator, Philharmonia Orchestra; Clive Smart, General Manager, and Stuart Robson, Assistant Manager, Hallé Orchestra; Edward Smith, General Manager, and Beresford King-Smith, Assistant Manager, City of Birmingham Symphony Orchestra; Andrew Burn, Administrator, Royal Liverpool Philharmonic Orchestra; Laurie Lea, Manager, BBC Symphony Orchestra; David Richardson, Bournemouth Symphony Orchestra; Ernest Fleischman, Executive Director, Los Angeles Philharmonic Orchestra; Rick Lester, Marketing Director, Cleveland Orchestra; Paul Chummers, Manager, Chicago Symphony Orchestra; Mary S. McElroy, Assistant Managing Director, New York Philharmonic Orchestra; William R. Moyer, Personnel Manager, and Bruce Creditor, Assistant Personnel Manager, Boston Symphony Orchestra; Mme Janine Pontet, Administrator, and Mme Jacqueline Muller, Assistant Administrator, L'Orchestre de Paris; Richard S. Warren, Archives and Research, Toronto Symphony Orchestra; Professor Alfred Altenburger, President, Vienna Philharmonic Orchestra; Ellen McStone, Administrative Assistant, American Federation of Musicians; Colin Dunton, Orchestral Manager, Sydney Symphony Orchestra; and Warwick Ross, Administrator, Elizabethan Sydney Orchestra.

I would also like to thank my colleagues of the woodwind world: Kevin Murphy (Sydney) and all the other Australian friends, Anne Menzies, Terry Stirzaker, Neville Thomas (Sydney Conservatoire), Martin Forster, Don Westlake, David Hooper and Alan Vivian; Ray Carpenter (Bournemouth); Ed Warren (Liverpool); Colin Bradbury (BBC, London); Ian Herbert (Royal Opera House, London);

Michele Zukowsky (Los Angeles); Larry Combs (Chicago); Alfred Prinz (Vienna) and others, who have gone to the trouble to write to me with their views. I am most grateful.

PHOTOGRAPHIC ACKNOWLEDGEMENTS

page 2 – top: © G.MacDomnic, supplied by Philharmonia Orchestra; *bottom:* © Hallé Concerts Society; *page 3 – top:* © Mary A. Goodman, supplied by the Royal Philharmonic Orchestra; *bottom:* © Royal Philharmonic Orchestra; *page 4 – top:* © David Weiss, supplied by Los Angeles Philharmonic Association; *bottom:* © Royal Philharmonic Orchestra; *page 5 – top:* © London Symphony Orchestra; *bottom:* © *Daily Telegraph,* supplied by the Royal Philharmonic Orchestra; *page 6 – top:* © Hallé Concerts Society; *bottom:* © Farrell Grehan; *page 7 – top:* © Cleveland Orchestra; *bottom:* © John Mills Photography Ltd, supplied by the Royal Liverpool Philharmonic Orchestra; © *page 8 – top:* © Mail Newspapers plc, supplied by the London Symphony Orchestra; *bottom:* © Hallé Concerts Society.

The original of the very first programme of the London Symphony Orchestra was kindly loaned by Neil Watson.

PART ONE

Amabile Colla Parte
('Friends Play Well Together')

INTRODUCTION
Amabile Colla Parte
('Friends Play Well Together')

Now that the time has come, after a whole lifetime of unquestioning devotion, for me to say farewell to the strange occupation of orchestral playing, the hoary old jest about the famous concertmaster who was asked by his well-heeled hostess 'What is your daytime occupation?' doesn't sound quite so odd. Seen from outside the profession, the whole activity of concert-giving and audience attendance does seem a strange and possibly inexplicable ritual.

Why do so many thousands of intelligent people every day leave the comfort and security of their own firesides, to struggle through fog, ice and snow, so that they may sit in serried ranks and pay rapt attention to the antics of a hundred penguin-garbed instrumentalists, directed by one supreme being whose function is reputed to be his ability to breathe life into the printed thoughts of a long-dead and far distant composer? There is obviously some vital force in this corporate worship which gives a satisfaction not to be obtained from the most perfect mechanical/electronic reproduction of exactly those same sounds, or the perfect visual replica which comes from video-tape or film. There is also the same sort of dedication in the attitude of the players; otherwise they would undoubtedly turn their reasonably high IQs to more profitable use. Instead, they mostly play together, if they can, because that is regarded as one of the great virtues of their calling. Just occasionally they have the delight and privilege of being out on their own, playing solo for a few blissful seconds or even minutes. It is then that they become 'messengers of the Word', and at such moments are dependent not only upon their own capacity, but also the ability of every one of their colleagues, whose good-will, attention and support are essential to survival. That's how things would seem if they thought about them anyway. In practice it is rather like moving from car to car on a roller-coaster – tricky at all times, satisfying if you make it, but a sad experience if you don't.

Orchestral playing is a way of life which has vivid reality when you experience it; the examination of its validity and doubt as to its importance can be disturbing, especially after a long life spent at it. It may be a slightly unreal way of making a living, but it has one real advantage – you are part of a very big team, and act accordingly for hours at a stretch. There's no need to pop into the next office to find out what old Jones has been up to all day. You *know*, because you've been doing the same thing, and thinking the same thoughts – well, almost – ever since that first 'down beat' of the day lurched its sickening way sideways. You've been playing *together*.

With me, ensemble playing started very early – as the dawning realization of a nine-year-old that playing along with others was as big a thrill as that first high dive, that nicely potted black or that pass that almost got the winning goal. It was a *jolly* experience, and far better than playing on one's own, if only because some of the brighter lads could get all those black-tailed notes with obvious ease, and it was good to be carried along. It all seemed so *natural*. Many years later, it came as a surprise to hear a famous colleague at the end of a long day in the film-recording studio express his doubts: 'It's a strange occupation, when you think of it – sitting all day in a soundproof box and spitting down a little black tube, all for sordid gain!' As an adult, it was just possible to agree with him, though grudgingly. As a small boy it wasn't a bit like that.

It was in the medium-sized seaside town of South Shields at the mouth of the Tyne that it all began for me. A windy, bracing, and I'm sure in those days a dirty place to be in, even though by the 1920s the industries upon which the prosperity and smoke depended for their continuance were in decline. My first ensemble experience was in a tiny darkened room in the tram depot, sitting on a bench with about six other clarinet-blowing members of the DLI First Cadet Battalion Military Band – boys of all ages from nine to seventeen, of all sizes and shapes: a wonderful experience, and not only from the musical point of view. To the younger ones among us, with knees accustomed to exposure to sea-born gales, the touch of rough khaki was sheer torture, but at the same time thrilling and with the promise of manly things to come. There was also the testing of musical muscles in the inevitable comparison with the technical superiority of others; and this was without doubt the most important factor of any. I have no idea at all how good or bad these young idols may have been, but they did without doubt provide the inspiration necessary for a child to progress. *Playing together* had started, and it is probably the only way to lay a foundation upon which a successful orchestral career can be built. Sixty years later those first days still carry their message. The factors which made for success had already become operative, and the rest was a question of time, devotion to an ideal and a real belief in the reality that persists in spite of the strange nature of the occupation. What follows in this book is no attempt at autobiography. That has been tried before, elsewhere.* It is partly a series of recollections of those long years in many orchestras and in many lands, and of the events and personalities encountered on the way. Happily most of the people in it are, or were, very good friends. It has been a great pleasure, in preparing to write, to recontact many of them to get their views on our chosen profession and how they feel about it. That is the other purpose of this book – to find out what they really feel about their activities, and to compare and contrast the lot of orchestral players in many and distant lands. It would be possible to do this purely on a fact-finding basis, by comparing figures gleaned from orchestral accounts, or by finding out the contributions made by the Arts Councils where these exist, then adding these to the help given by sponsors, public, private and individual. But to do only this, without prying into the lives of those who are thus benefited, or trying to discover the direction in which they are being pushed or coaxed, would be both tedious and misleading. The only way to come to some sort of conclusion, or even to get a reasonable basis of comparison, is to examine orchestras known personally, with friends whose lifestyle one knows, and whose job satisfaction or lack of enthusiasm is clear. This I have tried to do. My friends do the job I have always done, and I understand them; but they do it in a set of circumstances and in conditions I have not necessarily experienced. Along the way there will be digressions, because remeeting them all is certain to remind me of events we have enjoyed (or not) together, of people we have met, and of works we have played. I hope that these digressions will not overshadow the more serious thoughts about the industry and the prospects of

* *From Where I Sit*, Cassell, 1979

those who are involved in it. There are several facts about orchestral life which I consider to be too little known, many of which will come as a surprise to anyone interested in our work. We are all, even internationally, just one huge orchestra, and nowadays one gigantic audience as well. The orchestra in all its guises is a vast subject. I hope I may be able to throw some light upon it while introducing you to some of my very best friends.

1

Con Spirito
('They're a Lively Lot')

I wonder how it seems to you, the start of a symphony concert and what goes before it? I've always felt it to be one of the most exciting of life's experiences. The empty platform; those special chairs carefully spaced out which seem to have no other function in their design than that of allowing the tails of an evening coat to hang naturally while sitting; music-stands carefully arranged according to instrumentation, with closed and often crested folios upon them clearly containing precious and carefully marked material which was probably in Berlin last Saturday and may well be in Tokyo next Thursday. Always, it seems, odd instruments simply left around at the whim of their players – very few violins, violas or cellos, but always a shoal of contrabasses left stranded on their sides like abandoned whales, or propped carefully against the tall bar stools which are used only by their proud owners; gleaming copper kettledrums in circular groups of four, polished tubas, monstrous plumbing achievements, upended and at ease; the occasional trombone left perched on its slender stand looking eager to be up and active; and the mysterious bric-à-brac of the percussion department, which may not be required until the second half of the concert, but may well be in full view during the Mozart, Haydn and Beethoven of the first. This can include anything at all, from the immense gong known as a tam-tam, to a set of tubular bells which can vary in height from six to about fifteen feet (if Berlioz is showing off his *Dies Irae* today), and the smaller debris of the section – castinets, tambourines, cymbals, whips, rattles and even the odd bird-call.

All this is potential drama, at present at rest, just awaiting the arrival of the actors in the plot – the players – to arrive and breathe life into it. All very exciting and certainly all part of the show. It even looks like this to the players themselves, and is part of what makes a concert a quite special occasion, however often it has been experienced. It is at this point, however, that the impressions on the two sides of the podium begin to diverge.

From the stalls, the arrival of the players looks serene, orderly and even leisurely as they emerge from the mysterious nether regions bearing Strads of various sizes and hues, or immaculately tended golden flutes, gleaming oboes, or bassoons of that startling red colour which no billet of maple wood has ever naturally attained. Obviously they know everything is going to be alright, because many of them don't even glance at their music-folders but simply chat as they warm up or tune the strings in that wonderful cacophony which is even more exciting than expectant silence. Then, casually, they fix their attention upon the tuning 'A' given by the first oboe. (This is a tradition of long-standing, and a disastrous error, because any first-class oboeist can vary his or her pitch by as much as a semi-tone at will, and most of them check carefully with an accurate tuning-fork before committing themselves to a final pitch.) Finally, with the arrival of the leader (who is really the principal first violin, but also has some other important duties we'll talk about later, and therefore a separate entry and bow of his own) we have that expectant silence; we are ready for the maestro. Here one can expect almost anything from a scuttling little run followed by a hurried nod to the audience and a dive at the down beat just when you don't expect it, to the slow and dignified entrance of the Great Master or the smiling ambiance of the Video Image. Quite often it's an unsmiling and pensive approach, because he really is a man with a lot on his mind, and if he's wise he's already thinking about the possible thrills and probable disasters which are to come. He raises his baton, carefully adjusts the speed of his up beat to the tempo of the first bar (because that's the only way his orchestra can have a clue to the right speed), brings it down with all the confidence he can muster, and hopes that everyone will do his duty.

Already there are different impressions of the same concert: from the audience, who must always be kept comfortable and confident, from the orchestra, who must be fairly sure it will be all right but will none the less by wary, and from the conductor, who has every reason to know how things can go wrong, and is trying to make sure through every fibre of his being that they won't.

It's a fascinating experience for all three parties, and a pleasurable one, with the adrenalin flowing nicely and a feeling of achievement in the air; but what looks from the audience to be quite a complicated affair is quite different when seen from the other side of the podium, as a player. It's simpler, and at the same time much more complex. Simpler, because it becomes a personal issue first and foremost, and the overwhelming necessity to succeed in one's own part is obvious and clear-cut. The fact is that if you are good enough you can do it; and if you can't, because you aren't, you shouldn't be there, and soon you won't be. There remains of course the necessity to do it at the given moment, and also the fact that this is a famous orchestra means that you're really running in the Olympics this Thursday evening or Saturday afternoon: most of the audience will have the LP of this work at home, with Karajan and the Berlin Phil, and unless this is just as good it's not worth bothering about. So the issue is simple, even though the solution may not be so easy. The complex part of the operation is that one's own part is just a thread – maybe a vital one, possibly not – in the huge tapestry of the musical score about to be tackled; and it's a tapestry seen from back to front, or one-sided, with the colours possibly exaggerated and the perspective distorted. It takes imagination, time, and a superb sense of hearing to make sure your thread is correctly woven into the fabric, and this is only one of the factors in a complicated experience, because it assumes that all the other players are thinking likewise, and that all their instruments are behaving normally. This is most unlikely to be so at any given moment, human nature being what it is. Besides, all these other people have their own very complicated lives, have just struggled through the second London rush-hour of their day, spent a hectic half-hour trying to get into their splendid tail-suits in overcrowded and overheated dressing rooms in which a dropped cuff-link is either flattened or lost, and where white bowties become dark gray if released for an instant. There is also the fact that those lovely instruments, so perfect when seen from a range of ten yards, may not only suffer from leaking pads or weak needle-springs, buzzy strings or cracked bridges, but may be objecting to the weather, the air-conditioning, or the lack of humidity in the hall, which in any case has the poorest acoustics for a hundred miles around.

So the experience of the orchestra is different from that of its audience, and it can quite easily be different from the experience at the last concert or the next, because an orchestra is many things of many sizes, and the prelude to a performance of Strauss' *Ein*

Heldenleben with a Beecham or a Karajan is very different from that preceding a concert which includes Mozart's G Minor Symphony with a Menuhin or a Monteux. It must be remembered, also, that the sudden revelation at the start of either of these concerts is no revelation at all for the members of the orchestra. They have rehearsed this performance, and upon how they have rehearsed depends whether they know exactly what is about to happen, or not; and many of them would tell you that they are happiest when they are not *quite* sure. Rehearsals can be valuable, even incredibly so; but they can also be destructive, boring and pointless, and can vary in their character from country to country in a most remarkable way. Certainly what does for Berlin, or Tokyo, or Vienna may not be at all suitable in London, or Paris, or New York. This international aspect I'll come back to a little later, but the British attitude to rehearsals is perhaps worth looking at now. British orchestras, in my opinion, have a character of their own, and this can be puzzling and upsetting for conductors used to the way things happen in many other lands. The basic principle of our own players seems to be that there is only one show, and that's the concert. On the rare occasions when they have been tempted to give their most heartfelt rendering of a great work at the final rehearsal, the concert has invariably been an anti-climax. Those who played in London for Arturo Toscanini on his memorable visits tell me that it was markedly so in his case; and I can recall vividly one rehearsal in recent years which was like that. It was in Salzburg, with the LSO, and the conductor was Karl Böhm, a man whose music-making we found both awesome and heart-warming. His discipline was first-class, probably because of the respect we had for him as a great musician rather than as a person, and this enabled him to produce, at the final rehearsal, the finest performance of Strauss' *Death and Transfiguration* anyone could recall. I swear that many of us – and there are few members of that excellent orchestra who could be called thin-skinned – were in tears at the end of it. It was an unforgettable experience, and should have resulted in an incredible performance that night. What it got was an excellent one, just as it *should* have been at rehearsal, but it was without the tearing passion of the morning. You can't do that twice with a British orchestra. What you must do is leave it just short of culmination, and let it bloom at the concert. If you do this, music can be what it has always been intended to be – a *happening*. It is difficult to arrange this always. It is usually the case that rehearsals can be too many for the orchestra and too few for the conductor, and the views of both parties are firmly held and immutable. Rehearsals can also be uneven in character – concentrated or sloppy, revelatory or dull, or simply a waste of time because they happen in impossible acoustic surroundings like Bishopsgate Town Hall, where you simply cannot hear anything, said or played. Then there's the possibility that a key member of the orchestra may fall ill or have a tumble between the first rehearsal and the final one, or be absent for a reason which is perfectly plausible but none the less fatal to the progress of preparation for a concert.

This takes me on to one of the worst aspects of the whole orchestral rehearsal pattern – the working of Parkinson's Law. That's the law which says that the amount of work you have to do expands in proportion to the amount of time you have allotted to its completion. Given that the work is Beethoven's Fifth Symphony, and the time allocated is six hours, there comes a problem. Any first-class orchestra could give a performance of this work without rehearsal (I won't say without a conductor, because this just happens to be one of those works that can't even start without a fairly convulsive beat of some sort). The trouble is that this has got to be recognizably the Beethoven of Dr X or Prof Y, Signor A or Sir William B. It must therefore be taken apart, examined, reshuffled and then reassembled in the shape in which any one of these luminaries wishes it to be heard. Parkinson then takes over, and the result can be completely devastating. Any orchestral player will recall a dozen occasions when at the end of six hours none of them could play the thing at all, and the concert was saved only by a resolution on their part to go back to the things they knew as young men and women. It's exactly the effect of taking a finely balanced watch apart to see if you can alter the tick – you may never get it together again, or it may develop a hiccup if you do.

It's possible that you may think of this as an exaggeration. Of course it is, because a truly great conductor can show you aspects of a work you have missed in all those years. Rudolf Kempe used regularly to point out dynamic markings in Beethoven to the Royal Philharmonic which we genuinely found most revealing; but this is a very rare experience, and most rehearsals when

Parkinson is present are quite disastrous. There is also the danger that if there is plenty of time we will all start to look for perfection, that passion born of the long-playing record, and about as rewarding as an attempt to balance the curves of a Grecian urn. The real trouble arises when correct balance, perfect unanimity and nicely judged phrasing have all been achieved, because now we come to the last refuge of Parkinson – Intonation. Here, unhappily, the ghost of an old adage no longer seems to walk. I mean the old saw which says that in polite society there are four forbidden topics – Religion, Sex, Politics and Intonation. Nowadays Intonation is all the rage, and the more it's tackled the worse it can get. The best way to resolve such a problem is sorting it out in the tea-break or at the end of a rehearsal, when the section can get together. It can be even worse when the intonation of a particular phrase or scale played solo comes under the microscope, because personal methods of correction become involved; the conductor may think a note is sharp when the player knows it is flat, or even when they agree, methods of correction may be entirely different in each case. There was a particularly glaring example of this in London recently when the final *pianissimo* D flat in a tiny clarinet interjection in Beethoven's Fifth came under the magnifier. It was sharp – predictably, because that's what happens to a clarinet when you do a special *pianissimo*. The player of course knew this, and next time Parkinson came around he played it just a reasonable *piano* in dynamic – in tune. The conductor (not a wind player of course) wasn't happy at the solution. He wanted *pp*, so he got *pp*, and sharp. He then made the obvious suggestion of any fiddler – taking another 'A' from the oboe. What this was supposed to achieve was quite obscure, because the fixing of that 'A' on the clarinet could bear no relation to the D flat, which is an overblown harmonic on a part of the tube and not affected in any way by the adjustment of the 'A'. The player knew this – it was his job to know it. The conductor didn't, nor could he be expected to have the intimate knowledge of acoustics of an overblown cylindrical tube with an attached single-beating reed, which was the basis of this little problem. So Parkinson did his worst, and a lot of valuable man-minutes were wasted on a problem which in fact needn't have existed, because the solution was quite simple. That afternoon, all the player had to do was to remove a couple of keys, clean out the tone hole for D flat, and insert carefully a tiny patch of sticky medical plaster before replacing the keys. The D flat could then be played really flat, in *pianissimo* – and upon such simple but far-reaching remedies do those Heaven-sent performances depend. This was of course no permanent solution, because the note D flat was then too flat to be played decently *fortissimo*. That was a problem for another day. Every player of any instrument could tell a similar tale – cellists about the impossibility of keeping pace with the piccolo as they thrash about the open acreage of their A strings, trombones trying to get suddenly from B flat to B natural with five feet of slide to move between them, tympanists with quick changes of pitch to make in dead silence, oboeists with impossible low notes to attack as softly as swansdown, bassoonists with lyrical tenor solos which go right off the top of the instrument, trumpets who have to play off-stage who can hear the chat in the bar but not the orchestra, and who play in normal pitch but sound flat because of the distance. The list is endless, and it all goes to make up the unlikely miracle which is a symphonic performance.

Having given a hint as to how one player might set about solving his or her instrumental problems, this seems to be the time to recall one or two further tricks of the trade which have been resorted to at times. These get no publicity to speak of, so I think I should reveal them now. They are very private happenings, and by no means the sort of thing one learns at a college or from a professor. I learnt my own tricks at school in the woodwork room, using a lathe to remake the joints of the terrible clarinet I was learning to play, and turning a high-pitch A clarinet into the low-pitch B flat I needed. It was all an adventure and a series of experiments, and taught me more about how the clarinet works than anything since. The fact that *short* means *sharp* was only the start; the real revelation was that a bigger hole also means sharp and rather vague in sound, and a smaller one, achieved by filling the rim with Plasticine, means flatter and much duller in sound. Other players of my acquaintance have gone further in this direction, not least because the things they play are in many cases not really instruments at all, but complicated contraptions which are no more than the raw material of music-making, having to be shaped, coaxed and bullied into making those pleasant sounds. I remember Leonard Brain the oboeist (Dennis's brother) once having a discussion with some of his less adventurous colleagues,

and insisting that he could take a key off his oboe in a sixteen-bar
tacit passage in Beethoven's Emperor Concerto (slow movement,
of course) and get it back in time to play the final chorale. His
point was that success as a wind player can easily require one's
success as a mechanic, something certainly demonstrated by the
rest of the section from time to time. Such mechanical or acoustic
experiments are all done in cold blood and often in a situation
which might suggest despair, but they all have the same aim –
artistic perfection, or as near to it as this life ever permits us to
reach.

Still on this topic, one of the most notable experimenters in my
experience is Gwydion Brooke, the superb first bassoonist of those
great RPO/Beecham days. His instrument was an Adler, dating
from the 1920s, but hardly recognizable by the late 1940s when I
first saw it. By that time it had sprouted a whole host of new and
somewhat exotic keys, all brightly chromium-plated and many
with strategically placed ebonite rollers to enable the overworked
thumbs to glide sweetly from one to the other. The bulbous 'bell'
had been firmly lathed to a parallel contour and the heavy ivory
ring (which has always been traditional) removed, while the
mouthpipe (usually called a 'crook' because of its gracefully bent
shape) had been replaced by a straight tube which, incredibly,
seemed to work better. It looked superb, modern and streamlined.
Unhappily it was nothing of the sort, because it was in serious
trouble from dry rot in the tenor joint and one or two other places.
This was bad – almost as bad as the woodworm I once saw at work
on a bass clarinet, and whose activities, heard through a
stethoscope, sounded like feeding-time at the zoo. Anyway, as a
result of its decrepitude, Gwyd was kept very busy during our
exhausting 1950 American tour. Every afternoon we would book
in at a new hotel, and before setting off for rehearsal he could be
found with the Adler submerged in the bath, a piece of rubber
tubing attached to the mouthpiece, furiously blowing down it to see
where the bubbles emerged from his leaky bassoon. These were
easy to detect because they came from almost everywhere, and
through the body of the instrument, not the pads. The instrument
still played – just – and the whole tour was achieved, somehow;
but when we got back to London at Christmas it was with the
knowledge that we would have to rely upon a deputy player for
about six weeks while Gwydion was at work upon the dry rot,

removing it completely. This done, very little of the original maple wood remained, so the gaps were filled with successive layers of Araldite, a remarkable plastic composition which sets like cast-iron and has to be in its final shape before it dries, since it will never be workable again. This was a conspicuous success, and the magnificent Adler was better than ever. It certainly seemed to give no more trouble for thirty years or more, but it still continued to have a remarkable life, being the subject of many experiments during its remaining years. I wonder what it's doing now, that magnificent old instrument and product of so many hours of trial and error? Unfortunately it was stolen in the early 1980s, and with its loss came the end of an era in bassoon-crafting. It could of course never be replaced.

Enough of mechanical complications and back to the orchestra itself. Obviously, with players in his orchestra going into such detail to find out how to make music, the average conductor – even the genius – cannot be expected always to know how to get the results he wants. He has to learn to leave the detail to the people who actually make the noises, and he would be a very worried man if he decided otherwise, because an orchestral performance depends upon thousands of human factors coupled with an element of mechanical perfection and just a touch of sheer good luck, all of which may not always happen together. And if this is unhappily the case, then the performance must just get by without this happy conjunction. The players know this, and if the audience can be blissfully unaware of it, that is because part of the business of an orchestra is an awareness of 'show-biz' and all that implies. The Show Must Go On. It is surely no coincidence that attached to the Barbican Centre in London is the seat of learning where many of the players either teach or have been taught: the Guildhall School of Music *and Drama*. From it emerge musicians skilled in the art of acting away like mad, smiling in the face of almost certain disaster at every concert. To add to this delightful uncertainty there is the fact that whereas a concert can, and often does, start without a leader, a principal second fiddle or a leading cello or bass, it cannot do so without any member, however humble, of the brass, woodwind or percussion sections. Such players do not hunt in packs but are unique in their contribution to the musical tapestry. Like the others, they have to get from place to place, often – no, usually – at the most trying of times, complete with tail-suits, instruments and spectacles, if worn. This uncertainty of arrival can be even more trying outside the strictly symphonic world, when orchestras are required for the very expensive pursuits of recording or film-score synchronization, and delay cannot be tolerated. Needless to say, it sometimes happens; and there the good sense of the conductor (who in such instances is very often the composer) comes into play. However, this good sense is unhappily sometimes not very much in evidence, like the time about five years ago at a film-recording studio in Bayswater right in the heart of London. Not a good place to try to start at 9 am on a frosty, foggy November morning, which is why one important player was absent, even by 9.05. He also happened to be a vital protagonist – the first trumpet, a stalwart by the name of Stan Roderick whose bright roulades have been heard in many a famous film for decades. Stan had been in a taxi incident at Victoria, ending in a punch-up which he avoided by leaving precipitately, trailing coat, hat, scarf, trumpet case and bag of mutes and hailing another cab after some delay. It was in this condition that he arrived in the studio at 9.20, all set to startle us with his usually brilliant playing. On such occasions there is usually a flexible attitude on the part of the maestro, who can easily decide to do a recording of one of his smaller masterpieces –say the little love scene 3M4 – (they're always 'M' for 'music') which he has scored for cor anglais and string quartet. Certainly the big 1M1 – the title music, with all those famous names in glowing capitals over the scene which contains the drawbridge and the castle behind – is out of the question without Stan or one of his brilliant peers of the silver trumpet. This time the maestro, for some reason, was adamant. 1M1 it had to be. As a result there was a sulky, sullen silence for fifteen minutes before the culprit arrived. Then, instead of the usual ironic applause reserved for such late arrivals, coupled with the ding-dongs of wristwatch alarms and the Big Ben chimes from the percussion, there was a quiet hiss of disapproval as he entered and made his way to the podium. It didn't seem to worry Stan. He just embraced the sullen maestro warmly, saying cheerfully, 'Give us a kiss!' and proceeded to his seat at the back of the studio. How right he was, because he had put his finger right on the principal difficulty we all face – the impossibility of everyone being ready 'on the dot', with no excuses allowed, with everything working – and still in the right frame of mind for music-making.

The last point is worth noting, because although nobody would be stupid enough to become a professional player without a real love of music *and* an affection for his or her instrument, there can come a time when enough is enough. I remember Nick Tschaikov Senior, the well-known first clarinet of the BBC Symphony Orchestra before and during the last war, once telling of such an experience. Before he arrived on that hottest of 'hot seats' at the BBC, Nick used to play in some of those splendid orchestras which accompanied the epic silent films, often playing scores especially composed for big combinations of players. Monday morning was the only rehearsal – three hours of concentrated effort to rehearse this score, as well as fitting in a few light pieces for the comic film and some unexpected bits for the newsreel. There was also invariably a ten-minute orchestral interlude for lovers of icecream, usually Jonny Heykins, Wolf-Ferrari or Waldteufel. One day, Nick, the first clarinet, was well tucked into all this at rehearsal when he was puzzled by the complete silence of the second clarinet, who was sitting white-faced without even touching his instrument. The conductor was also peeved, and he finally stopped orchestra, film and stopwatch to inquire somewhat frostily what was amiss. The pale one was full of remorse. 'I'm sorry, Mr Conductor,' he said, '– it's just that I feel sure that if I put this thing in my mouth I'll be sick!' I wonder if there is a single busy professional player who wouldn't at times like to say just that?

But I digress. Such incidents simply show clearly that it's very different, from where we sit. Even the conductor looks different from our viewpoint, and later we'll see how and why this is. He can even give a different impression, according to the sort of orchestra he's involved with, the country of his origin or the country from which the orchestra comes. Certainly in my own lifetime the attitude to conductors in general has varied tremendously, in almost inverse ratio to the immense increase in their wealth which has occurred over the past thirty years. The maestro is richer now, but he is less of a tyrant. All this can wait for later discussion, but meanwhile let's focus on the mass of material which is at his disposal, the raw material of his craft – the orchestra.

One thing is certain about any orchestral player. He will never know his job. He may carry in his memory the details of Bruno Walter's Brahms' Fourth Symphony, Stokowski's *Petroucshka* or Beecham's *Così fan Tutte*, but these he must learn to ignore when he is instructed in the mysteries of these works by the latest of the whiz-kids freshly hatched from the Academy (and I don't necessarily mean the RAM!). This is certainly a fact and can even be just, because it is the bounden duty of any conductor to get only his own reading of even the most familiar work, and anyway he may not like the way it was performed by the aforesaid Bruno, Sergei or Sir Thomas. Worse, he may not even have heard them, even on wax or tape. So the young conductor starts out with a clean sheet, and if he keeps it so one can honestly say that he will get cooperation from his orchestra. It must really be remembered that even the toughest of orchestras (Vienna, New York Phil, Berlin Phil, LSO and Orchestre de Paris to name a few) are really only looking for a conductor to love. You would be amazed at how many excuses are made before a final 'thumbs down' verdict is reached; and while the dictatorial attitude of the maestro of the past would certainly not be tolerated anywhere nowadays – or, nowhere I know – there is quite a lot of tolerance shown to his tantrums. If a new conductor approaches an orchestra with obvious knowledge and respect for music, he will succeed. On the other hand, if he tries to feign such attributes, he will suffer like the newcomer who once fell foul of the redoubtable first oboeist of the Philharmonia Orchestra, Alec Whittaker. 'Young man,' he thundered, 'one more remark like that, and we'll follow your beat!'

It all has to be a question of give and take, because even the most experienced of players knows that fashions in music change over the years, and that musical ideas he thought had been discarded long ago are coming up again, and being hailed as the *nouveau frisson* of the day by all the best critics. Of course there's always the consolation that everyone changes opinions over the years. If you doubt this, just listen to a cherished recording of twenty years ago, whether you played it yourself or not, and see how it seems now. Music isn't only completely subjective. It's alive; it's *now*! One is, as my flautist friend reminded me on my first day in the profession, exactly as good as this morning's performance, not last night's!

The most important ability of the truly valuable orchestral player is something you can pick up only slowly. It's a skill you are never taught at school or college, because it can't be taught, and must be absorbed quietly, slowly and almost unconsciously. It is the ability to *listen* while playing, to correlate what you are doing with what others are doing, so that it reaches the ears of the audience in due proportion and in perfect balance, as well as in exact synchronization. One lovely example is in the slow movement of Brahms' First Symphony, where a solo violin and solo horn are playing in octaves, accompanied by the whole orchestra, marked *mf*. This is of course nonsense, because first of all the horn solo must be played *p* to balance the *mf* of the solo fiddle, and the orchestra will drown both of them if playing more than *pp*. Then the horn dries up and the solo clarinet takes his place. By then the orchestra has shut up enough to make the balance easier, but still the clarinet must be certain he can *just* hear the violin, which will mean he is playing equally, but not too loud. At this point he must also entirely ignore the anxious conductor and fix his eyes on the bow movements of the solo violin – if he waits for the beat he will be just too late. This is the sort of skill one arrives at with many years of humble endeavour, and is best started in childhood.

At first that small boy in the band is too absorbed in the little 'chug-chugs' of his own third clarinet or second fiddle part to do much listening. He hopes he can do it, and if not is delighted if he can get away without being able to; but soon he's aware of the achievements of others around him, and before long he realizes that he can actually do it better than the lad next to him, who is holding the thing wrongly anyway. He must therefore show them all, and play it all just a little louder. A dread mistake. Soon he learns that those 'chug-chugs' are important, but only in context and in balance. He then gets moved up the line, and has more of those nice black-tailed notes to play – and some high ones too. Surely this is where he can begin to shine? Alas, no, because it is quickly pointed out to him that this is a cornet solo, and what he is blowing so furiously is a counter melody of secondary importance. He must then work even harder, so that finally he is *the* solo clarinet, and playing that lovely solo line himself. He does so, only to find that some young genius has started on the 'chug-chugs' and is drowning him in the usual ridiculous way. It is a moment of revelation and education, and the real start of the road to stardom. From that point on, it's simply a question of the long climb through musical refinement, the realization that Brahms requires a different approach to Beethoven, and that Mozart is the composer ninety-five per cent of us can *almost* play, but nobody can *really* play. The player has developed that ability to listen while playing, which is his greatest achievement. All this may sound simple, but it has its difficulties. You may not always be able to hear everything you need.

As a string player you start in the very worst seat of all – at the back of a huge section, whether you play violin, viola or cello. (The basses are usually few enough to obviate this difficulty.) You have a very poor view of the conductor's beat, and although you can just see what the players in front of you are doing, you can't really hear them because of your own sound. In the woodwinds exactly the reverse is true, as there are usually only two each of your instrument, whether it be flute, oboe, clarinet or bassoon. Every note you play is important, but may not seem to be since you are usually submerged in a welter of string tone on all sides and often assailed by a deluge of brass attack from behind, until suddenly all this stops without warning, leaving you alone, naked and ashamed of the puny sound you are producing. It's exactly like that embarrassing remark you make in a pub – it always coincides with a dead silence from the assembled company. Nor is it much better for a brass player, because the use of brass in an orchestra is very different from that in a brass band, where you play all the time and have tremendous fun in *William Tell* or *Zampa* trying to sound like a violin section in full flight. (You also play in treble clef only, whether you're a soprano cornet or a double-bass contra-tuba, but that's another story.) In the orchestra you may sit for ten minutes in rigid, timid and finger-counting silence before having to play three notes in perfect octaves with your partner. And just as you prepare to do so you suddenly realize that you are now supposed to be a 'tromba in Doh', or 'Si bemol', or 'Fah' when what you hold in your hand is unmistakably a B flat trumpet. It is, indeed, 'horses for courses'.

In spite of all this, everything finally sorts itself out, and that all-important skill, the ability to hear the whole score from the *inside*, with a sense of balance which makes it intelligible from *outside*, is achieved. It is the knack of playing as a sensitive member of a team most of the time, but also of becoming a telling soloist instantly when the music, not the conductor, asks for it (if you wait for the conductor, it is too late). Still later comes the ability to make those solos sound balanced within the acoustic surroundings you are dealing with – making a sound like a gentle *pianissimo* while actually playing quite a lot louder, with enough sound to give it the essential 'presence' which the audience needs if they are to be aware of it. A generation ago this was a question of instinct. Now, with the wonderful work which is being done by youth orchestras the world over, this is no longer so. This is because these young people are not only better taught than their fathers and mothers, and play on better instruments; they have also *heard* more, and absorbed more of the message of music. Not only that, but on most of the courses which precede their important concerts and tours, they have seasoned and skilled professionals advising and coaching them on these very points, balancing and moulding their parts in the scheme of the performance in a truly musical way so that by the time they start to study at our universities and colleges many of them have already absorbed these all-important skills. There are old heads on their young shoulders because they have learnt to *listen*. They are part of an orchestra.

2

Allegro Non Troppo
('You Can't Get There in a Hurry')

Having been advised what it is like to be in front of a conductor rather than behind, it is obviously up to a youngster to decide whether or not this is a reasonable, viable way to spend the greater part of one's waking hours. Astonishingly in these days when it seems to us oldies that most young people exist and wander around in a dense cloud of deafening pop 'music', there are still many who are anxious to take up this challenge, and are willing to suffer quite a lot to succeed in it. It is a constant source of amazement to me that while the dress and habits of many of them proclaim them to be the serious young people they are, there are quite as many who look like anything other than the disciples of Mozart, Arne or Vivaldi, but are none the less deeply, intensely involved with the music of these fastidious masters. There is many a punk coxcomb to be seen bent over its owner's cello or viol da gamba in the production of Baroque sounds nowadays, and many a vulgar T-shirt to be seen in string quartets busily engaged in unravelling the mysteries of late Beethoven. The musical results are the same, whichever school of dress is favoured, and this tends to indicate that aural damage by Walkman decibels may not be so serious as one feared.

Can one who has reached the end of his time in orchestras advise these admirable young men and women as to the best way of attaining their goal? I hope so.

There are several ways of becoming an orchestral player, if that's what you really want. All of them take time, patience, devotion and can cost money, but finance need not be a problem if you're really bright, because scholarships and grants may be had if you really look for them. Leaving this aspect aside, as being something better left to discussion with your nearest Director of Education, let's see how these methods work out. There would appear to be three of them.

First, we have university courses, culminating in a degree which oddly enough need not be in music. Next we have courses in our national music schools, ending in either diplomas or degrees which display one's ability in the chosen path. Finally we have the quite rare player who seems to have been at it all his life, who graduates from the lighter side of music, be it in theatres or bands, in jazz or light music, and comes to the more serious side of music much better prepared for its demands than one might expect.

There is little advantage to be gained from a choice of any of these three methods of entry, at any rate in Britain, because here the real test is the way you *perform*; in other lands, succession and pedigree may play its part to a more marked extent. A little later we will be comparing this aspect of orchestral entry in other lands.

The foundations of success must be laid long before any of these three entry points is tackled, starting with the simple process of meeting up with the instrument for the first time. This can be a haphazard affair, often being dictated by circumstances: like there only being one instrument left in the store at school, a horn, say, or a cello, which may well finish up in the hands of potentially the greatest flautist we might have had. It can also work in reverse, and happily so – as in the case of John Fletcher, whose instrument was the horn while he was at school, but who found they needed a tuba at his university, and just happens to be the most gifted of any player I can think of on that strangest and most multi-shaped of instruments.

With luck, and finding the right instrument, the earlier the start the better. The basis of later excellence may not start in the cradle, but it is true to say that many successful instrumentalists simply cannot recall a time when they didn't play, any more than the rest of us can remember learning to speak. The incredible results of the Suzuki method of violin-playing in Japan is consciously based on this phenomenon, with tiny tots wandering around playing diminutive violins which look as if they had been born with their owners. I myself was lucky enough to find an ancient pawn-shop clarinet at home when I was four years old, and that toy simply grew up to be one of the important factors of youth, and perhaps the dominant factor of mature existence. To have instrumental utterance as a deeply subconscious means of communication is probably the key to success in a performer – which is just another way of saying 'play the thing – people may like it'. This early acquaintance with an instrument applies to them all, except of course the big ones. With percussion, perhaps the less said the better, because Santa Claus usually provides the first tormenting paradiddle long before school age. With woodwind and brass there is some doubt about an early start, because from the orthodontic point of view there is some risk of damage, unless the jaw and teeth are already well formed and set. A brass cup-mouthpiece may well push the teeth inwards, and the more solid members of the woodwinds, especially the clarinet, may well lever them outwards. Perhaps a check-up with your dentist is a good idea if there is a worry. Many of us have seen no ill-effects from very early starts, but it's a good thing to be certain.

I think I need hardly say that once the school pattern has been established the future of a young player shapes itself. There are now so many players around that natural selection invariably sorts the wheat from the chaff, and the worst possible action of parents at this point is interference. It is simply of no use at this point to show anxiety as to the progress or future possibilities of a child. To do so will simply cause tension in a sensitive child, which is the worst possible thing for such a beginner. In an insensitive child it will have no real effect, but then this one would never make it anyway. There are many parents who still believe that forced, long hours of concentrated practice will lead to adult excellence. I am not so sure. A player *can* be produced in this way, and maybe even a good one; but is he/she going to be able to give the whole of life to something so deeply hated? The best advice which can be given to a child who asks how much practice should be done is surely 'As much as you like – and make it plenty. If you don't like it, you won't be any good, and then you can sit around and listen to the good ones.' This usually means that the ones who resent listening to better players will try to compete – and the ones who don't will give up, which is the best thing they could do, given the crowded world they are trying to enter.

The whole experience of a young player at this stage is inevitably tightly bound up with gaining a wide knowledge of the instrument and its possibilities. This will make him or her a good player, but to be a complete and useful member of an orchestra a youngster needs more; he must be a complete *musician*. To achieve this, he must make music his staple diet – and that means music of all sorts. It need not even be good music, though I must confess that nothing I have met since has had such an important impact upon me as my first acquaintance with the string quartets of Mozart, Haydn and Beethoven, which might seem a strange take-off point for a lad who wanted to play the clarinet.

So, let it be music of all sorts. I can recall many sorts of music I experienced as a small boy which I thought were fun – jazz, light music, brass band concerts, circuses even – obviously not of use in later life, I would have said. There is not a single one of these which has not been of great value to me professionally many years later. An incident illustrating this happened with the arrival in London of Elie Siegmeister, a composer from Hollywood. When we met he asked me to record his clarinet concerto, which I said I would be happy to do. In fact I was quite delighted, because at first glance I could see that this was far and away the best jazz clarinet concerto ever written – but without both a misspent youth in local jazz outfits and a later career playing the standard clarinet concertos, I would never have been able to bring this off.

Equally, playing at home when young with a piano which was only a semi-tone higher than the pitch of my B flat clarinet (instead of a whole tone higher – like any respectable instrument) was an advantage, as it taught me the valuable art of transposition – first a semi-tone higher, then, when at last a decent piano arrived, a full tone. I now find I have to teach such skills, as a professor at one or more of our national academies, to young people whose fine natural gifts should have been extended by such an experience years before. So I am thoroughly convinced that there is no musical chore, however humble, which is not useful in the mature player who has acquired its habits in his youth.

Having reached the age of eighteen, a musician can be almost completely prepared in some ways, but woefully lacking in others. To hear the results of many of the magnificent youth orchestras now, as well as the youthful brass bands and big bands which seem to be blossoming as never before, one might be forgiven for doubting whether either a university or a music college can add anything to their achievement. Incredibly, both of these institutions have quite a lot to offer, because the sum total of one's knowledge or the profundity of one's ignorance does tend to shine through the sounds one makes, and at the very highest level it really isn't enough just to play well. You'll do this anyway, when young if you have talent; but I must say that hearing a slice of Weber I recorded as a young man is an experience I suffer with mixed emotions, because although there are quite a few things in it I have never been able to do since, and will never now achieve, there are quite a few I certainly wouldn't wish to do now, with possibly a little more knowledge of Weber the man, the great operatic composer, and the intense sufferer who died in London in despair while working himself to death for his family left behind. This is what education is for – and the choice of obtaining it has to be faced at this juncture. At eighteen, should one choose a university, a music college, or just keep music as an extra-curricular affair, making a living in some other way, while making a 'diagonal' attack upon the profession?

The obvious plan must be to let one's own talents decide which is the best course of action. If all those Os and As are right, then the university is the place for you: a good university, and in this case that means one with a first-rate music department. This has proved to be the wise choice for many of the finest of all orchestral recruits in recent years. Many of our players can now boast a degree of sorts (most of them not in music!) but few of them have ever used it. There are lots of excellent physicists, chemists, mathematicians and geographers, to say nothing of the occasional lawyer or accountant, all daily sitting with oboes, clarinets, tubas or trombones in their hands, and delighted to be so doing. I believe they always meant it to be that way. As a result they are very complete people, and used their university years to pick up all sorts of musical experiences: playing in orchestras, chamber music ensembles and opera productions; conducting madrigals and modern music; meeting important Establishment personalities as well as the most 'way-out' and even wild musical innovators. It is a rich time, and can result in a rounded musical personality who can turn his or her talents to many fields of music.

What of the others? Here there is no need to despair, because the bigger purely musical colleges are now much wider in scope than they were even twenty years ago, and the late developer in an extra-musical sense can easily grow in stature in the four or so years he or she is attached to one of these. It is largely a question of one's own ability to make opportunities, to expend every possible source of energy in finding things to do, whether it be string quartets, sonatas, wind quintets or small combinations which will be welcome for little tours abroad, to Paris or Vienna. No college can give one quite enough orchestral experience to be ready to emerge as a competent professional, so it is up to individuals to find other amateur or semi-professional combinations, or start one of these themselves if they can. Nor need they be so terribly good. I can recall the amazement I felt when I first joined the great wind section of the Royal Philharmonic Orchestra, and discovered that I could really play quite reasonably in tune. I had been playing for years with players of a rather lower degree of skill, and constantly 'bending' things to fit in with their intonation. The ability I had developed to do this was absolutely invaluable when at last I did find myself thrust into the limelight in this most dramatic of ways.

But the fact is that the two well established entries into the orchestra – the university career and the similarly wide-reaching graduate course at an academy of music – leave one in exactly the position, so far as the management of any orchestra is concerned, as an individual who may have followed neither. The criterion is quite a simple one: can he/she do the job as well, better or less well than the others available? A good audition can show quite a lot of the absence or presence of the necessary ability if it includes the sort of skills necessary to the job in question: sight reading, transposition, following a wayward beat, carrying out the odd outrageous instruction without actually blowing up, stamina and unflappability, in addition to the more obvious excellences of tone, intonation, phrasing and knowing the difference between late Beethoven, Pergolesi, Brahms and Bartók. (The *avant-garde* may or may not be required, according to the orchestra's demands.) None the less, an audition cannot really indicate the final potential of a player, especially if he is to be a soloist within the orchestra. The only possible course is to have him playing either at a rehearsal or a less-than-crucial concert, and see if he satisfies his section, and of course the conductor and the rest of the orchestra. This may sound unlikely, but it works quite simply. Within a few minutes the really fine artist is obvious, and after an hour the satisfactory orchestral worker has so settled in that it seems a shame to move him.

Perhaps, after hearing the young aspirant play, one can begin to consider his or her other characteristics. Is he or she the student of a great teacher, and likely to carry forward the traditions of his or her mentor? Has the young player studied widely outside the narrow field of music in which he has now been heard, so that he will know what Paulo and Francesca are up to (and have been!) in that bit of Tchaikovsky* which is probably soon going to overtake *1812* as the one to fill the Albert Hall each Sunday? This nugget of knowledge may not be vital to the job, but it and others of its ilk can illuminate the daily task as nothing else will. Further, can his last job as solo cornet of Black Dyke Mills Band, coupled with a youth spent in that dazzling world of virtuoso brass playing (and also in the art/craft of bricklaying) possibly give him the edge over one or two of the less robust artists under consideration? This is the third method of entry I was talking about – and a potent one: learning the art of ensemble playing simply by *doing* it for many years in increasingly excellent company, while at the same time learning about life and all that it can be said to mean by experiencing it through travel, and finding out about the world, its people and its music. This is obviously a fairly haphazard business and can be unproductive, because there are so many wrong turnings one can take, and so many bad musical habits one can pick up. In spite of this danger, which causes a large proportion of wastage, a fair number of useful orchestral players have emerged from this school. They are so varied in experience and approach that there are as many stories as there are players in this section of orchestral entrants. Some, like the great horn player Alan Civil, came straight into principal positions from the Army, having studied with many admired senior professionals while carrying out their military duties. Indeed, Alan was probably the first musician ever to face a charge because he was seen on TV by his director, playing first horn for Beecham and the RPO, when he had no permission to do so. Others, like the magnificent trumpet players Harry Mortimer and Jack Mackintosh, have graduated from the great brass bands. Present representatives of this group are two of the LSO brass section, Maurice Murphy and Willie Lang. In addition there are a few string players who desert their office desks after a few misspent years, to do the job for which they obviously have a greater penchant. The odd schoolmaster like myself can just occasionally be found, though it must be said that this could almost certainly never happen these days, and would not have been possible at all but for the unique genius of Sir Thomas Beecham, who always did things his own way. It's an old story, so I'll spare you most of the details, but one well worth the

* *Francesca da Rimini*

telling. Briefly, having spent all my youth playing in bands, jazz outfits and the odd weekend municipal orchestra in the north-east of England, I left it all in 1933 for London University, to study the teaching of general subjects, with no intention whatever of using music, or at any rate the clarinet, as a fully professional occupation. This seemed a reasonable thing to do, as in the early thirties there were unemployed musicians on every street corner, ousted by the newfangled talking-films which required no pit bands for their success. My chosen profession was therefore a scholastic one, and my choice of Alma Mater was Goldsmiths' College (now famous as the home of the National Centre for Orchestral Studies, but then entirely innocent of any orchestral activity except that of the Evening Institute, where a symphony orchestra under the baton of the redoubtable and sympathetic Frederick Haggis met each Tuesday and performed once each term to my intense delight and enlightenment). It was here that I met for the first time players who had been my idols for years – members of the London Philharmonic like the flautist Gerald Jackson and oboeist Horace Green, the horn player Charles Gregory and bassoonist Cecil James. To play with them was a revelation, and far more advantageous than study with any professor, however famous. They of course came only for the final rehearsal, but it was an event worth waiting for. As I've said, the way to learn to play in an ensemble is to play in one . . . I also did a lot of listening, of course, and the great clarinettists of the day – Charles Draper, his nephew Haydn Draper and Frederick Thurston as well as Reginald Kell – would have been astounded at the things they taught me, without a penny piece changing hands. I had no desire to be a carbon copy of any of them, fortunately. There is no sadder fate for any musician than to lose his own identity in this way. Then came the Ernest Read orchestras, which were weekend affairs: the London Senior Orchestra, an amateur combination, and the Ernest Read Symphony, supposedly composed of young professionals, but containing one or two people like myself who hadn't even a union card at that time. Ernest was wonderful. A true gentleman, he somehow got us through a tremendous repertoire with ease, and with never a really sharp word to anyone. He was one of the kindest men I ever knew, and his obvious love of music was communicable and an inspiration to us all. He was a great admirer of Sir Henry Wood, and so were we all; but for me just then there was only one conductor – Sir Thomas Beecham. I knew then that he was the only one for whom I really would have worked for nothing. But I'm jumping the gun. For the present I was content to bask in the presence of the brightest of my young contemporaries from the Royal College and Royal Academy of Music – Dennis Brain, then just sixteen and already among the greatest horn players in the world, his brother Leonard, a chemist turned oboeist and a pupil of the celebrated Alec Whittaker of the BBC Symphony, and Gareth Morris, the favourite pupil of the great flautist Robert Murchie, who in his will bequeathed to him his wonderful old Rudal Carte flute as his natural successor. Then there was the great Archie Camden, master of the bassoon, and a joy to play with.

Who can say that this was not an obvious preparation for a life at the hub of London's orchestral life? Certainly I had no thought of any such thing, nor did any of my celebrated friends. I was just a young Croydon schoolmaster by that time, who spent all his time and his spare supply of money in indulging his passion for clarinet-playing. Besides, there was a war coming, and all these young men were to find musical billets, most in the magnificent RAF Symphony Orchestra, but some, like the brilliant young clarinetist Bernard Walton, in the Guards. There was one exception. Sadly, Alwyn Kell, brother of the more famous Reginald, but with as great a potential, joined the Royal Navy and was never seen again. Otherwise, most of us seemed to survive pretty well. I myself went into the RAF, but as a physical training instructor. Even here, preparation for an orchestral career seemed to continue with a will of its own. Most of the time I was happily stationed at Morecambe, that charming seaside spot in Lancashire where one could glimpse most of the Lake District while putting the lads through their paces in the pathetically poor physical training syllabus, which was the best the RAF could at that time boast. (This improved later, in about 1944, when at last the group captain in charge of it made an exact copy of the 1933 Board of Education PT syllabus and taught us all to do it – again, for that is what we had been learning at Goldsmiths' and elsewhere.) As a result of this relaxed posting, I found that instead of being a Music/PT/English teacher in Croydon, I was now a PT/Music/English instructor in the RAF, because all my spare time was spent in leisure activities which either involved talking about, or playing, music. There was jazz, a lot of it, played with some of the finest of the young players of the day who were 'passing through' at the time – people like Kenny Baker on trumpet and Ray Ellington on drums. There was chamber music, with the odd fiddler from a famous orchestra or quartet now in uniform: Leslie Hatfield from the LSO, Harvey Philips the well-known cellist, and on a course at Uxbridge the famous Griller Quartet, now all in RAF blue for the duration. There was also some conducting with the string orchestra, and the playing of solo items not only with that but with the famous Boyd Neel orchestra on their way through on an ENSA tour. As a result, with demobilization there came a sense rather of anti-climax in musical terms. But a return to Croydon, to Goldsmiths', and to Ernest Read were very welcome and as advantageous as ever.

It was obvious, though certainly not to me, at the time, that all this was leading somewhere. A year later it all became clear where this was to be. It seems that Beecham, faced with the loss of Reginald Kell to his great rival the Philharmonic Orchestra, decided that he would find his own clarinettist rather than honour established opinion. The post was never advertised, nor did I apply or even know of its existence. He simply rang my home and asked to hear me play the 'clarionet' the next day. Within three days I was his principal, and during the happy sixteen years I spent with him he never told me where he obtained my phone number. Looking back it was obvious that my whole life had been spent in preparation for that first memorable day in EMI Studios, with Beecham in front, the fabulous RPO all around, and an old man in a raincoat leaning over my shoulder to mark the part of his *Heldenleben* – Richard Strauss in the last year of his life. I had found a way in.

So there are several ways to join an orchestra, and the only things these different methods have in common are the necessity for a lot of playing, a lot of listening, a natural talent, a good ear, and an aptitude for the job which will carry one through the stickier moments. To this end I must say I commend the work of such institutions (if there is in fact more than one) as the National Centre for Orchestral Studies, the brain-child of Basil Tschaikov (who was, incidentally, my sub-principal in that wonderful Beecham section, and a truly great orchestral player). As I've said, this is based at Goldsmiths' College, in south-east London, and is simply to provide a postgraduate year for the finest of the young players from all parts of the country. Here they live a full professional life, with two concerts each week, difficult programmes rehearsed with famous conductors, and excellent coaching from widely experienced teachers. They also have the opportunity to play in all parts of their various sections. (Believe it or not, there are times when the second or third player has the 'sticky' bits – ask any woodwind player who has ever tried to play Ravel's *Daphnis et Chloé*.) The sad fact is that at the end of the year they can suddenly enter the vacuum of the overcrowded world of young orchestral hopefuls, and life can suddenly seem empty without the excitement of their recent activities. I'm not sure there is anything one can do about this. In the USSR I believe they have solved this. They take into their conservatories only the known future requirements, plus about twenty per cent. That twenty per cent is weeded out during the college course, so the remainder may be sure of a job – but possibly geographically incredibly remote, and without any certainty of it being the sort of post they would wish for. In Britain, one faces the usual haphazard affair of auditions, interviews and applications while making a living at teaching or clerical work, and a quite soul-destroying affair it can be. At the same time it must be said that there is a remarkable number of players who are as busy as beavers all over the country; and in London the scene is quite amazing, certainly without parallel in the world. The reason for this is that instead of having a Hollywood at one end of a continent and a Broadway at the other, with a vast dispersal of concert halls and recording studios, university campuses and TV venues throughout a huge country, everything seems to happen in London. It's true to say that things also happen in other British centres such as Manchester and Glasgow, but not to the same extent, nor is it quite like that anywhere else in the world. The result is a tremendous pool of busy musicians in the capital, and far less activity than there ought to be elsewhere. This is not by any means an admirable state of affairs, but such is the bustling activity in London that it can truly be said to be the musical capital of the world, only a couple of generations after it was reputed by the rest of Europe to be the 'land without music' – and this is a most hopeful state of affairs for the young orchestral aspirant to contemplate.

PART TWO

ANDANTE
Con Meto
('Keep It Going Somehow')

3

Tema Con Variazione

('Some Are Different From Others')

Not only can an orchestra seem different because it exists in a different country: it can seem different, as seen by a visitor to any land, from the impression of those who live there. In addition, there is a divergence of view between the orchestral members and their managements – I know several cases of genuine changes of opinion which have occurred where players have become managers. This complexity has always fascinated me, and I think the whole question deserves a slow and detailed survey from all these points of view. Wandering about the world among orchestras has been one way of making this survey, for thirty years or more, so this chapter will be a series of impressions that a visitor has received, with a few friends met on the way making their personal contributions. Then it will be revealing to carry out a careful survey of the conditions which truly exist, statistically and in detail, in several countries. Such detailed information can certainly contradict one's own long-held views, and it may be possible to reach a conclusion only after an intimate examination of the rights and wrongs, the joys and frustrations of members of orchestras.

For the present, though, just let us visit a few foreign climes and see how things seem, on a purely superficial level. Obviously one has first to beware of the fact that the grass seems greener on their side of the fence, and try to make allowance for that. It probably isn't.

My very first impression of playing with a foreign orchestra, strangely enough, was at Haringey Arena in north London, in 1948, when for the first and last time in my experience two important orchestras played together as one: the French National Radio Orchestra from Paris and our Royal Philharmonic. The idea was Beecham's brain-child, and it worked remarkably well. We simply 'sat in' together – six of each woodwind player, ten horns, eight trumpets, trombones to match, and over a hundred string players. I can't recall what happened in the percussion – probably not a lot, remembering the easy-going attitude of most of ours. In some dramatic Wagner, which was by no means the natural musical utterance of either orchestra, but very much the *métier* of our maestro, the winds all played together, with incredibly brilliant results. Otherwise the French played in the Dukas piece, the British in the Elgar, and there was a lot of toing and froing in Beethoven's Fifth Symphony concerning who would play the solos and who would simply double the loud bits (a circumstance which had some interesting results, and managed to end in one entry being missed altogether through a misunderstanding, and the whole orchestra having to lurch ahead a full beat to catch up with a solo which had come too early because of over-anxiety on someone's part – possibly mine).

Interestingly, there was very little jostling or juggling for position in spite of the many famous names in both orchestras. The four horns of the RPO, led by Dennis Brain and including Norman Del Mar, happened at that time all to be playing French instruments, while the Parisians were all playing wide-bore German horns. Surprisingly, the resultant sounds were the exact opposite, with the French players giving their typical *cor de chasse* attack and the Londoners sounding much closer to the Viennese or Berlin schools of production. Obviously, the sound you can get is the one in your head, not the one in your hands! In the woodwinds it was exactly the same, except that the French clarinet sound came from French small-bore instruments, while the British were obviously of a bigger calibre, giving a contrast between the mercurial Parisian technique and the possibly more lyrical London sound.

It was, however, in the bassoon section that the greatest contrast existed. The French were playing *bassons,* the small-bore Buffet bassoons, with soft reeds and a direct, quite buzzy and reedy sound. The British were unquestionably on the side of the *phagots* or *fagots* from Germany – the well-known Heckels and Adlers, with their more open tone and even vocally-vibratoed production. The twain, in this case, ne'er met. In spite of such differences, the surprising fact was that the attitude of both teams of players towards their work was identical. In off moments all of them read newspapers or did crosswords from the *Telegraph* or *Figaro,* and in coffee breaks the conversation was normal – what's in the diary, how much for this or that concert, and *sacré bleu*, did you see what the so-and-so conductor did in the Berlioz last week?

Even in the audience at the Opéra in Paris it's the same sort of thing. You can, if watching, actually see the trombones coming into the pit during the last act, putting their instruments together as they come, obviously straight from a job at the Folies Bergères or from a local bistro. This is a sort of professionalism shared by no other two nationalities. It was, at Haringey, an unexpected pleasure for us to discover that such exalted names as Gaston Hamelin and André Dupont were in fact very much the same sort of orchestral players as those with whom we associated daily – just clarinettists, like us.

Looking further afield than Paris – say, in Cologne – the general atmosphere can at first seem quite different. Here, music seems to a great extent to centre around the opera house, and this is a new attitude for us. Not that I do not love opera – my sixteen long and lingering summers spent with my family in the lovely Sussex countryside deeply immersed in the Glyndebourne scene are among my happiest and most precious memories. But to a majority of British orchestral players the opera is only one aspect of music. To many Germans it can, and must remain, very much the main feature of the foreground. No bad thing, if you can have well over forty opera houses spread all over the country, each with a well-proportioned and perfectly balanced orchestra, properly funded and prosperous – just different. And it naturally makes for, and produces, a different sort of player. As a result there is a generally high standard of orchestral playing in all parts of Germany, but perhaps less opportunity for the many other sorts of playing which one might like to explore: when you are very busy at one thing, you obviously can't bother about the others. The German musician is, of course, thorough and painstaking, and generally a very well-turned product. This is quite admirable but it is just possible to be too secure, too certain of one's infallibility, and this can at times lead to a blandness of performance which fails to excite. There was one occasion (as it happens not an orchestral one) which it always delights me to relate. We were in Hanover, that most dignified of northern German centres, and giving chamber concerts. 'We' in this case were the members of the Tuckwell Wind Quintet – apart from Mr Barry Tuckwell himself, the members were Messrs Lloyd, Wickens, Gatt and

Brymer, all very experienced orchestral players, which means that each of us had a fair idea of what the others could and were doing, what they couldn't (or possibly weren't), and also how much you can get away with. These luminaries were joined in the magnificent Poulenc sextet by a most distinguished pianist – nameless because I honestly can't remember his name, but his was a name at the time which stood for all that was worthy, well-prepared, solid and admirable in this sort of music (although possibly Poulenc, a most mercurial man and pianist, enthusiastic rather than accurate, might have disagreed). All went well at the final recorded public concert, until the last few pages, when a sudden 5/8 bar followed by a quick turnover can give an understandable flutter to the best ensembles. It certainly did so in this case, resulting in our pianist being just one beat ahead of the quintet; not a serious blunder, because it often happens at rehearsal, and in such a case just a series of raised eyebrows from the wind players, who are still in unison, brings their keyboard friend back to the fold. On this occasion eyebrows were duly raised, but after about ten bars it was obvious that Herr Professor was not going to be so tempted. Eyebrows were therefore wagged, bottoms shuffled on seats, and the quintet neatly reversed its 'oom-pahs' into 'pah-ooms' to fit into the new and unplanned rhythmic pattern. The audience seemed to love it all, and after the dressing-room congratulations were over, Barry suggested that perhaps we should re-record the last movement to make the broadcast more acceptable, 'as none of the wind players thought they had given of their best'. The pianist was most generous – certainly he would be prepared, however much trouble it might be. We did it again. Predictably, exactly the same thing happened, and due apologies were made by the wind players for the poor ensemble. It was at the third attempt that the final explosion came, and it was pointed out that a 5/8 bar sounds 'ra-ta-*ta*-ta-ta', not 'ra-ta-ta-*ta*-ta-ta'. It was quite a revelation to the professor, and I don't think he believes it yet. I don't think we ever went back there, anyway.

All this doesn't give any real impression of the patterns of German *orchestral* playing, however. What everyone seems to admire about German orchestras is their smooth roundness of sound and the polish they seem to give to all music. This may possibly have something to do with the fact that from infancy German musicians have all played in delightful acoustic surroundings, in which music sounds beautiful naturally – and as the sound you carry in your head is the pattern you naturally follow, the whole business of tone production is more mellow than in those places where the notes tend to fall on the floor as soon as you've played them. There must surely be more excellent concert halls in Germany per million population than anywhere else, and this certainly has its effect, even in opera houses, where the pit conditions may not be perfect, but are usually better than in most other countries.

Further East, behind the Curtain, you meet an intensity of purpose which can at times be a little unnerving to those of us who tend to laugh off the whole serious business of music making. There, be it in Poland, Czechoslovakia or the USSR, life is serious for the orchestral artist, and he never quite seems to forget it. I recall with great pleasure a solo tour I once did, playing several concertos with the Royal Liverpool Philharmonic Orchestra and Sir Charles Groves in seven or eight towns in Poland. Music really seemed to mean so much to these people; it was, at any rate at that time (about 1968), one of the few bright spots in what seemed to be their drab lives. One can easily feel the emotions of an audience when great music – especially Mozart – is played. Here it was almost unbearable. The members of the orchestras in every district were always around at rehearsal time, anxious to chat; and in spite of their inevitable similarity in musical outlook and experience, they did seem to take their work seriously, and were most anxious to know how their music was regarded in the West. Happily we were able to convey to them our great admiration without at any time having to admire the administration they themselves so revered – or seemed to. Just once, in 1966, we suffered a little from this officialdom when the four clarinetists of the BBC Symphony, in Moscow, were invited to supper at the flat of one of the Moscow Radio Orchestra clarinets – an apartment which, it transpired, also contained two further members of the section, as lodgers. It was a great party, with home-made cakes, plenty of vodka, delightful salads and generous cuts of meat supplied by the motherly wife of the senior player. In such German, French and English as we could muster we were all starting to get to grips with the real issues, things like rates of pay, conductors, days off, taxes and the black market. Then in came the man wearing a Party tie, and in a trice we were all drinking to 'the glorious BBC, the wonderful USSR radio service', and trying hard to find topics of conversation which might not lead to World War III. Suddenly we remembered that all this had happened just a year before, in London, when the venue was Colin Bradbury's house and there was the same little group, but a different fourth member of their party. We *nearly* made natural contacts on each occasion; and if only such official snooping could be avoided I am certain that musicians would be more likely to be able to get to the heart of things than any diplomats or experts in protocol could ever do. One happy thought in this connection is that the actual printed parts we play from, the raw material of our international music message (which is what music can claim to be), are possibly the only bits of completely intelligible communication which regularly pass between the nations. We sit down on a Monday morning to play from the parts of a Shostakovitch Symphony which were played from in Moscow on Saturday, and have been brought to us by Gennadi Rozhdestvensky or one of their other excellent and friendly conductors – and those printed dots mean exactly the same to us as they did to the Russians. On such occasions we all take delight in signing the final page of the copy, with dates and details. Some of these documents could be collectors' items, if you like that sort of thing, as they contain as many as a dozen quite famous signatures. I suppose I do enjoy them, but can honestly say that some of the names one sees there could be regarded with a hint of suspicion. I don't mean Martin Gatt's bassoon parts of the Mahler symphonies, which are signed without a name but just the effigy of an emaciated bassoonist hanging from a spectral gallows, and the dates and venues of all the thirty-six performances given with Claudio Abbado of the work in question. These and other signatures are authentic enough. What gives rise to some doubt is the name of one J. B. Snodgrass, who appears to be the first clarinetist of the Empire Theatre in Penge, south London, and has signed most of Pierre Boulez's most abstruse works with great aplomb; and two renowned clarinetists of the Madagascar Symphony Orchestra just could have played the Brahms and Dvořák symphonies, but one has reason to doubt if their names really are Thyti Goloshi and Lucy Bütte! In spite of these strange characters, the international orchestral world is a fairly tightly knit community, and I think a model to the rest of the world through its understanding and tolerance. It can even foster trade in a remarkable way. I once helped out the distressed first clarinetist of the Moscow Radio Orchestra, who was lamenting loudly that the barrel of his British Boosey & Hawkes instrument had cracked disastrously, by an instant replacement from my own case. Who knows how many sales that saved from the wily French Buffet-Crampon represent- atives who were hanging around Moscow at the time? (Not that it mattered in the end – the British company finally bought up the French business, stopped making their own magnificent clarinets, and from then on simply imported the products of the very French factory which had been their deadly rivals. It's a strange life, and just occasionally slightly unreal.)

To get back to surveying the international orchestral scene, one might expect to find that the English-speaking countries (USA, Canada, Australia and New Zealand) would have many common aspects. Nothing could be further from the truth. The reason is perhaps that so many physical factors are entirely different: vast distances, more extreme climates, different disposition of orchest- ral forces, sponsorship and standards of audience appreciation. The players are more or less alike, but have different day-to-day lives as a result of these factors. For the present, a survey of just the American and Australian orchestras should illustrate this.

The first thing we all noticed in the USA on the big 1950 RPO tour in which we had an opportunity to visit forty-nine different musical centres, each with an orchestra of its own, was that every one of them was so isolated from all the others that it really did seem to be an outpost, with its own unrepeatable set of conditions and demands. Most of them, for a start, appeared to have quite a short season – about thirty-six weeks in the year instead of our fifty-two, so that during those long happy summer months they could all look forward to doing something else for a while. This clearly gave everyone a lot of satisfaction, and also an important place in their surroundings, because although musical jobs were few and far between in most of their centres, they were at least prestigious, and gave their owners quite an important influence upon the musical life of the town. Quite certainly this pattern has changed greatly during the past twenty years, and most big orchestras in the USA have working conditions which are the envy of the rest of the world. None the less this pattern still exists in the smaller centres, and it is difficult to see how it could be otherwise.

One factor which must be the envy of most British players, leaving aside the purely monetary side of this American scene, is the adventurous nature of the programmes they are able safely to present. The reason for this is the subscription tradition of most of their concerts. Because there is only one central musical organization, even in some of their biggest cities, there is no real competition for an audience – either they come or stay away; they cannot decide to go on Thursday instead of Wednesday to hear an equally good orchestra playing a programme they like better. In London such 'voting with the feet' means that unless the same well-known works are presented often (but not *too* often) the hall can be empty even with a fine conductor and a really excellent artistic programme. In America it is not only possible to fill the hall with 'regulars' to hear a fairly 'way-out' programme (which is also an excellent one to hear and play) but you can repeat this concert possibly more than once, so making the vast amount of expensive rehearsal really worthwhile. In London, as the LSO can testify, this is a recipe for bankruptcy, and something we will come back to at a later point.

At the same time, this local interest in, and to some extent control over, orchestral activities in the USA can have its disadvantages. It can seriously hamper the work of an excellent conductor, unless he has a really good rapport with his audience and their chosen representatives. Almost always he has this rapport, and is an idol who can do no wrong. On the odd occasion when this is not so, his days are numbered. I recall with horror the fate of the greatest of them, Rafael Kubelik, whose stay in Chicago was a short one, in spite of the wonderful concerts he was producing with their truly fine orchestra. (Yes, it was one of the greatest, even in 1950, in spite of later statements by others who claim to have brought it to its present peak!) Somehow, Kubelik had fallen foul of Claudia Cassidy, the most acid-tongued critic of them all, and everything he did was torn apart the next day. In time, this sort of criticism inevitably has its effect, and the maestro, instead of being a local idol, becomes a hunted man, and finally finds he must leave. When he *is* an idol, however, the boot is on the other foot, and this too can have its problems for his orchestra, because then he is so all-powerful that it becomes important to please him, all the time. It's a long way out of town to the next union locale if you don't work for him, and in any case you must live there for six months before you can work, so it is a good idea to please your conductor.

So the general pattern of orchestral life in the USA is different from our own; but there are excellent posts to be had there, and they are tenanted by some remarkable people like Sol Schoenbach, who was the famous first bassoonist of the Philadelphia Orchestra, who once left my house after a party without a shirt; he insisted upon leaving his own behind for me, just because I had admired it in passing! This sort of bonhomie and good-neighbourliness is quite common among the members of American orchestras. It's the casual side of their personalities, and not to be confused with the more serious side which epitomizes their attitude to their occupation. I've known many players in America who can make one humble through the sheer enthusiasm and dedication they display. This can be quite tiring on tour. I remember spending the whole of a long post-concert night in Washington DC at the apartment of Bob Marcellus, their first clarinet, and all we did was to try – for five hours – to find a decent reed to go with the latest highly-advertised mouthpiece, without success, then or later. Then there's the story of one Willard C. Snapp, who was instructor of woodwinds at Bloomington, Indiana, when I first knew him, and who apparently taught one dedicated young clarinet person who insisted upon observing my digital technique (if any!) through a pair of binoculars, and who was most ambitious to have the same sort of thumb-support I was using. This was easy. It was just a piece of heavy-duty medical sticking plaster bound tightly round to allay the pain of an old Rugby football dislocation – of some fifteen years before! I thought perhaps such serious dedication deserved something a little more technically advanced.

Certainly in the USA each state, every city, and even every university has its own characteristics. Several Fulbright scholars I have enjoyed teaching at home developed both quickly and with apparent pleasure, and seemed ready to take back to the USA the fruits of our work together: a new style, a new approach maybe, certainly an individuality they hadn't brought over with them. Yet when it was suggested that they were in a position to set the State of Carolina afire with this, the reply was always 'Well, I dunno – I guess the maestro might not like it. He isn't *used* to it!' That, in spite of the fact that the very maestro in question had been dashing about London kissing on both cheeks the sort of player he now has returning to his fold. Happily, the new approach of some British teachers to the clarinet is starting to take effect, and many American orchestral artists are displaying joyously the only thing they ever lacked – real individuality and powers of invention; and that just at the time when we in Britain are tending to iron out those very characteristics, and worshipping the conformity which is so popular with the average producer of compact discs. But let us get back to the survey of American orchestras.

Whether or not the players are individual, there can be no doubt that there are almost as many ways of running an orchestra in the USA as there are orchestras, because the functions they have to fulfil are so different from each other. Playing to a mid-western campus audience twice a week is entirely different from the mad whirl of putting on concerts at the Lincoln Center and Carnegie Hall, New York, and the desires of an audience in Los Angeles can be entirely different from those to be found in New Orleans or Chicago, Boston or Baltimore. The USA is a varied scene, and fascinating. Even as seen by a casual visitor it is a bewildering and wide spectrum of achievement and intent, fed as it is by not only the great music colleges like Julliard, but by a wealth of university faculties which seem to go into the instrumental side of musical education in a very thorough and searching way. To take part in one of their instrumental Congresses, which are held every summer and attract hundreds of players from all over the world, is a startling experience. You suddenly realize that you are playing a Brahms sonata in front of not less than five hundred full-time professors of your chosen instrument . . . So it's hardly surprising that any definite opinion as to the sort of life an orchestral player enjoys in the USA cannot easily be formed. It can be many sorts of life, many sorts of orchestra – and as we'll see later, when assessing the essential data, many different ideas and aims.

In Australia, by contrast, there is a much greater degree of uniformity. In fact at first sight the visitor might well think there is complete unity, because unless you look into it you can conclude that all their orchestras are working under the same umbrella – that of the ABC (Australian Broadcasting Corporation), which is pretty much the same as our BBC, but in some ways even more powerful and all-embracing. The truth is that they are out-numbered by, but possibly better known than, the others. The

ABC orchestras are the Sydney Symphony, the Melbourne Symphony, the Adelaide Symphony, the Queensland Symphony and the Western Australian Symphony. All are full-sized orchestras, varying in size between about sixty and one hundred players. The Tasmanian Symphony is smaller – less than fifty; but all these orchestras are heard almost daily in broadcasts and seen frequently on TV, and several of them record with some success. The others, the non-ABC orchestras, appear to keep a lower profile, but do vital work and provide a valuable service. The Elizabethan Trust Orchestras, in Sydney and Melbourne, both employ sixty-nine players, and are full-time employers for opera and ballet. In addition there are the Australian Chamber Orchestra, the Adelaide Chamber Orchestra, the Queensland Theatre Orchestra and the Western Arts Orchestra, all smaller combinations of under forty-five players; but of these only the Queensland can be said to offer full-time employment. In addition there is the Canberra Symphony, a mixed professional/amateur organization of eighty-five players, providing about ten concerts per annum, and the Melbourne Philharmonic players, whose principal function seems to be widespread tours with a wide variety of repertoire from light classical to oratorio and rock concerts. A pretty mixed bag, and one which is enlivened by the extremely individual personalities of the players.

The ABC orchestras, in spite of their common background, somehow manage to retain separate and recognizable personalities. All these orchestras are excellent, but somehow this achievement doesn't seem always to completely satisfy their members. Several members have told me that their remoteness from the rest of the big musical world makes them feel isolated, and impels them to take trips to European centres to test their skills against those to be found there. When they do this, it is almost always with success, and can result in a welcome addition to the talents of our own orchestras. There have been, and are, notable principal players in several of our best sections who arrived in just this way. Barry Tuckwell, Nelson Cook, Douglas Whittaker, Russel King and John Kennedy (who came and returned) are sufficient evidence of this. For the most part, though, these artists return to the Antipodes once their curiosity has been satisfied, and I was startled, upon one of my widespread solo tours, to find my own pupils in important posts in Sydney,

Adelaide, Hobart, Perth and Canberra. It was also a surprise to realize that they are almost as far from each other as I am from many of my American students. They once flew the excellent accompanist Beryl Potter all the way from Sydney to Perth to join me in a recital – and it was exactly like asking her to come to London from Chicago. As a result of this far-flung spacing the Australian orchestral player really does feel he is out on a limb – and many of them, with time to spare because there are no extra orchestral possibilities, find that a secondary occupation is not only financially rewarding, but also socially fascinating. This is certainly so when they run a stud farm (sheep, not horses) but is even more interesting in those instances when they decide to own a 'winery'. One very bright boy we managed to run to earth in the vine-covered hills north of Adelaide had worked a quite remarkable feat of transformation. He had found a derelict chapel at the very top of a south-facing ridge, planted some very special vines and set about rebuilding. The stained glass was still there, as were the Gothic arches and the heavy oaken doors. Nothing else was left, except the entry to the crypt, which at the time I visited him contained casks containing 36,000 bottles of sherry: what type I never discovered, because his process of maturing was going to take ten years to complete! At the end of those years he would presumably become a rich man. Meanwhile he was living with his wife in a Nissan hut nearby, a place full of buckets, tubes and, for some reason, tins of Seccotine (the mind boggles at this – but it was probably an innocent enough store). He still played the horn, and well; but his life as an orchestral player obviously wasn't at all like that of the suburban London player who makes his way to Maida Vale every day for the BBC, however similar their professional duties may be. I am not saying that this sort of background is typical of Australian players any more than one could say that Dame Edna Everage is typical of their ladies(!) – but Ashley Arbuckle, the excellent sub-leader of the LSO whom I first met as a leader of ABC, Perth, once said 'Of course you must remember that in Aussie everyone's got an aunt like Dame Edna!'

The rather remarkable fact about Australian orchestras is that although the ABC management makes them similar in administration, the sort of life each orchestra enjoys is entirely different from any of the others: the sophistication of the Sydney Opera House; the rather more old-worldly and English scene at

Melbourne; the pride of the Adelaide orchestra in their own Festival Hall, built at a fraction of the cost of the 'Sydney sail-plane' and in their opinion far better; Perth, with its far-flung Fremantle feeling, where you can buy a few acres of gum-trees cheaply enough to enable you to employ someone to clear the first acre for your dwelling, and then spend the rest of your life felling the rest and sorting it all out as real estate (which is what one of their distinguished conductors, David Measham, was doing, bare-handed, when last I was there).

In addition to these differences, on successive days some of these Australian ABC orchestras can have experiences which could spring from different ages, and certainly from different lands. Take concerts in Sydney and Newcastle for instance. To work in Sydney Opera House can be a weird and quite a scary experience. To start with, everything inside it was put there – and even planned – *after* the outside shape had been decided and approved. It's such a magnificent-looking place that this could well be worthwhile, but it has one or two snags, like the impossibility of getting from the stalls to backstage without a very long walk on the outer deck, followed by an equally long climb up the gentle inside slope of the wasteland which is inside the stage door. No lifts – just a pioneering determination and a lot of time, as well as will-power. Then there's the fact that the main opera hall is too small to put on a big opera – Wagner or Verdi, even – but is a fine symphony concert hall. The 'concert hall', on the other hand, is an excellent small opera theatre – Mozart, even Puccini and Rossini are happy there. The recital room is too dry for its purpose acoustically, but is an excellent recording studio. The recording studio makes a good small chamber music room, as does the lecture hall – so it all works, somehow, in an exciting way. For me, one aspect of it is *too* exciting. You sit in your subterranean dressing room, about three hundred yards from the platform, listening to the overture, which lasts nine minutes, on a tinny tannoy system. As your concerto follows, after six minutes or so it becomes necessary to gird up the loins and proceed up the ramp outside – a narrow, airless affair, horribly soundproof. Logic asserts that the concert is still going on, but can one really be sure? The steps quicken, the pulse becomes the only audible thing in the world, and the arrival backstage is indicated by a simple iron spiral staircase, only some twenty steps in height, but a veritable Everest in the circumstances. At the top, all seems quiet and orderly . . . but should it be? Surely some sound of a final *crescendo* should be audible from here? Apparently not, because although one can observe some quite hectic bowings and blowings through the special window at the prompt side, of sound there is no evidence. Finally it all seems to stop, and there is just the faintest tinkle of applause coming around some corner or other. They all sit around, obviously expecting something – you, in fact! Suddenly a door opens, and with a firm push you find yourself in the midst of it all – blazing lights, searing heat, clamorous noise, the whirr of TV cameras and the cacophony of orchestral tuning. The mouth goes dry, the face becomes wet, the eyes peer helplessly and the memory goes blank – which, with thirty minutes of concerto to remember, is not a good idea. Yet the next day, only a couple of hundred miles away up the coast at Newcastle, a repeat of this programme can be completely relaxed, comfortable, elegant and unhurried. You fly there in a small eight-seater plane or take the leisurely train which stops at every clump of gum-trees, and before settling down to a rehearsal you watch the clifftop bowls competition which could easily be taking place on Plymouth Hoe. The Town Hall is obviously a copy of our own Leeds example, complete with cast-iron Victorian nudes, but in this case with the concert hall as part of the administration buildings, and very much an all-purpose affair with scenery lift and a noble proscenium arch. The dressing rooms are predictably shabby, with their myriad naked bulbs around the mirror, and of tannoy there is none – because here you can hear the orchestra at work, and you needn't leave until they begin that final *crescendo*. You can then stand coolly in the wings watching your friends at work, and marvelling at their combined skills and composure. It's all like balm to the soul, and needs only one final touch to make the relaxation complete: just as the downbeat is due to descend, the very loud but musical notes of the Town Hall clock start to chime – and as it's eight o'clock, they go on . . . They are of course heard on every radio in Australasia and simply remind us of what everyone should always bear in mind – that life is going on, all the time, even during concertos.

The basic fact remains, after wandering around orchestras for the best part of a lifetime, that the raw material from which an orchestra is made is a constant, wherever or however it exists: just people – and quite remarkable people, with great resilience and strength, covering up a not-too-thick skin and a sensitive ego. Vulnerable people. All different, though possibly, as we shall see, all shaped by their devotion to their own particular musical environment.

4

Molto Deciso

('. . . But They Still Form a Definite Pattern')

It seems obvious that the preoccupation with a given instrument for most of one's waking hours and about three hundred days in any year must show in the formation of one's character. That character is bound to reflect some of the characteristics of the instrument – or so one might suppose, just as people are said to be like their dogs. Occasionally this can prove to be dramatically incorrect, like the soft spoken, bespectacled principal trombonist or the lumbering, macho piccolo player, the foul-mouthed oboeist who plays like an angel, or the dashing young-lady-killing drummer who is just about the world's best natural businessman. These are the exceptions. Most often, orchestral players seem to fit into their chosen scene, which is why most of them, on a foreign tour, are to be found in gregarious groups, making contact with others of their kind from the local orchestras with varying degrees of linguistic facility, but with almost invariable social success.

The approach of such groups varies greatly, and is by no means always serious, as seen by others. Bass players, in particular, tend to be less respectful to their instrument than one might expect. The celebrated Nick Chesterman, principal with Beecham for many years, invariably introduced himself to the great players he met abroad, be it in Vienna or Los Angeles, quite simply as 'Chesterman – Dog-House', using the dreadful pet-name of many of his colleagues for his large and kennel-like accoutrement. All bass players, however, are proud of their craft, and when four hundred of them congregate on the Isle of Man for a great summer convention they are happy to line up along the prom to be photographed in full flight, even though the caption in the paper the next morning is bound to be 'Isle of Man in danger of sinking'. The other thing is of course the fact that inside every bass player, whose life is inevitably spent in the mastery of perfect placement of the odd 'tonic' and 'dominant' rather than the drawing of a smooth melodic line, there is a frustrated soloist – and by virtue of the fact that solos usually happen rather high up the musical ladder, that must mean a frustrated cellist. This you must never so much as breathe to any of them, as it is the biggest possible insult; yet they spend most of their practice hours in playing *The Swan* and like masterpieces, and the best of them really *do* sound like cellists. None the less they retain their sturdy individuality, and are proud of the fact that the moment they cease to double the bass line in a Mozart or Haydn symphony, in which cellos and basses almost always play together, the bottom drops out of the whole performance. All this leads to a very healthy contempt between the two sections, probably best epitomized by the attitude of one great maestro towards another, some years ago. Toscanini, who was a cellist, was asked if he knew Koussevitsky. He looked vague for a moment, then showed dawning comprehension. 'Ah,' he said, 'you mean the *bass player*!' He could hardly have demolished his conducting rival more neatly, or completely.

Cellists, in their turn, tend to be of a romantic turn of mind and to run to expansive gestures. They take up a lot of room on any platform. Fourteen of them – which is a full orchestra-load – seem to need about a fifth of the total area, giving them a sense of dominance which permeates their general attitude to life. Theirs is a lovely fate. They sit on the very edge of the stage, admired from their shining shoes to their romantically drooping hirsute heads, and playing together, as one great united tenor soloist, some of the finest tunes of all. This can sometimes make them 'stretch' the melody a little, like the backwash of a great ocean wave behind their perspiring leader (which means that the solo bassoonist, whose instrument is of hair-trigger swiftness, and who often has to play in unison with them, can rarely be found in the bar with them afterwards). If from this description of the average cellist you conclude that he can be something of a dreamer, you're probably right. But of course the exception once more proves the rule: the best administrator and managing director the LSO has yet found, Clive Gillinson, walked straight out of the cello ranks. Talking of cellists walking out of orchestras reminds me of the strangest method of getting the sack ever achieved – at the Royal Opera House, Covent Garden, in the immediate prewar days when the Russian Ballet season was the big event of London's cultural activities. The orchestra was the London Philharmonic, and among the brightest of all the bright lads was the principal cellist,

Anthony Pini. He was quite young, and like many other members he felt a keen frustration sitting in that quite deep pit with his back to the stage, especially when everyone else seemed to find complete enchantment in watching the poetic movements of the most attractive *corps de ballet*. Finally, after a week of this treatment, and finding that even by twisting his neck to its limit he could not avail himself of this delight, he hit upon a solution. A keen cyclist at the time, he removed his driving mirror from the handle bars, found a convenient place and the correct angle of attachment on his music stand and was able to enjoy in full his forward view of the exotic limbs of the dancers. Not for long – a member of the management reported the incident, seeing it from the grand circle. It was considered to be a let-down to the House; and possibly the finest cellist ever to play there left in deep disgrace and considerable haste. One wonders if this could possibly happen now without a cessation of all music in every orchestra pit in the land, but happen it did. There is, however, a happy ending to the tale because Charlie (as he was always known in the profession) not only returned to that orchestra, but also to its successor the Royal Philharmonic, for many years; even later he returned to the Royal Opera House as principal, and stayed there in great splendour until he was well into his seventies, still playing as superbly as ever, but without the aid of mirrors. Cellists are obviously an interesting race of people.

Viola players also seem to fit into a recognizable pattern, and often this pattern is one which one might expect from hearing their chosen instrument. I sometimes think they have a real love/hate relationship with it. Many of them, who love the rich, dark sound it can make, are saddened by the fact that most of the time their glorious efforts are submerged in a welter of orchestral sound. Others honestly seem to be uncertain as to the true beauty of the sound, and do not seriously rebel when the old joke about the 'two coldest things in the world' being 'an eskimo's nose and a viola solo' comes to the surface. Certainly it's an instrument which can depress its players if they cannot find other releases for their energies. Dvořák, who played the viola for about sixteen years at the Prague Opera until he was made famous by Brahms (who championed his compositions), apparently hated it. A couple of years after he left the Opera, when he came to conduct perform- ances of his works in Birmingham, he wrote home to his mother (always his most intimate confidante), 'You cannot imagine the thrilling sound of the orchestra here. They have fifty-four violins, eighteen cellos, twelve basses and woodwind and brass to balance.' The violas were notably absent! This may have been a Freudian slip, but it is significant. Love or hate notwithstanding, viola players are at the very core of the orchestra, and often to be found branching out into management, publicity, finance in addition to their orchestral duties, as well as literary endeavours such as Bernard Shore's *The Orchestra Speaks*, Thomas Russell's *Philharmonic Decade*, etc. As a slightly harassed first violinist once put it to me, 'No wonder they can do so much writing – they haven't got so many semi-quavers to play as some of us!'

Talking of first violinists, the very same applies to them as to 'seconds' – they just want to be *leaders*. It's true that *the* leader, the concert master, has other duties, other responsibilities, and other honours in addition to being just the 'first of the firsts'. The leading second violin is equally – well maybe not quite equally, but certainly similarly – important in the string scheme, which means that behind him he has a cohort of capable, conscientious and clever colleagues who are ready to take over at the drop of a hat, and can be heard at any rehearsal preparing to do so, by practising all those gorgeous solo bits that come all too rarely in any orchestral string player's life. They also spend every spare moment in every band room exploring the wonders of the Brahms, Beethoven and Tchaikovsky concertos: and it's amazing how many of them sound as if they could take over Isaac Stern's role at any moment. It must be a very saddening life if you take it seriously, because I honestly can't say I've met many who are bread-and-butter violinists, and are just clock-watching and piece-working players – a few, but not by any means the majority. Perhaps I haven't been in the right sort of orchestra for this. There's the story of the second violinist in an opera orchestra who retired, was his gold watch and went home. He showed his watch to his adoring wife, who admired it, but still seemed puzzled. 'But what's in the case?' she asked. 'Oh, that! It's my fiddle!' was the reply. During all those years she had never seen it. Seeing a series of racks full of discarded violins and violas ready to be picked up by their owners at the next performance in an opera house in Germany, I can vouch for this possibility at least.

But what of the leader, the player who has weathered all this, come through the ranks, proved his superiority, and is now the supremo not only of the strings, but of the whole orchestra? Is he or she really so special, with superb technique, great solo potential, leadership in plenty, tact, understanding, sympathy and the ability to placate and even control a recalcitrant maestro? It's a pretty tall order for any human being, but happily, in my experience, the answer is quite often 'Yes'. During the forty years in which I've been sitting at the very centre of one or other of London's most magnificent orchestras, in the perfect position to observe every sort of player, the many leaders have always been the focus of attention. They have all been excellent, and all vastly different. Some are natural soloists with a real style of their own, some have to force themselves to be soloistic. Many have personalities which permeate the whole orchestra, others simply become ghosts of the stronger-minded conductor. All of them are fine players and it is quite essential that they be so much on top of their jobs that they can spare time to be aware of all sorts of currents of emotion which are running around them all the time. It is a far from simple job and one, I suspect, which has almost as many solutions as there are leaders. The first time I noticed this complexity of approach was when I studied the work of Paul Beard, then of the London Philharmonic. A dominant player whose style seemed to galvanize the whole string section, he looked immense on the platform, in spite of his average stature. He also played his solos with complete mastery and great élan – yet a student of his assured me that in working at Rimsky's *Scheherazade* with him only a day before a most important concert, he had great doubts and difficulties. The performance was, as always, a triumph. Obviously he was a great leader. My next encounter was with the diminutive Oscar Lampe who led for Beecham from 1946 to about 1948, and was one of the greatest technical wizards of the violin who ever lived. Beecham taught him every note and every nuance of the *cadenza* in Strauss' *Heldenleben*, with Strauss himself in the background. He recorded this so perfectly that when I played it to some of the members of the Philadelphia Orchestra they said, with one accord, 'It's gotta be Heifetz!' Yet Oscar seemed to lack all enterprise in his own powers of invention, and while he was certainly capable of leading with great skill, somehow never stamped his personality on the section or the rest of the orchestra. I wonder what would have been his fate had he been around thirty years later: he was sacked on the spot for smoking and drinking a bottle of beer over the High Altar of Canterbury Cathedral, which I feel would probably be regarded nowadays as scarcely a mild idiosyncratic failing.

Next in the succession of Beecham's leaders came one of the ripest of all the characters who occupied the supreme orchestral position for most of his life, David McCallum. It's hard for many of us now to recall the time when he wasn't known better as the father of the film star of the same name, once typecast as the Man from Uncle himself, Illya Kuryakin. David Senior was of a very different type, a tall thin man of granite features and a puckish sense of Scottish humour which lay very near the surface. I have never known a player whose personal appearance so contrasted with his musical capacity. He made the most gorgeous sound, soft and rich, the absolute equal in many ways of that of the great Fritz Kreisler. This sound he used to superb effect in all his solos, but he was also able to project it into any section he led, and I sometimes feel that under his leadership the Beecham orchestras achieved their finest string sonority. In private life, David was individual in the extreme, and, in spite of the obvious prosperity his position must have brought, seemed to wish to underline the traditional thriftiness of the typical Scot. While the rest of us were to be found tucking into fillet steaks between rehearsal and concert, David would be found quietly nibbling at a packet of sandwiches backstage. In the matter of tobacco, too, he tended to be just a trifle eccentric. There was a nice touch one morning at EMI Studios when Sir Thomas, always expansive in that particular, ran out of cigars. He turned, as any maestro does in such a moment of need, to his leader, asking if Mr McCallum could oblige him with a cigarette. The response was immediate. David dug out the old Bruno Flake tin which was his cigarette case, raked inside among about ten 'dog-ends' which he was saving for later ignition, and finally proffered it saying, 'Have a *whole* one, Sir Thomas!'

In spite of this canny approach to matters of money, David could and did 'splash' quite often on the purchase of old and famous fiddles, which was his great passion in life, and I believe he brought off some remarkable coups in this department. He did tell me once, however, of one of his most adventurous excursions into this sort of transaction. He heard on the grape-vine that a rather special Guarnerïus violin had somehow got into the hands of a humble crofter in the Shetlands – a man not given to the study of the works of the great masters, but rather to the more rudimentary tucked-under-the-armpit fiddling of his native habitat. It seemed too good an opportunity to miss, and David made the journey thence in high spirits and some glee. The old man was delighted to see him and thrilled at his playing, so they drank together far into the night, toasting the ghosts of famous fiddle-makers and players alike, and playing the odd duet from time to time. Finally David broached the vital question – would he care to part with his old fiddle? No, he didn't think so, really, because he quite liked the sound. So there were more toasts, more duets, and finally, at about 3 am, the crofter relented. He would part – though it broke his heart – and for exactly the price which had been quoted to David as being acceptable by the famous firm of Hills in London. It seemed that the telephone had reached the outer islands some time before!

From these three examples I think it can be seen that it is quite impossible to categorize leaders, even though there may be an underlying trend. The same contrasts can be found between the personalities of all the other concert masters in London, just looking at those with whom I have worked – Hugh Bean, Hugh McGuire, Manoug Parikian, Arthur Leavins, Stephen Starek, Bela Dekany, Michael Davis, John Georgardis, Jean Pougnet et al. There is scarcely a personal characteristic in common, yet unmistakably each of these is a violinist first and foremost, and bears the marks of his profession.

If the contrast between personalities of string players is great, it is when one begins to explore the 'winds' that some truly marked contrasts start to emerge. Starting at the bottom of the woodwinds with the contra-bassoon, it immediately becomes obvious that there is something different about these players. They no longer belong to a gang of co-workers all playing the same notes. They are responsible for a unique noise in the orchestra, and they do it *their* way. Sometimes this way may be to the dismay and disappointment of the maestro of the day, but there is little he can do about it because such players have always been a fairly rare species, and in most orchestras you either have to take them or leave them. Like every other orchestral department, this one, the contra-bassoon, is on the up-grade, and some very bright young men are taking it over; but a generation ago things were very different, and in almost every orchestra there was an individual specialist on the most basic of woodwind voices. In the RPO it was Cuthbert ('Cuts') Harding, the robust uncle of the celebrated TV personality Gilbert. He was ex-Royal Marines and proud of it. His most notable characteristic was his famous Sherlock Holmes 'coming-and-going' hat which he wore with his heavy tweed Ulster coat, and in which he was quite often to be found fast asleep in the middle of afternoon sessions or rehearsals. He once made history by waking up just in time to record a famous passage from Holst's *Planet Suite*, which he played throughout in 6/8 time instead of the normally required 5/8, to the great disgust of the aforementioned Nick Chesterman, who led the basses and kept shouting 'Shut-up!' all through the recording.

Cuts's eccentricity, however, was surpassed easily by that of Jim O'Lauchlin, who played the contra with Harry Blech and the London Wind Players for some years, and made his own contra-bassoon at home, because it was impossible, at that time, to get such an instrument into Britain without smuggling or paying thousands of pounds in duty. Another bassoonist fell foul of this difficulty rather sadly, and was as a consequence never heard of again. He was known as 'Buzzer' because of the quality of sound he made on his normal Buffet bassoon, and therefore not in great demand for the more refined endeavours of his profession. He decided to take advantage of the penalty paid by all smugglers by informing the Customs and Excise that the gleaming monster owned by one of his famous colleagues was contraband, a fact which was easily checked by simply looking at its maker's number. It was immediately confiscated and put up for public auction, the proceeds to go to the Customs and Excise. Buzzer was the only bidder, got it for a knock-down price, and spent the rest of his life wondering why he was never asked to play. Most people were quite happy that he remained silent. Buzzer's normal tone, when magnified by the acoustics of a contra-bassoon, would have endangered the walls of Jericho or any other city he graced with his presence.

There was another example of exactly the reverse effect in a famous Brigade of Guards band during the war, concerning a fine bassoonist, playing a superb instrument, who had no intention at all of making any sound. He was Tom Wightman, once principal of the LSO, and he soon found that trying to play his bassoon on the march destroyed his reeds as well as his embouchure. So he stuck a broken reed on to a piece of bent lead-covered lighting flex, attached it to his bassoon, and spent many happy hours simply going through the motions without being detected. There came a morning on parade, however, when retribution almost came to him. The director was walking along the ranks, carefully checking the tuning 'A' of each player in turn. Luckily he checked the second bassoon, in the front rank, first, so that he was able to pass his crook and reed back to Tom before that worthy had to play. When he did so, it was no 'A' at all, but a very resonant B flat – the very lowest note on the instrument. At that depth, there isn't really a lot of difference in the sound of any note, but the director had the good grace to look rather puzzled. 'Come on, Wightman,' he said, 'you know what's wrong – put it right!' Obviously it's necessary for a bassoonist, however good he may be, to develop this sort of sense of humour. The laugh is on him most of the time. It all has something to do with the fact that although the sound of the instrument is distinctive, unmistakable and indeed quite indispensable to a satisfactory orchestral wind ensemble, it is also quite a quiet sound, unless the player decides to make the sound of tearing calico his model. A beautiful bassoon sound can float enchantingly over the right sort of orchestral texture, but it can rarely cut through it. Yet almost every composer continues to use it in the full orchestral ensemble when even the first clarinet, who sits in an adjacent seat, finds it completely inaudible. That remark you see him make to his neighbour after the battle scene in Strauss' *Ein Heldenleben* is usually nothing more informative than 'Far too much bassoon throughout, I thought!' As a result of this frustration, bassoonists have to develop a sense of the ridiculous simply to preserve sanity. On one occasion this was demonstrated neatly by the bassoonists of Philharmonia, Cecil James and Peter Parry. Having been chivvied by one insensitive maestro, who should have known better, for their inability to match up to a choir of horns and trombones, they came to the next rehearsal dramatically equipped with large cardboard reflectors which they fixed to the bells of their bassoons, thus appearing to be deflecting the sound forward above their music-stands and over the heads of the viola section. Of course it really did nothing of the sort, but the point was made. The violas were packed a little less densely and the lower sections of the orchestra encouraged to produce a slightly less robust sound when the bassoons were expected to be heard – and soon the deflectors disappeared.

So if you think some bassoonists can be considered a little odd, maybe you're right. They seem to alternate between treating the bassoon with what amounts to awed reverence and laughing it off as a rather good joke. The rest of us agree with both points of view – and Archie Camden certainly did, in his book, *Blow by Blow*.

But what, oh what, can one say about clarinettists, the next notch up in the woodwind score, and without doubt the true focus of the orchestra? Theirs is the perfect orchestral position for relaxation, usually with horns behind, aiming their sounds backwards innocuously, with quiet bassoons next to them, and oboes and flutes in front, right in the slipstream of the forward-pointing clarinet bells. This can be seriously embarrassing, because it can be necessary, especially in Mahler symphonies, to really give it all you've got, and this must be sheer hell for the first flute and oboe, who can easily grow to hate the sight of a 'gob-stick', and possibly, by association, its player. It says much for the tolerance of these artists that reasonable relations are usually maintained, particularly as most clarinettists seem to be quite articulate, and their remarks, as well as their musical assaults, can be *heard* readily but *replied* to only with difficulty. From this sort of circumstance, clarinettists often become the lone wolves of the orchestra, spending much of their time standing aside from the passionate debates of their woodwind colleagues in quiet guilt at not sharing the suffering. They also, by their very nature, must become philosophical about their craft, because theirs is an instrument impossible to construct perfectly: an acoustic freak which can be wrestled with *almost* successfully, but never completely overcome. To others, the correction of its imperfections may seem obvious and simple. To a clarinettist, who knows that solving one problem merely throws up two more, a sad smile can be the only decent response, and as this is often taken as a pitying look, it can lead to serious misunderstanding and a further deepening of the lone wolf syndrome. Just being a reed player of any sort can cause moments of doubt and days of despair, because anything made from thinly-shaved cane is both unpredictable and unstable, and while it's true to say that the oboe reed is more fragile and expensive, the clarinet reed is only half of the noisemaker of the instrument, the other half being the mouthpiece to which it is tied. Mouthpieces can become a lifetime obsession, and many players spend their whole lives trying to find the perfect specimen which will give them that magic sound they all have in their heads. What is worse is the plight of the clarinettist who *finds* this masterpiece. It is the only one in the world for him, which means that he must guard it with his life, and if he loses it or damages it, or it just wears out, the searching of Dante's Paulo for his Francesca in the wilds of Hades is nothing compared with his frantic scrabblings to replace it.

So a certain deep sadness may be added to the rather stern attitude of some clarinettists (to be shaken off the moment he reminds himself of the sheer versatility of his chosen instrument, with the biggest and most important solo repertoire, both in concerts and chamber works, of any wind instrument). He can also lead huge concert bands, play in jazz outfits of all sizes and play whispering background music for TV plays or films. All in all, sad though it may be, the lot of a clarinettist can be said to have its compensations. That is probably why his is the most over-crowded seat in the orchestra – every time he takes a day off he is quite certain to be replaced by someone much better, who may have been waiting for just this opportunity for most of his life. The strange thing is that dog rarely seems to eat dog in this very competitive field, and many clarinettists, in spite of their lone wolf cachet, seem to get along quite well with each other. Incidents like Buzzer's bassoon skullduggery are happily quite unheard of higher up the page of the score.

This obviously means that even higher up, among the flutes and oboes, the level of artistic endeavour and the manners which go with it are more civilized still. The two instruments and their players are natural companions, and hardly separable as personalities. Romantic, serious and with an innate dignity not really to be found elsewhere in orchestral circles, these players float on top of the sound, the social strata, and the less down-to-earth aspect of the whole caboodle. Unhappily, they have two instrumental preoccupations which are so different that they diverge dramatically in their interests, and cannot possibly be expected to see eye to eye. In the case of oboeists this is the subject of reeds, a complex and testing field which is so crucial that without great care, attention, time and financial expenditure it is quite impossible to have any artistic success. Oboeists look, consequently, with a jaundiced eye upon the predicament of their flute-playing friends, envious of the fact that the simple embouchure hole across which a flautist blows his or her heavenly sound is invariable from day to day, whereas the fragile and moisture-sensitive cane of a reed can change within a couple of hours from being a friend to a relentless foe. This situation was summed up perfectly for me by my quite remarkable friend and second clarinettist Walter Lear. He was about to retire after some fifty years at the centre of London's orchestral life, and was off to the West Country to relax and enjoy music of a more intimate kind. 'I'm going to play the fiddle tomorrow,' he said. 'I used to play it professionally as a young man and I play it twice a year, on holiday. I know when I get it out of the case I can get a decent sound out of it right away. With this damned thing,' he said, holding up his precious clarinet, 'if I put it away tonight, it may be completely dumb tomorrow!'

It should, however, be noted that this is a double-edged argument, because it does just give a reed-player some sort of alibi if he finds, or it is found, that his playing has lost some of its superb lustre. The reed has obviously packed up. There is no such alibi for a flautist, so he obviously must invent one, and this he does quite conveniently by using a multiplicity of head-joints, some of rare material (be it gold, platinum or even a special sort of wood), coupled with an almost equal number of flute bodies, some with different 'scales' than others, and even occasionally with contrasted foot-joints to further complicate the issue. The permutations of these are endless, and provide the flautist with exactly the same sort of problems and possibilities as the other members of the woodwind section, to his great satisfaction. They also make excellent talking points at rehearsal and because the flute is the only woodwind not actually taken into the mouth it can be passed from hand to hand in a section in the twinkling of an eye, so that nobody is ever quite sure who is playing what. It gives a sense of adventure and romance which is the envy of every other orchestral player, and flautists live up to this image quite vividly – they are the Adonises of many an orchestra. (You will note that I speak of the male of the species. This is quite wrong, especially since the women have in recent years become at the very least the equals of the men in the woodwind world. The study of their characteristics is equally intricate, certainly contradictory, and must be left to someone of greater experience than I. It just happens that in forty years I seem to have worked with almost exclusively male sections most of the time.) In the past, that is to say in the first third of this century, flute facts were rather different. At that time the flute-playing community was beginning to show a distinct dichotomy of purpose. There were those who believed the thing was still a *wood*wind instrument, made usually of cocus wood or grenadilla, an African ebony, while others insisted that only a tube of pure silver could deliver the mercurial message of Debussy's faun or Stravinsky's firebird. This seemed to divide the players personally too, into the more staid and conservative wood enthusiasts and the more adventurous silver advocates. The replacement of one by the other could throw confusion into any orchestra, though oddly enough some of the best conductors hardly seemed to notice. We had very much this experience when, in Beecham's RPO, we lost the dignified chairman Gerald Jackson (who played the wooden flute) and gained the very exciting and younger Geoffrey Gilbert (who played silver). Sir Thomas, who certainly noticed the difference, never showed it. There was, at about the same time, a change in piccolo principals, the excellent and extremely quietly spoken Cliff Saville taking over from the real blarney-boy of an Irishman, Bert Hanlon. These were just about the only changes in that remarkable section for fifteen years, and had no dis-advantageous effects. We did, however, miss Bert's inevitable after-luncheon nap, piccolo in pocket, as it had been our joy (to his intense chagrin) to steal his instrument and hide it somewhere.

Similar comparisons between oboeists show even greater contrasts, because the finest of them seem to share no personal characteristics: Leon Goossens, that grand figure of London's prewar scene, every inch an elegant figure but full of fun all the time; Terence MacDonagh, very much the model orchestral player and a superb chamber musician, but at times withdrawn and almost shy until he began to project his wonderful solo singing-line; Alec Whittaker, a man of rugged exterior and quite brusque speech when he felt it necessary, but with a most marvellous hushed magic in his playing when he wanted it that way, which was rarely; others like Sydney Sutcliffe and Roger Lord, entirely different in character but sharing the capacity to focus the attention of a huge audience in a remarkable way, and therefore showing a mental unity with others of their kind. I think maybe the first oboe can claim to be the central focus of the orchestra, and the players who occupy this position are, in my opinion, as important as the leader – but don't tell them I said so!

So far I have been able, with reasonable certainty, to elucidate the characters of the string and wind sections; and these don't seem to have changed radically over the years. In a way this may be true of the brass section, but I feel that in very recent years they have changed quite a lot and maybe permanently. I'm not quite sure why this should be, except possibly that the ratio of Honours Degree graduates and public school products to the more earthy products of the great brass bands seems to have increased in favour of the former. The two schools still exist, side by side and in remarkable harmony, but the polish is more apparent than it was, and the use in recent years of a multiplicity of sizes of instrument seems to indicate a more informed and thoughtful approach. Thirty years ago it was next to impossible to find a trumpet player who could play the high clarino part in a Bach *Brandenburg* concerto. It was even played *octavo basso* by one of London's most famous players. Now you can ask this of any decent orchestral player and he simply reaches for his tiny F *tromba* (known to some because of its size as a 'Christmas cracker') and gives accurate and brilliant voice. It's a far cry from the Toscanini days, when he insisted that the only solution was to forget the trumpet altogether and ask Ralph Clarke, of the BBC Symphony Orchestra, to play on his E flat clarinet. The same is true of the trombone, which has become, with its extra tubing controlled by a thumb-lever, an instrument of much greater compass and flexibility, though I, for one, regret the passing of the old G trombone, that wonderful bass voice which required for its mastery the extension of the slide by the use of a long-hinged handle. Then there's the tuba, and now almost every tuba player worth his salt has a collection of big and small instruments, ranging from coffee-pot sized tenors for Mussorgsky's *Pictures* to immense *Vesuvius* specimens for the best of Bruckner.

So much for the instruments. But what of the players? Incredibly, similarity of technique and achievement doesn't seem to lead to equality in any other way. My own boyhood idol, the cornettist Jack Mackintosh, was the finest technician of his or any other day, and a remarkably upright, military-looking man who was never in the army. He was also a non-smoker, a non-drinker and a somewhat stern critic of those who were not. Others who graduated from the excellent northern brass bands to become pillars of the brass sections of great orchestras were just the reverse: plenty of fun and games and an apparent absence of serious intent – until the down beat, when suddenly they became serious, dominant and authoritative. There is, and always has been, a remarkable unity about brass sections. Perhaps it's because they don't really need much elbow room, and can sit close together. Often you'll find them working out chording and attack after the rest of the orchestra has gone home (even after the bar has opened) with great painstaking care; yet lift the lid off them for a moment and you get the real 'lads of the village' at work instantly. I suppose it is simply the euphoria of knowing that you can dominate any orchestra whenever you want. There have been several lead trumpets who became world-famous for this. For about forty years it has been impossible not to recognize the sound of the Chicago Symphony Orchestra because of the incredible sound of their first trumpet, Adolph Herseth, yet off the platform he has always been a most relaxed and restful individual, I hear. Talking about off the platform, one certain method of bringing the greatest of trumpet players to his knees is to get him to play one of the many 'off-stage' calls like Beethoven's third *Leonora* overture or one or other of the Mahler symphonies. Suddenly he is confronted with an impossible situation, even in these days of closed-circuit TV links which show him the maestro face to face and is in perfect synchronization. Always someone is wandering around, blowing smoke in his face or tripping over his feet, opening or closing vital doors which need to be exactly placed for perfect sound transmission. The old story about the uniformed attendant, who actually physically prevented a trumpeter from playing in case he spoilt the concert, really did happen, but there are many other sorts of possible disasters, and they all seem to converge on this familiar experiment, making even the greatest player appear less than lifesize. Worse, everyone knows that a distant sound always gives an effect of flatness – an extension of the well-known Doppler effect of the retreating police siren, but in this case puzzling because it involves no movement. As a result, the best players make an upward adjustment to correct this, and invariably sound sharp because they are nearer than they think. The great consolation for the artist involved is that he can arrive late, spend most of the time in the artist's bar, and leave early. He also need not change into evening attire, though these factors can lead to embarrassment at the end of the work when the maestro decides to reward his efforts with a special solo bow, when the public wonder who the little man in the sweat-shirt and shorts is, or why the open door refuses to reveal anyone at all. Such absence is of little consequence, because brass soloists are made of durable material, and won't be around until tomorrow anyway, and that probably only after their quite important round of golf.

The remaining brass instruments, the horns, are really a thing apart, because they don't belong to the normal brass chorus, and are even to be found in *woodwind* quintets. In the orchestra theirs is a very special function, because they are as complete a section as the forty strings, the eight woodwinds or the seven brass, and there are usually only four of them – or in a prosperous orchestra five, including the 'bumper-up' who chips in to give the first horn a rest every now and again. This is a luxury no other player is granted, and it really does give that worthy a very special significance which he is rarely slow to underline. Horn sections are in fact the most completely united of any, and many of them really do associate intimately in extra-curricular life, because they truly are interested in their job, and can be found discussing it most of the time. Like every other section they have all sorts of personal quirks, but underlying this they are horn players in character – men of few but well-directed words and the obvious characteristics of decision-making which could make them splendid business-men, and sometimes does. The greatest of them, the Dennis Brains, Barry Tuckwells, Alan Civils and so on, have taken the instrument to high flights of solo virtuosity outside the orchestra while still remaining in their orchestral posts; and often these artists have other talents which could easily have been used as main professional occupations: Dennis as an organist, Alan as a cartoonist, and at least one as a constructor and flier of light planes. From time to time about six hundred horn players consort at a congress here or in the USA, and it is a sound which has to be heard to be believed. There are still, however, more cracked notes on horns than on any other instrument (though usually these are not so comic as the squeaks emitted by a carelessly blown clarinet, which are so far from the intended note as to be funny even to the player). There has been a great improvement in horn playing over the past twenty or so years, and also a noticeable change in the status of the average player. But this is nothing in comparison with the change in the final section of the orchestra – the percussion.

The changes in the 'kitchen' department (as it used to be called) in the past generation have been dramatic, not only in the amazing improvement in the fortunes of the players, but in the quality and diversity of the instruments employed. Before and for some time after the last war, a glance at the back of any orchestra, even a famous one (at any rate in Britain), would reveal an assortment of shabby old kit which would have graced the back room of any junk shop. The tympani were usually quite reasonable, if unpolished, with their vellum heads opaque where the modern plastic heads give a clear view of the inner depths. They were manually tuned, by large turnscrews around the rim only, without the pedals which make the modern instruments so flexible. There the glory of the percussion section ended. The bass drum was invariably a shabby barrel of scratched wood on a rocky canvas stand, the xylophone a scarcely-resonating skeleton of unpolished slabs, the cymbals dingy, and the tam-tam (the huge gong which can majestically herald doom or mystery) usually undersized and tending to sound like a dinner-gong. The players, apart from the famous figures of the tympani world, pretty well matched their equipment – and who could blame them? Only about one concert in three used a full percussion section, and in our enlightened realm the vast majority of musicians are paid per attendance. At the same time it can be said that these players included some of the most interesting, amusing and deeply philosophical members of the profession. 'Bonzo' Bradshaw, the brother of the famous James, the master-tympanist, was a case in point. When not required, which was most of the time, he spent day after day in a tub of a rowing boat fishing a reservoir in north London, with great success. He had no scales with him to weigh the fish – a prerequisite of the licence to catch them, as only fish above a certain weight could be retained. The whole of the stern area of his boat was taken up with an immense barrel, into which he dumped the huge numbers of fish he hauled in. As the sun set he would look at them, tickle one or two affectionately, then tip them all back in for the night. 'I know most of them,' he once said. 'I think they just come up to say "hello" every now and then!'

Bonzo was joined in the section by another worthy of uncertain age but a very definite military past. He displayed this by wearing always a wide elastic belt with a snake-clasp, in the Grenadier Guards colours, round the waist of his ample grey flannels. A man of few words he was the despair of Bonzo because, in the latter's vivid language, 'He keeps on hitting that gong like a bleedin' fire-bell!' He was known, in spite of his virtuosity with the gong, to one and all as the 'Grand Cassa of Kennington' – the *grand cassa* being the Italian name for the bass drum. But all this is in the past.

Suddenly it all changed – and for two reasons. First, the generation of composers who became famous and ubiquitous in the sixties, but had been at work for some years before, decided that the symphony orchestra as it had been known for a hundred years was about as alive as the Dodo for them. New sounds were essential, new rhythms imperative – and this was before the days of the synthesizer and all the other electronic marvels liberated by the Chip. A whole battery of novel percussion instruments emerged in the orchestra, tuned percussion of all sorts, including marimbas, vibraphones, tuned gongs, tuned tom-toms, all the wonders of Latin-American rhumba bands, and even one or two instruments the composers thought out themselves. I swear one of these was the brain-child of Pierre Boulez – a thing we used to call the Play Pen. It was like a small boxing-ring, but of tubular steel, with players inside, and on the 'ropes' hung flat steel plates of various sizes, to be hit by a variety of mallets and beaters of varying degrees of hardness. A remarkable affair, so remarkable that to use it you had to take a van to Baden-Baden, where it lived, bring it to London for the event, and take it back afterwards.

Obviously such an explosion of activity had a marked effect upon the business of playing percussion instruments. The bright students at all the colleges decided to get in on the act, and hardly a conductor has emerged since then without spending time studying this most important aspect of orchestral sound. No rehearsal is now complete without a learned discussion between conductor and percussion section as to the sort of beaters or tymp-sticks essential to the work in question. Possibly more important, a player has to be prepared not only to play all these things, but either to own them or know where to get them. Certainly no orchestra in my experience ever owned enough of them, which means that it is now wonderful if you own them as a player, because (a) they must employ you, and (b) they must hire the instruments. Furthermore (c) they must pay you a lot of porterage to get them to the hall, and it's surprising how many odd instruments will go into a basic 1600 cc estate car. If you don't own them, of course, it's a pity, but all is not lost because you can always hire them. At least two famous players have built up huge commercial firms for this purpose, and their vans can be seen daily, rushing around the studios of London, delivering tree-bells and wind-chimes, thunder-sheets and temple-blocks as well as the larger and more complex requirements, like the composite Dies Irae bell which Claudio Abbado insists is the only possible climax to Berlioz's *Symphonie Fantastique*.

Another factor which has led to the unparalleled prosperity of the percussion player is the emergence of what can only be described as the double/treble/porterage/hire/overdub/buy-out world of films and TV recordings which now occupies the foreground in the mind of any young aspirant. Why work for one fee as a violinist of some skill and experience, when by taking along a whole bag of assorted oddments you can earn three fees, and by adding the porterage, hire and on occasions staying behind to superimpose a cymbal crash on the track, you can make five times as much as the leader? Logically it pays to just let it happen, and it has been said of one of the pillars of percussion in London (or did he say it himself?) 'His car cost rather more than the houses of most of his colleagues'. It's a far cry from those far off 'kitchen' days, or even from the wartime days of James Blades, whose recording of the doom-laden tympani V-signal from Beethoven's Fifth Symphony earned him practically nothing, but had a profound effect upon the spirits of resisters and collaborators alike when they heralded the news on the all important BBC World Service.

Tympanists, as distinct from percussionists, are of course quite special people. Sitting as they do in the very centre at the back of the orchestra, surrounded by acres of gleaming drums, it is hardly surprising that they feel very much in control of the situation. They can, after all, drown the whole orchestra at will; and although the conductor may think he is setting the tempo, you may be sure there's nothing much he can do if a determined tympanist decides otherwise. This is probably a subconscious reaction with most of them, but just occasionally it surfaces, as it did with Jim Bradshaw on the very first appearance of Herbert von Karajan in London, conducting the Philharmonia Orchestra. The concert had been exciting, to say the least, the more so since it included the very first appearance of Dinu Lippati, the wonderful pianist who died tragically a few years later. It had not, however, been without its moments of doubt or disaster, and James reflected sadly on this the next day. 'He wants watching, that Karajan,' he commented. 'He got away from me more than once last night!' He wasn't joking either!

It can be seen that the sort of instrument you play does have some effect upon both your disposition and habits, which means that if you are a multi-instrumentalist you are possibly a very complex character indeed. Such talents are displayed less vividly in the symphony orchestra than in the lighter spheres of music, but most players have a second instrument of some sort, and some 'doubles' are rather surprising, like the horn section in the LSO, which still boasts a first-class pianist. My favourite memory in this respect is of the bassoonist Edgar Williams, now a stalwart pillar of the academic musical world of Scotland, but once principal of the renowned Bournemouth Symphony Orchestra. There's a short passage (four bars only) in the finale of Beethoven's Fourth Symphony which is a noted stumbling block for bassoonists – fast, staccato, and requiring very nimble thumb-work indeed. One morning at rehearsal Edgar didn't quite pull it off, and decided to stop and have another go. Unwisely, one of the back-desk first violins, in the silence which followed the chuckles of the orchestra, played the passage by ear, and quite neatly. Edgar said nothing. Taking reed and crook off the bassoon, he placed his instrument on its stand with meticulous care, rose slowly, and made his silent way around the back of the orchestra in the direction of the offending fiddler. There was menace in his movements, and for one of such short stature this seemed a rather rash excursion; but reaching the player he courteously excused himself, requested the violin and bow, and gave a perfect rendition of the passage in question before returning to his seat with the remark, 'Now *you* can play it on the bloody bassoon!'

But, multi-instrumental or not, there seems little doubt that in many cases there is very often a capacity in addition to mere orchestral talent in many players. There are soloists to be found – lots of them. Oddly enough this solo ability isn't always realized, because at any rate one of the greatest of all orchestral wind players, now retired, used to shrink visibly if he emerged as a concert artist. He always took his music on with him, not, as he explained, because he couldn't remember it: it was something to hide behind, a blessed barrier between him and his listeners. As a result he was never a big solo name, and he should have been one of the biggest. With others the effect is exactly the opposite, and they emerge from the orchestral chrysalis in the most gorgeous of hues and to the manner born. When they do this, it is often with a sense of balance and a stability not shared by their more famous soloist colleagues. Without going into names of colleagues of my own orchestras, I feel sure without even asking him that Isaac Stern had orchestral experience when young, and to hear such players as the viola player Frederick Riddle, the violinist Stephen Starek, and Anthony Pini the cellist is to realize that the artistry of the best players in orchestras compares well with that of the well-known soloists from other spheres. Orchestral playing is much more than just a job – it can be a vocation. A job it remains, though, and now I'd like to explore in detail what sort of job it is in several parts of the world.

PART THREE

SCHERZO
('The Joke's On Us')

5

'It All Started With The LSO'

Any comparison of things orchestral in Britain with those elsewhere is certain to lead to the rather interesting statement, 'We have more of them here – but they have much more, there'. It all depends upon what those 'mores' mean. The first one means more orchestras, more concerts, more activities such as recordings, films, TV and video and light music, to say nothing of pop, in Britain. The second means more money, more prestige, more leisure, more local support, but possibly not more fun, in other lands. The contrast between those two 'mores' can be almost alarming, and it's interesting to try to find reasons for this.

As the first reason in each case is a question of history, perhaps the best way to start is with a quick look at the history of our own British orchestras, and in particular those to be found in London. Why are there so many, and where did they spring from? In addition to the fully-contracted salaried orchestras – BBC Symphony, Royal Opera House, English Opera and BBC Concert Orchestras – there are no fewer than four full-sized and quite famous symphony orchestras in London – the London Philharmonic, London Symphony, Philharmonia and Royal Philharmonic. Rumour has it that these are soon to be joined by an enlarged Academy of St Martin in the Fields, making a total of nine, or ten if you count the National Philharmonic, a huge and successful aggregation of the finest non-aligned players, many of them soloists or chamber-music specialists, who are to be found daily hurrying from studio to studio and giving wonderful service of every kind. That makes ten orchestras – and eight of them working flat-out twelve months of the year.

Obviously there are critics of such a rich and crowded set-up, not least because in addition there is the famous English Chamber Orchestra and a number of smaller combinations like the City of London Sinfonia also doing their own special thing and providing valuable occupation to the multitude of musicians who are, or should be, our pride and joy. But are there really too many? Some critics think so. I do not, personally. All four independent orchestras have got where they are after long and arduous struggles. All are now well-managed, and are providing valuable employment at a difficult time. What is more, they are all *good* orchestras, certainly as good as most of the famous foreign competition which is constantly being held up as exemplary. If you doubt this, just try the experiment of choosing, blindfold, a record from a pile of compact discs. You may be able to tell the orchestra by the acoustics of the church involved, like the Berlin Philharmonic, or the sound of the first trumpet, like the Chicago Symphony. Otherwise there's simply nothing to choose between the great orchestras of the world – and we have four of them in London. Having played for all four, and with quite a few of the famous foreign ones, I am convinced of their claim of equality at least, and superiority in one important and unique area – that of spontaneity. But more of this later. There is no question that there is far more music in London than in any other city. Much of it is superbly played. There is also a great deal of less-than-first-class music, as well as a vast sea of commercially orientated rubbish. This last tendency is no worse in London than elsewhere – but there's more of it. There has to be, because in the present financial climate it is largely what keeps the four major orchestras alive.

It puzzles people that there should be, in London, such a plethora of musical activity in the second half of a century which began in abject musical poverty. There must be many reasons for this, but if one traces the roots of all four of the now independent and self-governing orchestras, there is one important name which crops up in the history of each – Sir Thomas Beecham Bart. (That Bart often puzzles people in the USA. I once heard Bill Lover, first trombone of the RPO, explaining it with great care in Baltimore. This was in 1950 on our first big tour with Tommy. As Bill explained in a bar at the concert hall, all titles in our realm are controlled by the role one is given at the Royal Levée which is held at 7.30 am each Easter Sunday, with decorations worn by all. The officials of the Order of the Bath have obvious duties, as do those of the Garter. The Bart, it seems, comes a little later – he's the bartender. . .) Anyway, a Bart Sir Thomas always was after his father's death – a Knight he had been anyway, so the title 'Sir' wasn't new to him. He flitted through the years founding orchestra after orchestra, always at his own expense, and while he was directly responsible for the founding of only two of the surviving orchestras, the LPO and the RPO, both of the others fell under his influence. The London orchestras are not old, as world orchestras go. The Boston Symphony was born in 1881, the Vienna Philharmonic in 1842, and even the Philadelphia as early as 1900, which means that our oldest, the London Symphony, founded in 1904, is quite a latecomer. Something like the LSO was very necessary in a country known the world over as the 'Land without Music' – a sad title, and one which the British fortunately have been able to reject in a most resounding fashion in the present century.

The story of the birth of the LSO has quite an amusing twist, because it was created for what now seems to be the worst of reasons, yet it succeeded in establishing a pattern which has proved to be an excellent one – that of the self-governing orchestra. There was at the time a large contingent of first-class *ad hoc* players in London who appeared whenever required as the Queen's Hall Orchestra under the long and graceful baton of the then Mr Henry Wood. 'Timber', as he was known to them all, was a popular figure who spoke the language of the common man and was always clearly understood. Unfortunately, what he said in 1904, though it made good sense to all others, was like the Crack of Doom to the members of his orchestra. He indicated in plain terms that he wanted an orchestra, not just a collection of odd players who happened to be free for a few hours. He would like to come to some arrangement so that his principals at least would always be the same, and that the other players should be encouraged to undertake not less than seventy per cent of the work. He would *not*, he emphasised, condone the existing 'deputy' system which meant that every time he took his eyes off the score he saw a new and untrusted face in his orchestra. There's a story in music circles, almost certainly true, of the day he complimented the first flute, with some sarcasm, as being the only woodwind soloist to have attended all the rehearsals for one of his concerts. 'Thank you, Mr Wood,' was the response. 'I'm rather sorry I can't do the concert!' This may seem a strange state of affairs to us now, but in a land where music was just starting to emerge it was probably the only way in which musicians could be certain of making a reasonable living. It was necessary to flit from job to job, so the members of the orchestra bitterly resented Henry Wood banning a system which nobody would now dream of condoning. As a result, forty-six members decided to set up a self-governing orchestra which would be able to decide working conditions, salaries and continuity of employment, and actually to *employ* the conductor they preferred, rather than being subservient to his whims.

The London Symphony was born. The orchestra was one hundred strong, and the conductor of their choice was the German-Hungarian Hans Richter, a man of very different character from Henry Wood. Where Wood was a workmanlike trainer of orchestras, Richter was a vivid interpreter of the music, and in the LSO-promoted concerts which launched the new venture he was sensational. In the years which followed he was joined by the Hungarian Arthur Nikisch so that by 1910 the LSO had begun to make a worldwide reputation, and it was obvious that their sort of management, difficult though at times it was, was working. Beecham, who was very young at the time, first appeared with them in 1908, aged twenty-nine. He was even then obviously not only as good as the other two, but much cheaper – and even richer at the time, so therefore looked to for financial as well as moral support.

Soon it became obvious that work abroad was of great publicity value for such an orchestra, and a big USA tour with Nikisch was arranged in 1912, Richter having retired in 1911. This was a most successful tour, but one which almost failed to happen, because the reservations for the whole party to travel on the *Titanic* were cancelled a very short time before the sailing date, and alternative berths found on a ship with a more convenient schedule, as well as, as it happened, a longer future.

With the outbreak of war in 1914, the first phase of the LSO ended. Nikisch was now *persona non grata*; the orchestra's chairman Adolf Borsdorf was sacked because of his German parentage, and so a great horn player as well as a really fine businessman was lost to London's music. He had been a founding member, and without him the atmosphere changed. It was Beecham's day. The temptation at such a time was to settle for a safe diet of Brahms and Beethoven, because it seemed that concert attendances had lost impetus. Beecham thought otherwise. Bizet, Delius, César Franck all appeared in his programmes, and it was soon clear that phase two of the LSO was going to be different from the early days. The board decided to offer Beecham the post of principal conductor, and he accepted, although strangely his name never appeared on a programme over that title. None the less he did the work of a principal conductor, as well as giving very generous and welcome financial support. There were many important charity concerts during the war, and in addition to Beecham Hamilton Harty also had a go at conducting (between bouts of mine-sweeping in the North Sea), as did young Julian Clifford. These less important conductors became very necessary in 1916, when Beecham's father, Sir Joseph, died unexpectedly, and Sir Thomas left the LSO to spend what was to be several years in sorting out the business affairs of the family.

Obviously such a loss affected the LSO seriously. They lost public support as well as the Beecham sponsorship, and in 1917 they suspended activities for the remainder of the war. In 1919, still unable to get the principal conductor they really wanted, they engaged Albert Coates, a British national born in Russia. He had a lot to offer and in the years which followed he produced excellent results; but Beecham, the man who could make any orchestra play fifty per cent better than their best (though possibly neither he nor they knew why) was their aim even then. He emerged from Chancery in 1923, was enticed back and is reported to have addressed the orchestra at the end of the first rehearsal with one of his most celebrated *bon mots*. 'Gentlemen,' he said, 'I am about to leave you for an interview with the Official Receiver; and for what the Official Receiver is about to receive, may God make him truly thankful!' Beecham was back and things began to improve, especially since recording was now beginning to become a more serious business, and worthy of the attention of such an orchestra, as an important additional source of revenue.

In addition to the growth of recording as a serious business, there was also another technological development – films. Not yet sound films, and not yet electric recording. Both of these events were four years ahead, and were to be a revolution for the LSO. But by 1923 there was a demand in London for a large orchestra in the pits of the super-cinemas to accompany some of the epic silent films of the day, and Gordon Walker, LSO chairman, became the organizer of this move, which later led to a very lucrative connection with the sound-film business. The Three Choirs Festival was another important prestige series, and the LSO, as the orchestra chosen for it, was at this time the nearest thing to a permanent orchestra London could boast. It was not really very stable, however, and in 1928 Beecham became restless at this aspect of his conducting life. He had many meetings with the board with suggestions for a new organization to improve the permanent nature of the orchestra, always without success. The LSO, scared at the thought of power slipping from their grasp, arranged instead of his plan a contract with Covent Garden Opera House, the Gramophone Company, and an agent by the name of Powell, for the equivalent of 151 working sessions (either concerts, rehearsals or recordings) per annum. This, so small in comparison with present-day output, was a big improvement, but it involved only seventy-five players, and a rota system for the others met with resistance. Beecham was still around, and conducted from time to time, but without real interest now that he could not be the boss. The LSO began to drift, and nobody seemed to be able to stop the rot. Disaster struck in 1929, when the BBC founded its magnificent new symphony orchestra on a full-time contract, and walked off with many of the LSO's players. As a result, playing standards of the orchestra slumped, and the Press were not slow to 'put in the boot'. A new conductor, Willem Mengelberg from Holland, temporarily stopped the rot, and was officially their principal conductor; but only his and Beecham's concerts seemed to be able to rouse the orchestra, and in any case Mengelberg was too expensive for a long-term contract. It was a crisis time, and with Beecham it had to be all or nothing. He wanted complete control in every way, and when he couldn't get it he decided to make his own plans. The London Philharmonic was the result, and we will look at their development later. The LSO didn't recover from the blow of losing Beecham again for over fifteen years, during which time they seem to have become, instead of London's number one, as low at times as the fourth choice. They carried on doggedly, helped first by Nettlefolds Ltd, with Coates again conducting, and the deputy system, once their watchword, now ironically revised – if you played for the LPO you did *not* play for the LSO! A new and very helpful occurrence was the formation of the Glyndebourne Opera in 1934 which happily engaged the LSO, although because of the tiny size of its opera house, it used only about half the players, and for only six weeks each year. The whole magnificent affair was sited in a fold of the Sussex Downs with a small theatre built by the owner of the Glyndebourne house, John Christie, in the same style as his house; and in those far-off days of idle summers in other opera houses, he was able to gather to it many of the world's finest singers, as well as some notable anti-Nazi Germans anxious to be anywhere but their native land, like the producer Karl Ebert and the conductor Fritz Busch. The result was a wonderful experience for the players involved – but not for the rest of the LSO.

The other aspect of extra-curricular activity, films, was possibly of greater importance. Gordon Walker continued to contract for the biggest of film companies, and the LSO spent many happy and profitable days between 1935 and 1939 at Denham Studios making such great sound tracks as *Things to Come*, specially composed by Arthur Bliss, and with some items which entered the concert repertoire right away. Again, the size of the orchestra wasn't truly satisfactory, and Muir Mathieson, who conducted, was ready to raise an eyebrow as soon as he saw any but the front-desk players at his sessions; but the orchestra survived as a unit by giving as many concerts as it could promote itself, and the final flourish of the pre-Second-World-War days was the London Music Festival of 1939, when they thrilled to the conducting of the great Bruno Walter.

Unhappily, the second wartime experience of the LSO was no better than the first, although this time at least they kept going. Jay Pomeroy, a well-known 'cosmetic king', took over the Cambridge Theatre in London, and his series of concerts was a life-saver. Films continued, mostly documentary but also some big features, and those of the players not in the Forces took part. Even so, losses were great, and the RAF Symphony Orchestra was full of players from the LSO from the start. (In my own training as a physical training instructor during September 1940 I was in a barrack room with the principal second fiddle on my right and the sub-principal cellist on my left; both were pretending not to know about music in case anyone said, 'Give us a tune mate!' Needless to say they didn't get away with it.)

As a result of the drain upon their players by war service, by the end of the war only the core of the LSO (the part used by the Crown Film Unit) was left. What is worse, after the war the orchestra again failed for some time to find the conductor it so badly needed. Beecham was no longer interested, there were no real concert halls other than the Royal Albert Hall, where snow used to descend from the roof in winter, and by this stage there were at least three other major orchestras in competition. The LSO was in the doldrums. Two factors saved them – the arrival of the long-playing record, with Decca needing a whole new catalogue of recordings, and Josef Krips joining as principal conductor for the period 1950–4. Krips was a remarkable conductor, steeped in the Viennese tradition and bringing much warmth to his work. The players called him 'The Goldfish' because of his wide-eyed and open-mouthed expression most of the time; but he got them to play, and even if it was at times a love–hate relationship it did produce the results. He undoubtedly wanted to be the boss, but the LSO remained self-governing – and illustrated it when after an actual punch-up with one of the players in July 1954, it was decided that Krips must go. He went.

1955 saw the biggest change of all, when the board decided to sack the principal clarinettist for absence without excuse. This was the final spark which ignited a powder keg of long-held grievances. The principals resigned *en masse* in sympathy, and went back to their films, becoming the Sinfonia of London and living more or less happily ever after. The remainder reformed the orchestra as a very young and vital combination. I remember it well, as seen from the outside. It was clear that this was going to work, because the choice of players was excellent. Roger Lord stayed on oboe, Gervase de Peyer came in on clarinet, and Barry Tuckwell, fresh from Australia, became first horn. Soon the Press realized that the LSO as a first-class orchestra was back, and the future would be exciting. Under a succession of excellent conductors, including Antal Dorati, Colin Davis and the remarkable Pierre Monteux then in his eighties, they became a worldwide success. Credit is also due to Ernest Fleischmann, a director-manager from Cape Town, who saw to it by his good judgement and forceful publicity that the orchestra went from strength to strength; and further successes under Istvan Kertesz (1965–7), André Previn (1968–80) and Claudio Abbado in recent years have consolidated this success. There have obviously been hiccups from time to time, and the start of the residency at the Barbican Centre in 1962 was one of these. This is a financial problem, however, and one we will consider later. Meanwhile, having traced the life of the first of our self-governing orchestras over its first eighty years and more, let's look at how the other three started.

6

The London Philharmonic Orchestra

The remaining three orchestras – LPO, RPO and Philharmonia – all came to self-government after several years of directorship by a conductor or an impressario – and each, as I've said, had a connection with Sir Thomas Beecham. It was in 1932 that Beecham's first successful creation which has stood the test of time burst upon the world – the London Philharmonic Orchestra. I first heard them in 1933, at the old Queen's Hall, and it was a startling experience. He had hand-picked most of the finest players of the day, in spite of the fact that the BBC thought that they had just done so. The members were mostly young players. Some of them, like Leon Goossens, the unquestioned king of the oboe, were obvious choices. Others were simply young discoveries who were to be the stars of the future: the cellist Anthony Pini, percussionist James Bradshaw and such remarkable players as the clarinetist Reginald Kell, who was twenty-six at the time, the flautist Geoffrey Gilbert, who was a mere eighteen, and the hitherto unknown Charles Gregory, who led a horn section with the most perfect blend of tone yet heard in London, all playing identical instruments by Alexander of Germany.

The birth of the LPO wasn't at all an easy one, and was Beecham's second choice. The LSO, for all its organizational faults at the time, had a sense of permanency about it which Beecham envied. Indeed, he and the fellow-members of the board of directors he had chosen – Samuel Courtauld, Viscount Esher, Robert Meyer and the Baron Alfred d'Erlanger – spent many hours in discussion with the LSO board of management, trying to get them to agree to what amounted to nothing less than a takeover. Beecham had been delighted when the BBC the year previously had started their own symphony orchestra as a permanent feature of the London scene and had conducted them with pleasure; but being denied complete control of them he felt that the time was ripe for *him* to create his *own* orchestra – one to be the equal at the very least of some of the superb combinations he had conducted abroad, in Vienna, Berlin and elsewhere. Once again, he glimpsed such a possibility in the LSO, but only if he could have had complete control, got rid of much of the 'dead wood' they were at that time carrying, and auditioned everyone so that the remainder could be seated in the right order. The LSO, with twenty-five years of independence behind them, failed to see eye to eye with him over this, in spite of the fact that they had the greatest possible admiration for Sir Thomas. Unfortunately (for them) they failed to realize that there were in London more than enough players of brilliant quality for Beecham to form a new orchestra (although it must be said that quite a few names on the first programme list of the new London Philharmonic had had to be hastily removed from that of the LSO). From the very start, Beecham's new London Philharmonic Orchestra was a triumph.

Much of Beecham's success in founding his fine orchestra was due to the sad economic climate of the time. Many musicians had little chance of employment now that 'talking films' were established, and to find anyone offering the glittering rewards, both financial and musical, that Beecham promised was an irresistible temptation, especially to the talented young specialists that he needed. This made him less than popular with his rivals in the concert world, and for several years there was a very real enmity between the LSO and LPO – a feud which ended only with the Second World War. It was during the preceding seven years, 1932–9, that the LPO achieved what many people today regard as their finest artistic heights. The critics raved about the new sound they brought to London – and not only with reference to the fabulous wind section, hand-picked as it was. Contrasting their string section, led at the time by Paul Beard, with that of the Berlin Philharmonic, Ernest Newman, music critic of *The Times*, wrote, 'Unlike the Berliners, who sound like a hundred men playing as one machine, on Thursday we heard a whole body of strings inflecting and phrasing exactly as a single great violinist would do'.

With such playing it was obvious that the orchestra would be in great demand. They toured widely in 1933, when every important centre in Britain heard them, and also took over the concerts of the Royal Philharmonic Society at Queen's Hall in London, the central focus of all London music events at the time. Sir Thomas, ever the master of the grand gesture, then started seasons of international opera at Covent Garden, bringing to London most of the famous singers of the world, and conducting such works as Strauss' *Rosenkavalier* and Wagner's *Tristan*, although leaving the whole of Wagner's *Ring* cycle to Robert Heger, who was famous for just that. Italian opera also featured largely, with *Aida* and *Don Carlos* conducted by Beecham, and *La Bohème* by the young John Barbirolli. It was a time of great expansion. Oddly enough, the orchestral playing seems to have been much better than the singing, in spite of star-studded casts. There was also the very sad question of the cost of all this. Nothing in all music can cost anything like as much as opera, and no expense was spared in these seasons, especially the later ones with greatly expanded and rare repertoire, including such operas as Gluck's *Orfeo*, Verdi's *Falstaff*, and Puccini's *Turandot*. These are common currency now, but at that time nobody had heard them, and rehearsals had to start from scratch. In addition, such works as Debussy's *Pelléas et Mélisande* were beyond the understanding of most of the audiences of the day, which made for poor attendances, and occasional experiments like the inclusion of Eugene Goossens' opera *Don Juan de Mañana* were financially disastrous.

There was also an element of overwork in all this, because Beecham also included in 1935 a season of Russian ballet which overlapped the opera season; he wanted the players for his *opera Prince Igor* to go straight to the more traditional Tchaikovsky *ballets* without any lost days. Those who took part swear that it was the worst ballet-playing they have ever heard – yet within weeks Beecham had his audience standing on their seats on a short Continental tour in Brussels after a programme of all-British music – or what would have been such a programme if the music had not been lost at the station, making it necessary for the LPO to play an unrehearsed programme of anything they could borrow, until the original programme was found, when they started afresh.

It was all hectic, all uncertain, and by 1936 things had come to a head. Two of the directors, Meyer and Courtauld, resigned. Lady Cunard, a close friend of Beecham's, was co-opted, and an appeal for £20,000 issued. This was only partly successful, and for some years the orchestra tottered financially from crisis to crisis, with some changes in personnel but a surprising number of stalwart and loyal members. Yet despite this, these were still years of great artistic achievement both at home and abroad – and included the triumphal German tour in 1936 during which Beecham refused to be present for the arrival of Hitler, when everyone stood rigidly to attention. Instead, he entered later to his usual applause. There was also the remarkable 1938 Sibelius Festival in London which brought to this country the works of a great symphonist whose music was unknown. This was a revelation to us all, and an experience I, as a member of the audience, shall certainly never forget.

The final crisis with Beecham and the LPO came, as might have been expected, in 1939. In spite of the obvious signs of coming war, Sir Thomas insisted upon continuing his plans for yet another season of international opera. By then Beecham's rich friends had had enough of the demands the sponsorship made upon them, and he was left alone to support this incredibly costly event. Moreover, there were serious tensions backstage, with two Italians, conductor Vittorio Gui and tenor Benjamino Gigli, on opposing sides of the Fascist fence; and two Jewish singers from the USA being insulted daily by the Germans in the cast. The season progressed, but not with the usual verve. The last performance was of Wagner's *Tristan*, and Beecham seemed far from well. His doctors subsequently confirmed this, and ordered him abroad for a year to recuperate – advice he could not immediately take. He had spent seven years in the most intense effort to create an orchestra of international repute. He had succeeded – and now failed. He had demonstrated a truth that should never have required demonstration – that music, real music, cannot ever pay for itself. His London Philharmonic was at the crossroads, being completely unemployed, and a second 'self-governing' London orchestra was the result. This hiatus in activity came, luckily, in the summer holidays of 1939. It was a simple fact that the players came back after their vacation to nothing at all, and the next move was up to them. They had to take over the management.

The War had started, and London incredibly remaining for the moment unscathed, a meeting of the creditors was held within a few days. Sir Thomas was at his most eloquent, and seemed to convince most of his creditors that it was right that they should get just what they were about to receive – nothing! He also owed quite a lot of fees to his orchestra, and it says much for their spirit that they failed to press for payment, knowing that in fact Beecham had spent his own fortune as well as those of several others in the venture now being wound up.

Obviously some very drastic steps had to be taken if the LPO was to survive, and there was no lack of ideas, including joining the forces as a unit and continuing as the LPO in khaki, which didn't really appeal to the War Office. Next came the election of a committee of five members to explore possibilities, chaired by Charles Gregory, the first horn player. They soon discovered that there was a very real risk of the LPO losing its players. Already the BBC, afraid of relying upon London in the coming blitz as a centre of music-making, had stolen several key members of the LPO to play in their superb Salon Orchestra – small enough to play in an air-raid shelter of reasonable size.

At this time Beecham took an active part, even paying for the new limited company which was being formed to carry on the management of the orchestra. He cancelled a longstanding Australian tour and took over some of the concerts with the LPO which Weingartner would have conducted in happier circumstances. The orchestra was reborn, and after a short and triumphal provincial tour it returned to Queen's Hall with delight; but all was far from well. This time there was no money to support empty seats in the auditorium, and orchestral fees suffered and dwindled. It was then that Beecham, at the end of 1939, decided to go abroad, leaving as he did so some very stringent criticisms of the way in which the orchestra was being managed. This hurt the orchestral committee considerably, but they recognized that they were mostly 'new boys' in this respect, and needed to be more selective. Luckily, they chose as administrator one of their viola players, Thomas Russell, who immediately put down his bow to become one of the ablest of that rare class of individuals. He could see that the Beecham days were over, at any rate for the duration of the war, and he planned accordingly. The Beecham emphasis was given a subtle *diminuendo* and the personality of the players amplified in a publication called *London Philharmonic Post*. The players took on a new dignity and importance, the conductor of the day a much lower profile. Programmes were planned to please the public and fill the seats; there was a new public now for music, since the war seemed to be making musical experience more intense for many people.

So, helped by such conductors as Sargent, Wood and Cameron, the orchestra lived on as a self-governing unit. There was much to do, and a lot to suffer, including concerts in music-halls for the impressario Jack Hylton, a warm-hearted and sincere musician from the lighter musical sphere who never once suggested conducting himself, although he must have been sorely tempted. The choice of conductor for these events was a perfect one – Sir Malcolm Sargent, whose looks and efficiency were the essential ingredients.

All this was during the Phoney War, that strange period of a year during which London was unblitzed. In August 1940 all this changed. The Blitz was on, and concerts in London became almost impossible. None of the players was hurt in the bombing, though of scares there were plenty – and it went on and on into 1941, when it seemed to die down a little. It was then that disaster struck. After finishing a performance of Elgar's *Gerontius* at Queen's Hall on 10 May 1940 the orchestra left for home. There was to be a rehearsal next morning, so it was obviously convenient for them to leave their instruments behind. By 6 am it was all over – Queen's Hall had been bombed to the ground, and most of the instruments had gone with it. Incredibly, the concert wasn't cancelled; it was played instead at the Duke's Hall of the Royal Academy of Music, a mile away, on borrowed instruments. *Nothing* was going to stop the LPO.

So, throughout the war years, the orchestra continued its public duties, and it was at this time that many people now feel that the public appetite for symphony concerts was established in Britain. Possibly its members looked upon their work as a form of National Service, playing far more frequently than they should have been called upon to do, but they had come to believe in themselves, and many of them looked forward keenly to the return of Sir Thomas Beecham, the man who had brought them to the summit a decade before, and would certainly do so again.

Alas, it was not to be – and oddly enough I may have been one of the first people in Britain to know it. At the time I was stationed as a sergeant PT instructor at Morecambe, Lancashire, and in close touch with an army unit in Lancaster, a few miles away. We used to swop players in all sorts of musical activities from jazz to chamber music, and it was in the latter that I met a young cellist called David Cherniavsky, the son of the well-known Michel

Cherniavsky, also a cellist, who ran a famous piano trio. One day in August 1944 David was very excited. 'Beecham's coming back,' he said, 'and he says he's going to start a new orchestra called the Royal Philharmonic.' This seemed highly unlikely, because everyone knew that Beecham was coming back to the LPO – but Michel had been with him in New York and was adamant that he was quoting Beecham's own words.

His statement seemed to be even more unlikely when Beecham did return a few months later, and one of his first actions was to make a truly superb recording of Schubert's Sixth Symphony with the LPO, drawing from players who had never met him the same sort of magic that he had inspired in pre-war days. None the less, history was to prove Michel Cherniavsky right. It seems that Beecham, happy though he was with the playing of the LPO, could not accept his place in a scheme which did not give him entire control – and by then the LPO knew exactly how to self-govern an orchestra, and intended to continue doing so. I am not privy to the discussions which ensued – but that these failed there is no doubt, and so London was left with its *second* permanent self-governing orchestra – and Beecham without his own.

Rather than following through the history of the LPO to the present day, as I did with the LSO, I think it's better to try to clear up the stray facts concerning the births of the two other London orchestras which are now self-governing, coming back to the histories later. Neither the RPO nor Philharmonia started out to be in this category, but both followed the LSO and LPO in their belief that in this form of management lay their salvation. There was a connection in each case with Sir Thomas, although in the case of Philharmonia this was a fleeting one. With the Royal Philharmonic it was all of fifteen years long – the last and probably the greatest association of Beecham's long career.

7

Beecham Makes His Choice:
Philharmonia's Early Days

Sir Thomas' short interest in Philharmonia came first, when the impressario and recording executive Walter Legge, a man of brilliant talent who left his mark on the musical world more firmly than most people admit, invited Beecham in 1945 to conduct his new orchestra. This was a splendid collection of most of the great London players, and included many of Beecham's old stars from pre-war LPO days – clarinetist Reginald Kell, bassoonist John Alexandra and James Bradshaw, the tympanist, together with the remarkable flautist Arthur Gleghorn and the quite incomparable horn player Dennis Brain, freshly demobilized from the RAF and still in his early twenties.

The start of Philharmonia was bound up quite closely with the disbandment of two other organizations – the RAF Symphony Orchestra, a collection of players who had made a tremendous reputation during the war, and the short-lived National Symphony Orchestra which appeared only at the end of the war and contained quite a number of erstwhile stars from the RAF. One of the creators of the NSO seems to have been the somewhat shadowy figure Sydney Beer – a businessman and racehorse owner reputed to be fabulously rich, although he denied this with fervour. It was his ambition to be a conductor, and the creation of a superb orchestra through the spread of this non-existent wealth seemed the obvious solution. He succeeded in part, conducting quite a number of worthwhile concerts. He had previously conducted the LPO free of charge and with financial support before the return of Beecham, and hoped to continue this career; but like others in this category he soon fell behind the professional conductors. (This often happens when too big a repertoire is attempted – the wealthy Sheffield cutler Herman Lindars conducted Stravinsky's *Rite of Spring* with the RPO in 1962, and it wasn't at all bad. In 1963 he succeeded in almost bringing the same orchestra to a complete halt in Tchaikovsky's Fifth in the

Congress Hall of the Kremlin. After this his image faded.) Certainly the best approach is that being shown now by the American financier Gilbert Kaplan, who in 1986 wanted to conduct only Mahler's Second Symphony, and does it quite superbly every time. The lot of the conducting amateur need not be an unhappy one, if he uses his intelligence. I myself neither met Sydney Beer nor heard one of his performances, so cannot judge his work in any way; but there's a rather nice little story which does indicate the attitude of some of his players towards him. It was at a concert in Eastbourne in 1945, and at the old Winter Gardens – a venue where, in those postwar days, the orchestra tuned up behind beautifully fluted satin curtains before being revealed *in situ* just before the maestro entered. This time all was hushed, and the curtains swished nicely apart showing the orchestra sitting comfortably and ready to play. All, that is, except one – the cellist Clarence Willoughby, a superb artist, but never known as the soul of sobriety. He rose somewhat shakily to his feet as the conductor approached. His coat tails were duly pulled, but he was adamant. 'I always shtand for the Beer,' he said, '– however bad!'

The title National Symphony was one which Walter Legge had no wish to adopt, so he spent some time casting around for names not already in use. Almost accidentally he hit upon the title Philharmonia, which was to become his most precious possession, while chatting with Herbert Downes, one of his viola players. It was the name of a quartet organized by the said Herbert, and included the violinists Henry Holst and Ernest Clement and the cellist Anthony Pini. The title was made available to Walter Legge as an orchestral one, a circumstance helped by the departure of Henry Holst to take up an important leader's post in Scandinavia a few months later, so that the quartet ceased to exist. So the Philharmonia Orchestra was born in 1945, and Beecham was to conduct it.

History would certainly have been different if Beecham had continued to do so, as I feel sure Legge had planned; but it was the old case of the irresistible force meeting the immovable object with two such strong men striving for the helm. Sir Thomas soon realized that yet again there was no possibility of his complete control of this orchestra, whatever it called itself, in spite of the fact that he had a great deal of clout with the recording company, EMI, who were behind the whole project. So two of the orchestras he had planned to dominate upon his return had slipped through his fingers, leaving a vacuum which he would inevitably fill immediately – and did, in 1946, by founding the Royal Philharmonic. But I am moving on too quickly, and must finish the story of Philharmonia, at least to the point at which it, too, became self-governing.

Philharmonia continued its happy and prosperous course as house band for EMI and a concert orchestra for some of the most famous of visiting soloists and conductors.

It seems possible that within a year or two the orchestra had established a bigger reputation abroad – especially in the USA – than it enjoyed here. By this time the long-playing record was giving a fair idea of what orchestras really sounded like, and this one was *good*. I remember in 1950 being asked countless questions in New York and elsewhere as to when they could actually meet this orchestra. It was only later that Philharmonia got around to foreign tours – but at such events as Expo 70 in Osaka, an event which made that city the business centre of the world in 1970, they were greeted as something quite special, and this is an image they have always jealously tried to guard. During Walter Legge's regime, 1945–64, there was a succession of famous conductors. Von Karajan stayed only a short time, but had a vivid impact – especially his first concert, at the Royal Albert Hall in 1948, which I will come back to later. Guido Cantelli might well have been a potent force had he lived. Unfortunately those of us who had enjoyed Beecham and Bruno Walter, and maybe were less impressed by the antics of Toscanini, found in Cantelli the sort of super-tension which seemed by that time outdated. His last session was a disaster. I can't remember the work in question, but it was being recorded at Kingsway Hall – a place of lovely acoustics, plenty of dust, a sloping floor and with the London Underground a frequent visitor below floor level. It could clearly be heard rumbling away in every quiet passage in the score. It was in a passage for strings at about 3 pm that this intruder arrived in force. For Cantelli it was too much. Tipping the score to the floor, he left the session without even saying goodbye. It was only a couple of days later that he was killed in an air crash, at the age of thirty-six.

There is no doubt that it was Otto Klemperer who really set the seal of success on Philharmonia. A German who had conducted (opera for the most part) in Prague, Hamburg and Cologne, Berlin and Los Angeles, he came to the orchestra as principal conductor in 1959, when he was already an old man in his late seventies, severely handicapped and without full movement or speech. Legge didn't seem to want him as an opera conductor at all – he was to be the great Beethoven conductor, with quite a bit on Mahler and some Wagner but with the nine Beethoven Symphonies as his great achievement. It worked. In a few years he was regarded as the greatest world authority on these works, and was made principal conductor for life. When in 1964 Walter Legge decided to disband the orchestra, because he felt it couldn't face the commercial opposition in London and maintain its standard, Klemperer was still its main moving force in artistic direction. Perhaps to Legge's surprise, the orchestra did not disband. Instead it became self-governing, the third to do so in London, and became for a time the New Philharmonia Orchestra. It was under that title that it gave its first public concert in March 1964, with Klemperer still its conductor.

We will see what happened to Philharmonia later – but for the present I'd like to take a look at how the *fourth* member of our happy band of self-governing organizations, the RPO, came into being. The RPO had in fact just arrived as a self-governing orchestra a year before Philharmonia, in 1963, but its history from 1946 to that date is a fascinating one, and Beecham's longest association with any orchestra in the world.

8

The Royal Philharmonic Orchestra

I recall the day well; it was a Sunday afternoon in late September 1946, and I was home at last in Norbury after leaving the RAF. For some reason the radio had been left playing quite loudly and crossing the room to turn it down I was suddenly halted in mid-stride by the incredible sound which came from it. It was Sibelius' *Tapiola* – and I had not heard such playing anywhere for some years. The wild winds of the northern forests of Finland were screaming through the rent pinewoods, wolves were howling in the dark depths, and Tappio, the god of all this, was on the rampage. I called to my wife, Joan, 'It sounds to me as if Beecham is back. Have you got the *Radio Times* handy?' She had, and it confirmed my diagnosis. This was in fact the *second* concert of Beecham's new Royal Philharmonic Orchestra, playing at the Davis Theatre, Croydon – a huge cinema which could stage this sort of programme adequately when not showing films. Not being a professional player at the time, I had missed the first concert, two weeks earlier, but was now able to catch up with the details of the new orchestra. Not unnaturally, the personnel was the result of a great deal of pilfering. Key players had been borrowed or stolen from several other orchestras, some of them permanently, like the oboeist Peter Newbury from the LPO and the excellent trumpet player Richard Walton who was still the property of the Brigade of Guards. Others simply played when they could, and then disappeared again into the Philharmonia Orchestra: Reginald Kell the clarinetist, James Bradshaw the tympanist and Dennis Brain, who somehow managed to sustain the activities of first horn in both orchestras for three years. The strings were a little less star-studded, but with Beecham in front and some very skilful leading in all sections they somehow became most convincing. The concert master was John Pennington, erstwhile leader of the London Quartet and later of several American orchestras which Beecham had conducted. Raymond Clark led the cellos, John Sylvester the basses, and both were among the world's greatest. It was further back in the sections that weakness showed itself, because there just wasn't a sufficient number of first-class players in London not tied down by other orchestras. As Beecham said to me at our first meeting, nine months later, 'I can assure you that in London we still have a few – a very few – people who can play wind instruments with real skill and artistry; but the Decline and Fall of string playing since I last visited these shores has to be heard to be believed.' He was right then. Today is another matter.

Obviously Beecham saw trouble ahead, because you can't have a world-beating orchestra without excellent back-desk strings, and he simply didn't have them, however good he may have made the string section sound. It didn't seem to bother him; he knew he would have one of the world's greatest orchestras before long – an orchestra which would well merit the title Royal which King George VI had himself approved a year earlier. Meanwhile he continued to use borrowed 'stars' as his key players, and to hypnotise some of the weaker string players into thinking they were all Heifetz's star pupils. With this orchestra he took on, successfully, the concerts of the Royal Philharmonic Society, possibly the most prestigious of all; he also landed in 1946 a huge recording contract with Victor Records of the USA, the parent company of EMI in Britain.

Without doubt, a key factor in the establishment of the Royal Philharmonic was the long series of sessions in October and November 1946 for recordings for the Delius Society. Beecham was the most powerful force in the world for the realization of the music of this strangely uneven but fascinating composer. He had established a firm foundation for his music in prewar days with the LPO, and now he set about consolidating this with his new RPO. As it happened, he was about two years too early. In 1946 recording technique was still 'prewar', or even identical to what had been established in 1930. It was still necessary to limit 'takes' to a maximum of four and a half minutes, and recording was still done on flat discs of wax which could not be edited in any way. Soon there would be tape recordings, splice editing and the long-playing record, making those 1946 records obsolete. This didn't really matter to Beecham, whatever the Delius Society may later have thought. These recordings paid his players enough to make them identify with his new orchestra, welding them into a superb team (and, as a side issue, it gave Delius enthusiasts the sort of recorded performances they had always dreamt of; the fact that they had them all done again on LPs a few years later was merely a bonus!).

In spite of this success with the RPO, Beecham was soon to realize that permanently trying to use an orchestra which contained borrowed players was no way to succeed, and not to be tolerated. A bare nine months after he had started the new RPO he therefore decided to put it into a more permanent shape, with players who could be with him every day, and so make themselves into the team he needed for his special music-making. It seemed natural for him to start with the wind section, as this had been his pride and joy from his earliest days. Obviously he had no need to change the first flute, Gerald Jackson, who was devoted to him and his orchestra, being orchestral chairman and general spokesman. Gerry was an amiable man in his fifties, and a superb orchestral flautist as well as a natural section leader. He really wasn't a soloist in the international league, but his Bach playing was superb, and he played the odd Brandenburg Concerto better than anyone I know, although I don't think he took this too seriously: I once heard him chatting with the celebrated harpsichordist Thurston Dart as they came off the platform at the end of one such event, 'You know, Bob', he said, 'I enjoyed that. It's good to hear the old packet of pins again!' Bob Dart was not, I think, particularly amused.

So far as the oboe situation was concerned, Sir Thomas now saw his opportunity to enrol a new 'star' in the shape of Terence MacDonagh, who had just left the BBC Symphony and was exactly what the new RPO needed to give it international lustre. This didn't mean the loss of Peter Newbury, the original first oboe, as he was a superb cor anglais player, and simply moved his chair. The clarinet position was more difficult, because Reg Kell, so long Beecham's favourite player, was also principal of Philharmonia, and difficult to get to sign on the dotted line. It appears that Beecham, who had been entertaining him to a sumptuous dinner with just that thought in mind, finally realized this. 'Mr Kell,' he said gently, 'in all our dissertations on matters of artistic advantage and the furtherance of musical excellence, there appears to be a recurrent thread of enquiry on your part. It seems to be . . . "How much?" ' The whole point was that Kell found the recording sessions of Philharmonia more lucrative than the concert-giving which was at the time the bulk of the Royal Philharmonic calendar; and to ask him to forsake this meant that his concert fee was going to be prohibitive. Obviously, Sir Thomas had to find a suitable player who would make no such demand, in spite of his admiration for Kell's artistry. He had a choice of about six first-class players, all of whom would have been quite suitable and very happy to join. He asked none of them. Instead he found, how it is not certain, a young Croydon schoolmaster called Brymer, and made him a principal overnight. It needed courage – but then Sir Thomas was never short of that.

There remained one further problem – the bassoon situation. The famous Archie Camden, who had held this post since the orchestra was created, felt he wanted to devote himself more to solo and chamber-music playing. Archie was a wonderful man to play with, always secure and full of fun, and with a noble sound which made his instrument a most resonant orchestral solo voice. Certainly, he was difficult to replace, and so Beecham decided he wouldn't try. Instead he chose a bassoonist of an entirely different school of playing, Gwydion Brooke, who had been the second bassoonist of the LPO in the early 1930s as a very young man – an ex-student really – and a brilliant player who was now ready to become a star. Having spent the war in the African desert he had been completely out of touch with the bassoon, but was at the time regaining his formidable technique while playing in the Liverpool Philharmonic. The sad aspect of his arrival in the RPO was that he had high hopes of working with his brother-in-law, Reginald Kell, and he missed that delight by two weeks. The said two weeks, incidentally, represented the complete time required to accomplish all these changes, and when they had been made Beecham was left with what many people remember as the best-balanced and most interesting wind section he ever had. The four principals were all of widely different characters in any other aspect of life than music, but in our work we seemed to have complete unity of purpose and the instinct to play together. We were also supported by four sub-principals of equal stature: Clifford Seville on flute, oboeist Leonard Brain, the second clarinet Basil Tschaikov, and the remarkable second bassoon Edward Wilson, who could lay a foundation which was always easy to build upon, and if necessary do it *pianissimo* – a rare talent.

This new section was to be a very permanent feature of the

Royal Philharmonic and was one of the orchestra's main delights during the remaining fourteen years of Sir Thomas' life, the only change being the replacement about half-way through of Gerald Jackson by the virtuoso Geoffrey Gilbert. Obviously the wind section was the one which loomed largest in my life. So it did, I think, with Sir Thomas; but the reorganization of the other sections affected us all, and vitally.

There were changes in almost every section as time went by. The leadership changed several times, the next being a brilliant virtuoso, Oscar Lampe, quite forgotten by most people now, but able to play Strauss' *Heldenleben* with all the magic of a Heifetz. Then came David McCallum for possibly his longest period with a Beecham orchestra, with his superb 'Kreisler' tone and his friendly but firm direction, then Arthur Leavins, moving up from second chair without any obvious difficulty, very much to the satisfaction of Dr Artur Rodzinski, that terror of the New York Philharmonic when he was Toscanini's second-in-command, but a friendly figure to the RPO; finally, the young Rumanian/Canadian, Stephen Starek, one of the world's great violinists, under whose leadership the last days of Beecham were never to be forgotten. Each of these leaders brought a new sound to the string section. Other changes were made in almost every section, and the names which came and went in the strings, horns and brass were almost a *Who's Who* of the London orchestral world. These were fourteen great years, during which one of the world's finest orchestras grew and flourished.

Perhaps the only weakness of this orchestra was that while it could play better than any other for Beecham, it seemed to have less impetus with some of the other great conductors who took over when Sir Thomas was abroad paying off his income tax. I think some of them – Stokowski, Sargent, Boult, Celibidache and Basil Cameron – felt this very keenly; but there were others like Vittorio Gui, Fritz Busch, Artur Rodzinski and particularly Rudolf Kempe, who awakened the orchestra with their own special gifts, and got performances which were certainly not those of Beecham, but superb in their own way. During these vital years from 1948 to 1962, the RPO also learned to be a great opera orchestra, having gained a contract to play each summer from early May to mid-August with the Glyndebourne Opera, starting in 1949, where they accompanied most of the world's best singers and were part of productions many of which have gone down in history as of special significance. I think this also prepared them as did nothing else for the future, which would obviously have to be without Beecham, who was now ageing. It made them flexible and able to satisfy every demand, so that after that memorable last concert with Sir Thomas at the Guildhall in Portsmouth on 2 May 1960 they could look to the future with the hope that they could at any rate survive. Rudolf Kempe became chief conductor instead of associate, and George Prêtre, an interesting musician from Paris who had been a jazz trumpeter before becoming a talented conductor, was appointed as associate. Work went on as before; but within two years of Beecham's death in 1961 there were ominous signs of uncertainty in future plans.

Lord Boothby, who had been appointed chairman, wanted to gain for the RPO a tie-up with Covent Garden Opera, but this came to nothing. He was so disappointed that he resigned. Kempe also resigned in 1963, feeling that the RPO had no future. The Royal Philharmonic Society felt the same, and decided not to use the RPO for its concerts in 1963, and to cap it all, a series of concerts of the other three orchestras – LSO, LPO and Philharmonia – at the Royal Festival Hall excluded the RPO from its programme. It seemed that without Beecham the orchestra had no entity, and Glyndebourne, feeling this also, decided that the 1963 season was the last in which they would engage the RPO. It looked very much as if the orchestra had no future. It was obvious that some sort of New Deal was urgently required, and to that end the members of the orchestra got together with Shirley, Lady Beecham, the Anglo-American Associates and its directors to see if a solution could be found. It was then decided that the players themselves should take over the management, which they did, at first as Rophora Ltd, a limited liability company, and later as the Royal Philharmonic Ltd, with the usual early struggles but later conspicuous success.

So London's fourth self-governing orchestra was started, as proud of its roots as any other, and as certain of its worthiness for support – and with this event we come to the state of affairs which exists in London today.

9
'Where Are They Going Now?'

Continuing to survey the histories of the four self-governing orchestras gives us a vivid picture of the world of music as it is now. All of them have recently had to struggle for continued existence, and the Royal Philharmonic at times looked as if it could not survive. It says much for the RPO's management that they now seem to have an assured future, wholly due to their own resourcefulness, and are not only successful but also seriously overworked, with over 600 three-hour working sessions per year (a working session is a rehearsal, a concert or a recording). They take in their stride pop records, TV series, video recording, jingles for television advertisement, and films of every sort. Sponsorship has now reached half a million pounds per year and is rising. The orchestra tours widely, both abroad and in Britain – the foreign tours with little profit, but great prestige, offset by commercial work at home which pays well. They have what they call periods of residence in Nottingham, and special series of concerts in Cardiff and elsewhere where they feel they can set up a productive relationship with the local enthusiasts. Their timetable thus is quite a jigsaw puzzle, and the number of changes they have seen over the past twenty years or more is breathtaking.

Their first task upon taking up the reins of self-government was to see if it was possible to salvage the big tour of the USA planned by Anglo-American, the previous administrators. This was a gigantic undertaking – sixty-two days with fifty-two concerts from late September to early December 1963. Somehow it was brought off in triumph, conducted by Sir Malcolm Sargent and George Prêtre. The new RPO had arrived, directed by six of its players, headed by chairman James Brown, the first horn, and including, perhaps cunningly, Charles Gregory as general manager, also Beecham's first horn from the prewar LPO, and its chairman in the early days of self-government. They found life different upon their return to London, because by then the Royal Festival Hall, now thirteen years old, was showing its defects, and had to be closed for nine months for extensive alterations, including such refinements as a few dressing rooms and a buffet for the artists *behind* the platform (but no lockers, instrument racks or wardrobe accommodation, which luxuries are still denied to them).

A new venue had therefore to be found for concerts. The orchestra had started its life at the Davis Theatre in Croydon, a cinema. Again it was a cinema, the Odeon at Swiss Cottage, which became the home of the RPO and cooperated excellently in the venture, installing a removable apron extension to the stage and a large sound-reflector which acted as a counter-balance to all that absorbent foam-seating in front. Luckily, by this time, 1964, the Fairfield Hall in Croydon was also in action, and was a superb hall, with warm acoustics if somewhat dubious air-conditioning on the platform. It is not big enough to make a large-scale concert pay at reasonable prices, but has no other vices, which means that in any other country it would be an obvious choice for properly state-supported events. The RPO found it useful for repeat concerts which had been rehearsed and performed elsewhere, at a decent distance and therefore attracting a different audience.

There is no doubt about the very thorough way in which the new management set about their unfamiliar task. In the following three years they gave eighty-eight concerts at the Odeon alone, with thirty different conductors including Sir Charles Groves, Sir Adrian Boult, Sir Malcolm Sargent and a host of others. It was at this time that Lord Goodman's committee, set up by the Arts Council to look into the desirability of supporting all four of London's orchestras, came down firmly on the side of the orchestras. All should be retained and supported, and should receive adequate subsidies. The Royal Philharmonic Society, encouraged by this judgement, took back the RPO as the orchestra for their prestigious series. This was a triumph, because the society had previously been willing to talk only to Beecham – and the continued use of the Royal title by the orchestra seemed to depend to some extent upon this series. It was, however, the Queen herself who finally settled the point, by conferring on the orchestra in July 1966 the title 'Royal in its own right' – a unique honour which was quite incontestable. So the RPO had won its battle for survival. Kempe, impressed by all this, returned to the fold that year, to everyone's delight – but not for very long.

It was a sad blow when in 1975 he again resigned. He obviously had to do so. He died less than a year later. One wonders what changes in history there might have been had he lived another twenty-five years. Those of us who played for him – and I had done so in the late Beecham days – felt that in him there was a very distinct sort of magic seen only in a handful of the greatest conductors. He was a very special musician, a great student of any work he conducted, and capable of white-hot passionate renderings of well-known works which were a joy to every player in his orchestra. Unhappily it seemed to end there, because he radiated *forwards* only – from behind, his audiences were aware only of excellent music unfussily obtained. For them he was not a star conductor, and he certainly should have been. I firmly believe that after a few more years Kempe would have been almost unequalled in popular esteem. As it is he is forgotten by many music lovers.

After Kempe's death conductors have come and gone quite quickly. Antal Dorati was principal conductor from 1975 to 1979; Walter Weller took his place until 1985, when André Previn was appointed music director. I am certain André's work with them will be as happy as the eleven years he spent with the LSO – his first major appointment in a global sense – and that he will bring them all the benefits and advantages of association with a first-class musician in every sphere of music as well as a person of tremendous charisma with the media. Things, however, are by no means as simple as they were when the orchestra expected Beecham or Kempe to bring them fame and fortune. There are now just about as many conductor titles as there are days in a week. Antal Dorati is conductor laureate. Sir Yehudi Menuhin is president/associate conductor. Walter Weller is, or was, principal conductor while André was music director elect. Sir Charles Groves is associate conductor, and Yuri Temirkanov is principal guest conductor. We have entered the age of pluralism – anyone who can help an orchestra is roped in to do so. The need is dire enough, and the orchestra must be kept with its nose firmly pressed against the grindstone.

It is unnecessary to go into the detail of all the sponsorship which has also been required to keep the RPO alive up to the present. Suffice it to say that there are no less than thirty-one full corporate sponsor members, some of them of tremendous financial resource. The annual turnover is now about two and a half million pounds per year, and the RPO is proud that it was one of the earliest pioneers in attracting sponsorship, in 1966, with a scheme of 'Music and Exports' especially aimed at publicity for its sponsors on tours abroad. But it's an uphill business in any orchestra and one constantly hears discouraging statements from members of managements in the know, like 'One regional orchestra on the Continent gets more than the total amount granted to our four London orchestras' and 'the Vienna Opera alone gets more than the whole Arts Council Grant for everything, musical and dramatic, in the British Isles'. Like the other orchestras, however, the RPO has learned to live with it and survive. They have in fact found an answer to it. It's one I personally hate, as do most of the players – but it may prove to have been both necessary and a life-saver, so the managements seem to think it is reasonable. It's called *Hooked-On-Classics*. Without wishing to give this enterprise more publicity than it has already had, it might be worth describing it as seen from a seat of any orchestra taking part. (It would in fact be difficult to give it extra publicity now, since the orchestra have proudly announced the sale of ten million copies of this strange album, with a profit to the orchestra of well over £300,000.) Briefly, the idea is one used sixty-five years ago in the sheet-music world, then called a 'musical switch', and there were about ten versions, starting with a bit of *Pagliacci* which swerved into *Rule Britannia*, which gave way to *Aida*, only to be swamped a few bars later by *Colonel Bogey* and *William Tell*. This was great fun around the piano after tea. Not really what the composers meant, of course, but at least at that time not accompanied by an invariable, loud and extremely boring disco beat – the thing which turns it into *Hooked-On-Classics* and makes the millions. It's bad enough in the studio, but at least you can't hear that beat, which is relayed to the conductor only. At public performances, like the one at Luton football ground, it must be quite beyond bearing, even if it leaves a lovely warm feeling around the wallet. I suppose I am glad it has brought prosperity to one of my favourite orchestras – the very first I ever played with, and one with the happiest of memories. But I'm certainly glad it happened after my day, although I could be wrong to dismiss it out of hand. Maybe this is the only future for orchestras in our country, putting them in line with the decline and fall of most of our past successes and enterprises. None the less one must agree with André Previn when he was asked what he thought of this money-spinner: 'I'd be willing to visit them in prison,' he said.

So, we know the history of the LSO up to the start of their Barbican days, of the LPO up to their postwar re-start in 1947, of Philharmonia to their takeover of the reins in 1964, and of the RPO more or less to the present. We've seen how the RPO survives. What about the others? Is there really room on the London and provincial scene, eked out by foreign tours, to justify their existences? Incredibly, the answer seems to be yes, even though the small government support they receive means that they must work harder than they should, and often undertake work of a quality which may not be desirable. Neither factor seems to seriously affect their standard of playing. The best of their performances compare well with the greatest – and there are a lot of these good performances. It must be remembered that in the case of each of the four orchestras the full burden of the decision-making falls upon the board of directors, a group of unpaid individuals who are usually, apart from the managing director, very busily active players. The skill they all show in making such decisions is quite remarkable, and at times compares favourably with that of many highly experienced businessmen. In fact when professional business personnel are called in, it sometimes happens that irons have to be pulled out of the fire by their amateur colleagues on the board, because the music business is like no other business, and even those who have been in it for a lifetime can be surprised. The LSO's debut at the Barbican is a case in point.

It was in October 1982, and an eagerly awaited event. It had been an awfully long time a-coming, and although the orchestra knew that when it did finally arrive they were to be in residence, it seemed a far-off dream even as late as 1979. I can't be sure of when the session in question took place, but I recall wandering out in the interval while we were recording some Nielsen symphonies at the Church of St Giles in Cripplegate. I was with Tony Camden, the chairman of the LSO, and as we walked along the parapet of the artificial lake between the towering blocks of apartments which are now such an eyecatching feature (for good or ill) of the St Paul's district, we caught sight of what looked like a very deep opencast mine across the way. 'That's it,' said Tony. 'Before long we'll be living there. I wonder how we will breathe?' The question was fair enough, because the lowest level of the Barbican – and the orchestra lives just twenty feet above this – is slightly below the *bed* of the nearby Thames. The structure seemed to grow remarkably, and when, in 1982, the LSO moved in, there was much to commend the place. True, nobody could find it then. Happily they now can and do. There was, it seemed, no Artists' Entrance. Finally, after a couple of weeks, we discovered we could get backstage without going through part of the audience: you went to distant Car Park 5, in through a door marked Emergency Exit, down to Level 3 in a lift (which sometimes worked), down a further set of stairs, and in through a No Entry door. You were then in the quite luxurious backstage area, and everything was fine. The feeling of belonging was certainly a happy one, the acoustics, at first rather dry, were improved vastly by the removal of about three hundred huge goldfish bowls attached originally to the ceiling (supposedly there to improve the sound!), and before long even the temperature was under control.

The work was interesting, too. Plenty of rehearsal, some concerts repeated a day or two later, lunchtime concerts which were just as good as anything in the evening but only an hour in duration; and occasional quite informative lecture concerts which were intended to whet the appetite for what was to come next day. There were interesting series of concerts too, with contemporary or early twentieth-century music, and famous conductors coming to conduct their own special favourites. There were also lunchtime chamber concerts, with solo or ensemble playing in the foyer to greet the audience as they drank or bought their tickets. It was something the poor dreary old City had needed ever since the Fire.

Unfortunately, it was almost totally disastrous for the LSO. I was never a member of the board, and so am not privy to why this should have been so, although the pattern was clearly un-profitable. For some reason, audiences fell off after the initial novelty of the venue faded. It seems you can't really repeat concerts in the same hall in London, whatever you can do in Boston or elsewhere. Lecture concerts may be alright with recordings as examples; with an orchestra they are wildly expensive with virtually no revenue returns. Programmes which may be Heaven-sent to a minority and truly valuable artistically are often losers with the wider public. And so on. As a result, the contract which looked marvellous in 1981, when audiences at the Royal Festival Hall were well over ninety per cent, could not break even when added to the generous guarantee from the City of London Authority in 1983–4, because the attendances at the Barbican fell to a miserable sixty-five per cent. When to this loss was added the loss on a prestigious but under-supported world tour in 1983 (£57,000) an orchestra which had seemed to be prosperous and with every reason to look to the future with confidence suddenly found itself over £400,000 in the red.

It was obviously a serious crisis, and changes had to be made in the management, some of whom were non-players. It was then that the playing members took over sole control of the finances, headed by Tony Camden, the principal oboeist, and the man who was before long to become the managing director, Clive Gillinson. New plans were formulated including popularization of programmes at the Barbican which raised the attendance to eighty per cent. Other engagements were undertaken only when certain profit was involved, to help meet orchestral overheads. The orchestra was 'sold' to all sorts of organizations for concerts, tours, films and recordings, and commission charged as contractors. The Barbican assistance was changed from a guarantee to an outright grant which meant that it was possible for the orchestra to help meet its overheads while at the Barbican. The players were also called upon to assist, and in 1983 they all took out four-year covenants giving £10 per week from their pay to help towards paying off the huge deficit – a move which still earns, after the reclamation of tax, £60,000 per year for the LSO. Sponsorship was also rapidly built up in order to enable the orchestra to present its more presitigious concerts. A quite surprising success was the plan to bus in audiences by providing a free luxury coach to transport anyone who could fill it with ticket-buying customers. This has operated ever since 1983. With all these new projects it was found that quite ambitious artistic enterprises could be undertaken with confidence – and series like the Mahler, Vienna and Twentieth Century Festival in 1985–6 were artistically rewarding as well as a huge success in terms of attendance.

It was also found that series of budget concerts occasionally discovered less expensive artists of unexpected merit, and even the 'Summer Pops' series had one or two major surprises in this way, and brought a huge new audience. The whole project is big business, and the annual concert costs figures show dramatically that the way to success is expansion rather than 'drawing in the horns', provided the expansion is in the right direction and at the right pace. The total concert cost was £532,000 in 1983, and £1,108,000 in 1986, the former being a disaster and the latter a great success.

In addition to such obvious symphonic activities, the LSO, like the other London orchestras, undertakes recording work of all sorts, from a Richard Strauss cycle to a complete series of Mozart piano concertos; and in addition during the last ten years it has made a successful excursion into the pop world, with a series called 'Classic Rock' which was a best seller and paid substantial royalties to the company. Like the RPO, they found that symphonies alone would not pay the rent. All this means a very busy orchestra, and possibly a very tired orchestra, but it may well not mean a very rich orchestra so far as the individual player is concerned. No pay rise for self-promoted concerts was granted from 1983 to 1985. There is still the plain fact that concert work is by far the worst-paid sort of activity, because of the present method of payment which gives a free rehearsal for each concert, sometimes on the morning of the event, thus halving the rate per hour and doubling the expenses involved. This is something for future improvement, not least because it compares very poorly with what happens in the rest of the world. Certainly a big improvement in hourly concert rates would be a solution for every London orchestra. At present the players have to subsidize their concert work (which is usually also their principal objective in life) by undertaking other work which is better paid but of much less musical significance, such as the examples above.

As a result of the lack of sufficient public funding there is no doubt that London, one of the great music capitals of the world, is living dangerously. At present quite a number of the world's great artists continue to come here, despite earning lower fees than elsewhere. If in addition caution in programme planning means that the work they are required to do is less interesting, many of them will in the end stop coming.

The answer is sponsorship, either public or private, and if the state will not provide this, the responsible authorities must make it possible for others to do so. The present hand-to-mouth situation must stop, and the sponsors would certainly make sure it did if they were encouraged to do so. Tax-relief on sponsorship would be the answer. It has been in other countries, and could easily be so here. At present, organizations add their sponsorship total to their publicity expenses, which gains them relief from tax. No such relief is possible for the private individual, and this is in contrast with the many thousands of people who delight in being 'Friends of the Orchestra' abroad, particularly in the USA.

The cost would not be so great, and how can we expect anyone to give generously large sums of money upon which they have already paid tax? Artistic support could be made a legitimate business expense, and in the opinion of everyone who knows the true position, should be. It could be made conditional upon the money being spent with care and intelligence. As shown above, it is certainly now being so spent.

But now let's get back to the story of our four orchestras. The position of the other two orchestras at the present time is very much the same as the RPO and LSO. The Philharmonia carried on in its quite dignified way after it became self-governing in 1964, and to the end of Klemperer's life in 1973 they were inseparable. There was something touching about the performances they gave, especially the symphonies of Mahler and Beethoven because the conductor they loved and respected was by that time quite incapable of the physical aspect of his work. His intellect was still at its finest, and communication somehow was kept going in quite a magical way; but I can recall taking part in several performances in 1969 when one had to have great faith, and some in which guesswork was essential. None the less, the public loved the results, and many felt that these were truly great days. The orchestra did of course still find other work, and films as well as music of a lighter sort had always been their lot – scores like *Henry V* by Walton did in fact get into the concert repertoire quite quickly, and concert-orchestra scores by some of the best American composers were very much their métier. After Klemperer, life couldn't be quite the same for a long time, but the orchestra was fortunate in being able to associate with a succession of excellent conductors without settling with any one; Giulini, Maazel and Zubin Mehta were among them, and all of them gave most distinguished performances. In 1974 Riccardo Muti was appointed principal conductor, and a more settled and equally successful period followed, with Andrew Davis as associate before he took up his post as principal conductor to the Toronto Symphony Orchestra. It was in 1977 that the orchestra reverted to its original name, dropping the 'New', and about this time they seemed to have entered the hurly-burly which is London's orchestral scene, with accelerated schedules and big important foreign tours. In the 1984/5 season, for instance, they gave ninety-four concerts in London and out of town, mostly at the Royal Festival Hall, and spent fifty-five days abroad in tours which took them to Japan, Italy, France, West Germany and Scandinavia – a total of no less than 523 working sessions. In all this they have been helped greatly by generous private sponsorship, first by a large firm of cigarette manufacturers, and lately by the Japanese Nissan corporation. As a result, most of their work has been of a high quality, although despite this they have had to interest themselves in any sort of commercial work which helps to pay the rent, including film scores and quite a few pop backing sessions which would certainly have raised the blood pressure of their founder Walter Legge more than somewhat. Philharmonia remains, however, possibly the least overworked of the London quartet of self-governing orchestras and with their present conductor, Giuseppe Sinopoli, are going from strength to strength.

The most recent phase of the London Philharmonic Orchestra, since Beecham turned his back on it in 1946, has been one of steady achievement and solid concert-giving both in London and elsewhere, as well as a quite distinguished recording career. Generally, there has been a reluctance to appoint a permanent conductor – the Beecham experience taught them the unwisdom of doing that with a self-governing background – but in 1949–50 Eduard van Beinum was much in evidence, and did excellent work. From 1950 to 1957 Sir Adrian Boult was the chief conductor; and in 1963, when the orchestra took over from the RPO for the Glyndebourne Opera, John (now Sir John) Pritchard became their chosen maestro, until 1966. Glyndebourne has been a great support to the LPO for the last twenty-three years, and during that time they have played with a great many superb artists and many fine conductors. One of these has unquestionably been Bernard Haitink, who was their principal conductor during the period 1967–79. He was followed by Georg (now Sir Georg) Solti in 1979–83, and when he left for his present post in Chicago, Klaus Tennstedt was appointed as principal conductor, with Sir Georg Solti as conductor emeritus, and they face the future with confidence. Like the other three orchestras, however, they find it essential to make excursions into the lighter side of the musical world. In their case it is usually the world of films, and not always in the studio. Often many of them can be seen as well as heard in concert, playing music from some of the epics of the silver screen, when they are heralded under the rather unusual and fairly painful title of the 'Film-harmonic' Orchestra. Like their friends of the RPO, LSO and Philharmonia they do have to work unduly hard, their session total for the past year being 573 with forty-eight days spent on tour. If I have spent less time on the recent activities of the LPO than upon those of the RPO and LSO, it is not because I have any less regard or affection for them. It is simply that I have been less frequently involved in their everyday music-making.

Perhaps it is reasonable, before trying to contrast the activities of the four London orchestras with those of orchestras abroad, to make brief comparison of their lot with the contract orchestras to be found in their own city – BBC Symphony and Royal Opera House. Certainly the posts to be obtained in these are of a very different nature, and are in some ways more attractive than life in the busy and highly competitive world outside. Many of us have experienced both sorts of activity, and some have very strong preference one way or the other. My own feelings have always been with the freelance orchestras, but the nine years I spent in the BBC Symphony were not without their moments of consolation. First, one could quite often choose the programmes one would like to play, or the conductors whose approach was empathetic, and leave the rest to one's fellow-principal. This was not, of course, applicable to the whole orchestra, but I believe it still applies to quite a few players in both the BBC and at Covent Garden Opera. The consolation is that if this is done the salary continues, whereas with a freelance orchestra it is a question of 'blood or money'. Also, the number of appearances one makes is incredibly smaller than with one of the other major orchestras, usually about eight per week, which is possibly half or less than 'on the outside'. There is the disadvantage that the salary may be smaller than it could be with the overwork to be found elsewhere, but life is certainly calmer. Furthermore, activities are now moving away from the hitherto quite claustrophobic studio activities of the past, to frequent foreign tours, longer Promenade sessions at the Royal

Albert Hall, and visits to various festivals in Britain including that at Edinburgh, which is always a pleasure. Naturally, a lot depends upon the resident conductor, and in the fifty-six years of its life, the BBC Symphony has had just nine: Sir Adrian Boult (1930–50), Sir Malcolm Sargent (1950–7), Rudolf Schwartz (1957–62), Antal Dorati (1963–6), Sir Colin Davis (1967–71), Pierre Boulez (1971–5), Rudolf Kempe (1975–6), Gennadi Rozhdestvensky (1978–81) and Sir John Pritchard, since 1982. Having played for every one of these and found them varying from bearable to decidingly pleasant and inspiring, one can honestly say that the job should be one to covet. Somehow I never found it so. Possibly it was having to occupy the same seat in the same airless studio, slightly underground and artificially lit, for so many days on end; maybe it was the choice of programmes, often of *avant-garde* music with so very many rehearsals and such a lack of job satisfaction at the end of it. Just as likely it was the feeling of being out of the mainstream of music, and the fact that at the end of any normal day one could never be sure if or when one's work would be heard by anyone. It was a job to do, rather than one to be proud of – for me, anyway; but I speak of fifteen years ago, and I have reason to believe things are much happier now.

The same sort of objections have been voiced by members of the orchestra at Covent Garden, as well as the same sort of appreciation of the advantages. In most ways these contract positions are nearer to their counterparts abroad, but as we shall see there is often an opulence on the other side of the fence which we can only envy and hope one day to emulate. I should like to make comparisons of these different orchestral lives now, and afterwards collect a few observations of the players themselves, including those in British orchestras not so far considered, but of vital importance to us all – the City of Birmingham Orchestra, the Hallé Orchestra, the Royal Liverpool Philharmonic and the excellent pair of orchestras still to be found, in spite of many difficulties, in Bournemouth. British orchestras have hard lives, but adventurous ones. They deserve to survive, and can do so if they are left alone to decide their future, but also given a little of the sort of help orchestras in other countries enjoy. This is essential if they are to cease to be dependent upon commercial activities which may dilute their artistic achievement – and writing in 1986/7 one finds a quite disturbing new element. Film work is declining seriously because costs are lower in Eastern Europe, and the recording business can best be described as volatile – the right sort of record, with a 'star' conductor like André Previn or Claudio Abbado, can be a great financial investment both for the recording company and the players involved; other records, possibly of equal virtue, may be a dead loss. Yes, there is no doubt that our orchestras need the sort of help others enjoy.

They have shown that they can pull through many difficulties, organizational and financial, and if they are given that help they will not fail to make excellent use of it. Let us see now how it is done in some other countries.

10
'They Have Much More, There'

We all know the generally accepted opinion of the veracity of statistics, of which it is said (a) 'There are lies, damned lies, and statistics', and (b) 'You can prove anything you wish to prove by statistics if you choose them with sufficient care'. How, then, can one arrive at an honest comparison of facts of life which may be closely related in spirit, but far-flung in geographical, human and financial factors? Orchestral lives in distant lands may look very like our own, sound very like ours, and contribute much the same to the world of art – but they are different. They are richer, poorer, busier or more leisurely, more or less satisfying as well as happier or more miserable; and a comparison certainly requires statistics – figures which must be checked, sifted and finally looked beyond if they are to give anything like a true basis of comparison. Conclusions must be equally carefully checked if they are to be of value, so before setting out to state them, we must examine carefully how they have been arrived at. Let us, as an example, compare the rewards of being a first-class orchestral player in London with those in a similar post in New York. Obviously one starts with the financial rewards, the generally accepted media of comparison. Before this is done, one must know something of the relative cost of living in each place. Recent experience suggests that there is not much to choose between living costs in the two cities. Food may be fractionally cheaper in the USA, travel less expensive. It seems possible that journeys to work are shorter in New York, because the Londoner loves his suburban garden and the New Yorker his Eastside apartment, and more players live near to the Lincoln Center than to the Barbican. Rents are prohibitive in both cities. All in all, there isn't a lot to choose between the two places so far as this sort of expense is concerned.

Having reached this conclusion, an examination of the rates of pay in the New York Philharmonic and the LSO (say a middle-desk string player who has been in the job ten years) shows that the New Yorker is earning per hour just *four* times as much as his

London counterpart. His gross pay per hour works out at £37.65 as against £10.56 in London. *Net* pay is what gives that quadruple ratio, because if travelling expenses and *travelling time* are taken into account, the rate becomes £28.78 in New York and £6.95 in London. You may well say that there is a catch in this somewhere, because just by looking at the London player and his family it is possible to see that they aren't so catastrophically deprived. That's because of the hours he works. I sometimes think the brochures of British orchestras should start with the catchphrase of many a corner grocery store 'Open all hours'. The London player actually works about twice as many hours as the New Yorker, and for this receives about half the money.

How are these figures arrived at? Are they trustworthy? I think it is important to stress that guesswork takes no part in the figures used in this chapter. The American Federation of Musicians is a most obliging body, and publishes financial details of the administration of every orchestra in the whole of the USA each year, with extrapolations of future years. A study of the two documents which contain these details – 'Wage Scales and Conditions in the Symphony Orchestras' (national and regional) enables one to compare their lifestyles with those of their colleagues – and also with those of orchestras of other nationalities. To keep the picture slightly clearer I have declared salaries and benefits in pounds sterling, usually at $1.5 to the pound or at current 1987 exchange rates for other currencies.

This is not the only source of information. All the major American, Australian, and European orchestras discussed have been contacted personally, and the figures supplied by their administrations quoted. Most of them have been remarkably helpful in this matter. Just a few, while wishing to discuss their artistic and social structures, are somewhat coy about financial disclosures. In these cases I have made this clear and drawn conclusions merely by external appearances or by conversations with my friends in their orchestras. I must stress that I do not try in Chapter 11 to throw light upon orchestras I don't know personally. This is a personal document as well as an analysis of cold facts.

The British orchestras need little analysis of this sort, since although the more distinguished members may be rather better paid than the rest, the vast bulk of the membership receives exactly the fees and works in the conditions laid down by the Musicians' Union, and such arrangements are known to every musician and by no means a secret from others.

I apologise if at this point a book which has been quite light-hearted in scanning orchestral life now comes down to earth and is serious, if only for a while. Orchestral players are just like that – flippant about some quite serious things, but quite firm in their opinions about fundamental facts of financial affairs. They take a fairly dim view of the sort of comparisons one can make between their own lot and that of people employed similarly elsewhere, and certainly a review of the hard facts of this aspect of their professional life can be most revealing.

Having amassed the facts, we are in a position to equate properly the lifestyles of the New Yorker, the Londoner and the Parisian with those of several others, at least as far as it is possible to equate lifestyles in different countries in any other job. First, the Londoner. A mean average of the work done by the four main orchestras suggests a working year of 629 sessions. Obviously these are not worked by every member of the orchestra. It is necessary to deduct ³⁄₅₂ of this total for the three paid holiday weeks, which reduces the total to 592, and by questioning most of those involved it seems that in addition most of them miss about a further twenty-five in a year (possibly from sheer exhaustion) leaving a final total of 567 sessions – and at three hours each (be it a rehearsal, a concert or a recording) this means 1,703 hours, excluding travelling time or breaks. The average total pay for all this works out at a gross £18,000 per annum including holiday pay, radio or TV relays, and with no allowance for expenses, which breaks down to an hourly *gross* pay of £10.56. If expenses are taken into account – not meals, but merely travel from suburb to centre, the cost of the 400 return journeys at £5 a time totals £2,000. If journey *time* is also taken into account at a base minimum of forty-five minutes each way, a further 600 hours is added to the total. Therefore 2,303 hours per annum, for a reduced salary of £16,000 makes the *net* hourly pay £6.95.

Now, moving on to New York. There, if you are at the top of the tree, you are a member of the Philharmonic – the only full-time orchestra they have. (The City Opera is quite a good job, but has a basic year of twenty-six weeks, and for sixty-nine players only.)

The New York Philharmonic has a full fifty-two week pay-year.

You work only forty-four, because there are eight weeks vacation at full pay. The guaranteed minimum salary increases every year, and in 1985/6 it was $48,000 plus radio relays to the value of about $3,795 – a total of $51,795. As the forty-four weeks worked have a maximum of eight appearances each, and as these appearances have a maximum duration of two and a half hours, the maximum annual hours worked equals 880; so, with a basic salary of $48,000, the hourly rate is $54.60, or £36.65. With expenses deducted for 352 appearances at $7.25 for travelling ($2,552) the salary is reduced to $49,243, and with the extra hours for the 200 or so journeys involved (say 300 hours) the total hours involved in work rises to 1,180. The net hourly rate is therefore $41.73, or £28.78 – against £6.95 in London. Perhaps even more interesting is that if you go to the trouble, as I have done, of collecting data from across the American continent and analysing it in the same way, the results are remarkably consistent. Leaving out the expense factor, hourly payments work out at: Boston Symphony, £34; Philadelphia, £33; Pittsburg, £31; Seattle (a forty-five week season), £21; St Louis, £33; Atlanta, £23; Baltimore, £23; Chicago Symphony, £33; Cleveland, £34; Los Angeles, £32. It is necessary to go well down into orchestras at a regional level, most of whom are part-time organizations, before anything like the London scale emerges. As a result, life in these orchestras is very different from anything we know in Britain, and one wonders if there is anything in common except dedication to the art, the repertoire, and the conductors, who are usually the same.

The vast difference is that all these American orchestras are salaried, with settled terms of contract, severely limiting the number of hours involved, whereas in Britain this is very much the exception. In Britain we are 'open all hours'. In recent years the LSO has played 629 sessions, the Royal Philharmonic over 700, Philharmonia 523, and the London Philharmonic 560 sessions. Not, you might think, the sort of workloads which leave time for anything else. Yet a considerable number of the players in each of these organizations can be found regularly at their professional duties, teaching at the many learned institutions in London for fees which would also be laughed at on the other side of the ocean. It is sometimes puzzling that they should do this. In the past, teaching seemed a good thing to have 'up your sleeve' when playing days ended – you could continue to teach as long as energy could be found (and for that job energy is certainly what is required). Now there are very few schools of music which allow this to happen. Orchestral playing life and teaching life are deemed to end together, which is where one discovers the next big advantage of living elsewhere – pension arrangements. In the USA these are really big benefits at retiring age, privately arranged with the player paying a proportion of the cost, but bringing lifelong pensions which seem astronomical in proportion to the outlay: £1,005 per month in Boston, £950 per month in Chicago, with totals per month of £690, £776 and £1,350 in Houston, Washington and New York respectively, assuming a membership of thirty years or more. Philadelphia is even richer in this respect, with £345 per month for every year of service with the orchestra, up to a maximum of £13,800 per year. London has smaller pension schemes, but only with the BBC Symphony and the Royal Opera House orchestras; the *ad hoc* nature of the work of the major orchestras makes even this impossible, because where pay is per concert and not as a salary, regular contributions cannot be deducted. Certainly the *richesse* of the American schemes is unknown here.

But, you may say, different nations have different values, and musicians in one land may expect to be on a different level from those in another. True, but it's an irony that not one in a hundred purchasers of a given record is aware of the incredible international links which exist between the people who can be heard making the sounds. Very often one buys a record made by people of different nations at different times, but put together and sold as one musical creation. And the rewards are different in each country. I don't mean cases like the award-winning film *Out of Africa* which has Oscars for the music (recorded in London) and the sound engineering (done 50:50 in London and the USA) – and uses my very own recording of the Mozart Clarinet Concerto as one of the emotional characters in the action. (It is a borrowing – or theft – which certainly happened without my knowledge, approval or financial betterment, but my name is used freely in the credits, and as the action involves listening to this record in 1913, played on a tin-horn gramophone of ancient lineage, it is a poor impression of my performance and hints at the fact that in 1985, the year of release, the old man could well be in his 105th year and so hardly worth asking to perform.) This is international effort indeed, but not quite the sort of collaboration I mean. I am thinking of the tapes which may well be recorded by a choir in Alabama in January, orchestrally over-dubbed in London in July, and have the star tenor soloist, a Golden Boy of a Hot Gospel group, added in Paris in November so that the record can be pressed, sleeved and marketed in time for the Christmas rush in the USA. This is by no means an enterprise which is restricted to the Bible Belt. Many a Pop favourite takes in a dozen destinations before it bursts upon an astonished world with its thirty-six-track digitally-modulated final product. Surprisingly, most of these hybrid productions seem to retain at least a modicum of consistency in style; but there can be exceptions. One of these happened in 1986 at a highly polished glossy new studio somewhere in Islington which is specially equipped for just this sort of musical junketing. This time we were recording a series of little-known Israeli melodies – very beautiful and quite unusual – which were being given the full treatment, with a British orchestra of forty-five, complete with two synthesizers and a motley collection of percussion, conducted by a *Canadian* specialist in this sort of music, in an arrangement by an *American*, who was in fact absent. The choir was also American, but to be added a month later. The soloist was *Israeli*, unseen by any of those involved and heard only if one wore headphones, as he was in another studio (a method used to achieve the remarkable separation which lets one accompany a quiet cor anglais solo with an octet of trombones playing as loud as they like, which is fairly *fortissimo*). The final international touch was given by the absent American arranger, who for some reason had a strong Iberian leaning in his orchestration. At times the accompaniment led one to believe that the soloist would turn out to be a flamenco celebrity, much nearer to Granada than Tel Aviv. It was too much for the first horn, who was very much involved, playing the main solo part. 'The trouble with this chap', he said, 'is that he doesn't know whether he's Carmen or Cohen!'

From this sort of close-knit cooperation it would seem clear that the world's orchestras contain very much the same sort of people working in very much the same way, however different national values may be. It certainly seems like that when you are taking part, with lots of good will all around, and quite delightful people in charge of the enterprise. With many of them one soon gets onto

top: Richard Straus *(left)* and Sir Thomas Beecham, 1947

bottom: The Wind Players of the Wigmore Ensemble, all of whom were principals with the RPO: Geoffrey Gilbert, Terence MacDonagh, Jack Brymer, Gwydion Brooke and Dennis Brain

top: Otto Klemperer, 1970

bottom: Sir John Barbirolli

top: When Pierre Monteux succeeded Josef Krips as Principal Conductor of the LSO in 1960 he was eighty-six. He insisted on a twenty-five year contract. He had also a long cherished ambition to become a fireman – the LSO obliged in both wishes!

bottom: Members of the RPO rehearse Handel's *Water Music* in the Thames, 10 July 1985: *(from left to right)* Peter Nutting (violin), Stephen Williams (double bass), Diana Carrington (viola), Joe Atkins (trumpet), David Herd (violin) and Gill White (violin)

top: The Hallé
Orchestra, 1911, with
Hans Richter

bottom: Berlin
Philharmonie, home of
the Berlin
Philharmonic
Orchestra

top: The Blossom Music Center, summer home of the Cleveland Orchestra

bottom: RLPO and Choir performing Elgar's *The Dream of Gerontius* in Liverpool's Anglican Cathedral

top: The LSO in Oman, 1986
bottom: On the move again!

top: Antal Dorati with the RPO, 1982

bottom: Andrew Davis conducting the Toronto Symphony, with pianist Ken Noda

top: Andre Previn *(left)* talking business with Ernest Fleischmann, Executive Director of the Los Angeles Philharmonic

bottom: Sir Yehudi Menuhin, President of the RPO, with Principal Guest Conductor, Yuri Temirkanov

first-name terms, and at times they seem so very much a part of the local scene that meeting them in their own setting seems anachronistic, or whatever the terms for geographical misplacement should be! They obviously are the same sort of people – but their rewards are different. Because of such international goings-on, there sometimes emerges just a touch of asperity between the members of the orchestras of the nations involved. Obviously there is a good reason for dodging about from place to place, gathering honey for an album as one goes. It is not only a pleasant way of life; it can be selective of the best there is on offer – and it can also be *much* cheaper. It therefore seems to the New York freelance studio player that he is being done out of a job when the 'backing' is recorded in London, Paris or Amsterdam, just as it seems a swindle to the Londoner who has being doing this for years and paid his mortgage out of it, when he finds that the centre of activity is now Prague. Unhappily such activities are a fairly essential part of the schedule of our London orchestras as well as their many freelance colleagues, because while the latter depend upon them to pay the rent, the former need them to subsidize their more seriously artistic projects, like the 200 concerts some London orchestras give each year. These cannot pay their way, and the deficit is covered by less serious activities.

A comparison with the USA also reveals a shortfall in every other humane consideration. Sick leave, non-existent except for small Benevolent Fund payments in London, is established at 365 days per year in Boston with hospital expenses paid, although in Chicago and Cleveland the player pays twenty per cent of medical bills, and in New York only 120 days per year are paid. There is also a fine incremental scale in the USA for years of service: in Boston £10 per week for every five years of service, in Chicago £15 per week for the same, and similarly in Cleveland and Philadelphia. This leads to a marked loyalty to the orchestra in the USA so that the average years of service, when examined at any time, add up to an impressive total: thirteen years in Baltimore, seventeen years in Boston, fifteen in Denver, sixteen in Detroit, fifteen in Los Angeles, fourteen in Washington, seventeen in New York and a full eighteen in Philadelphia. Obviously there is great security of tenure of office and therefore a continuity of personnel which inevitably leads to a marked individuality of orchestral style.

It is difficult to obtain figures of this sort from some of the big European orchestras, and conditions are in any case so different in opera orchestras from those which apply to symphonic activity that equation is impossible – and in the case of the Vienna Philharmonic we have an orchestra which has a world reputation in both fields, symphonic and operatic. Certainly continuity of employment is one of the most important factors in all European orchestras of any repute, and contact with both players and managers suggests that while the players may not be in the very top earning bracket of professional personnel in a national business sense, they are about as well-off as their American counterparts and also have working conditions of the same spacious and deliberately paced pattern. There is another quite charming aspect in many German and Austrian centres, particularly in Vienna. The distinguished player is deemed to be the sole possessor of his orchestral post until he wishes to relinquish it and devote himself to preparing the artists of the future, by teaching. When this day arrives it is a surprise to nobody, and causes few ripples, because his very finest pupil has been co-opted for a couple of years quietly to sit in and assimilate the duties. He is ready to take over smoothly, and expertly, and will do so under the indulgent eye of his mentor. An incestuous practice? Maybe, not least because it is possible to miss the odd errant genius in this way; but it seems to work pretty well, for them.

This does not happen in all orchestras, even on the Continent. Berlin is another matter, as is Paris, and there have been some hectic rows in both during the past few years over the replacement of key players. It is a subject over which conductor and orchestra may well disagree; and in these days, when many orchestras insist upon deciding their own destiny, it can lead to the resignation or replacement of the maestro in question almost as often as that of the unwanted player.

So, having taken a quick look at conditions in a few major orchestras, perhaps we should now look at their organization in greater detail, because although there are many similarities each one is very much an individual, living creation. This is not intended in any way to be a comprehensive catalogue of the history and achievements of the world's orchestras. There are many gaps, because it is my intention to limit the review to those orchestras I have met personally and can claim to understand not only on paper, but as people. I apologise for the fact that they are not geographically or alphabetically arranged. This is intentional and the order is not simply a random one. I find it instructive to flit from country to country in this fashion, because doing so emphasizes the remarkable diversity of conditions and the resulting lifestyles, so strongly contrasted in orchestral posts which are on the face of it so similar in importance and achievement. Comparisons can be made of finance, history, leisure time and artistic satisfaction, and these prove to be much more varied than they seem from a seat in the stalls. A real attempt has been made at accuracy, and all figures relate to the season 1986/7 except where stated otherwise, when extrapolation is attempted up to the present day. The order in which I have reviewed the orchestras can easily be seen from the contents page at the beginning of this book. It is a short list, but not, I hope, too short to reveal some interesting facts. I have attempted mere thumbnail sketches of orchestras about which large books can be or have been written. I think the intimate details of their organization shown in Chapter 11 may give you a glimpse not only of remarkable diversity, but also a marked consensus of outlook, as well as a similarity of ideals and solutions to problems.

11
'Some Do It Better Than Others'

The Boston Symphony Orchestra is a typical example of a American phenomenon – a large-scale artistic enterprise which i unique in the big city which supports it, and one which seems t inspire the sort of warm partisan loyalty one might expect in much smaller and more parochial context. To be a true Bostonia is to be a fan of the Symphony, to know its members and thei activities, and to take much more than a passive interest in seein that these are safeguarded. It is very much a large family affair and one which occupies its devotees the year round. The reason fo this is that when the dazzling days of the Winter Symphony seaso are over, the summer brings the Boston Pops, still in the sam rather remarkable Symphony Hall, but in a new guise, with th audience seated at tables for five (!), all able to face the orchestr while eating and drinking – usually a terrible-looking purpl beverage called Pops' Punch. To try to present these concerts 'o the air', as I have done, is a very testing experience. Crashin crockery and tinkling cutlery are a constant accompaniment to th quietest *Adagio*, and in the more rhythmic passages there is ver often quite a lot of clapping and not a little singing. Incredibly, i seems that many of those involved, both on stage and in th audience, are the same people who sit in adoring silence throug the most austere symphonic programmes during the Winte Season. At the Pops they *relax*.

This has been going on for a very long time, and the traditions i embraced have been handed down over many generations because this orchestra dates from 1881, and it has been in thi same wonderful hall since 1900. It is a hall the players believe i and enjoy to the full; and certainly in my own experience it i among the two or three finest in the world. It presents externally a grey, rather dowdy surface, and even internally it seems un remarkable until you play, when suddenly it comes to life.

In 1881 it was a Civil War veteran called Major Henry Le Higginson, a New Yorker, who painstakingly put together a orchestra and engaged a conductor called Georg Henschel, thirty-one years of age, to give the first concert. It was an act of courage, because the ground in which he sowed this seed could well have been barren. The early Puritans did little to cultivate music apart from psalmody, and even the Musical Institute of Boston, founded in 1837, supported only amateur music-making. As late as 1866 the Harvard Musical Association was still struggling to start a series of orchestral concerts. There were fifty players, and for five years they continued to struggle, but without success, probably because of the severity of their repertoire which gave rise to a popular saying 'dull as a symphony concert'.* Higginson changed all this. He had studied music in Vienna as a young man, and determined to bring its delights to his home town when the war was over and he was settled down as a banker there. He found seventy musicians, not all local players, and engaged them for no less than twenty concerts. He opened rehearsals to the public, and the local people found a new fascination in seeing music grow and blossom under their very eyes. Soon they were addicts – and the growth has gone on ever since. Conductors have come and gone, leaving their marks upon the programmes and the players. The orchestra has stayed – and so have the audiences. Georg Henschel conducted during 1881–4, Wilhelm Gericke during 1884–9, the redoubtable Arthur Nikisch 1889–93, Emil Paur during 1894–8, when Gericke returned until 1906, and Karl Muck took over. A notable period was 1919–24, with a youngish Pierre Monteux on the rostrum, and some very exciting ballet scores by Stravinsky and others given their American premieres. In 1924 possibly the most important conductor in the final development of the Boston Symphony took over. He was Serge Koussevitsky, and under his baton the orchestra became world famous. He certainly had tremendous energy, and though some of the local subscribers seem to recall the work of Karl Muck as being incomparable, most of the musical world have come to regard the rise to world status of the Boston Symphony Orchestra in the thirties and forties as his work. In 1949 Charles Munch took over, and he was able to sustain this intensity until 1962, by which time the Boston Symphony was established on very much the basis we find it today.

* M. A. DeWolfe Howe, *The Boston Symphony 1881–1931*, Riverside Press

Meanwhile the Pops had continued to be a most attractiv 'other end' of the market. Started in 1885, they soon established traditions of their own, and in spite of a determined 'popular' bia they soon began to include music from the winter seasons repertoire, with success. The conductor who firmly put his marl on this series was Arthur Fiedler – through radio, TV and som tours he made the Pops world famous. In all he was in charge fo fifty years, from 1930 to 1980, when John Williams, composer o *Star Wars* fame, took over, and he has continued the tradition witl conspicuous success. It all adds up to a very busy life, even thougl the principal players are normally excused the Pops – because tha simply means that they take part in the activities of the Bostoı Symphony Chamber Players, formed in 1962.

In addition to all this (as if it were not enough), there is a *mélang* of activities for most of the players at the other end of Massa chusetts at Tanglewood, which is the name given to the Berkshir Festival. This festival is completely owned and operated by th orchestra, and started as long ago as 1934. It now takes in eight ful weekends in the summer in ideal country-life conditions, starting in July. At first the only concert venue was a large tent, but in 193 this became flooded, with disastrous results. The new plan, for aı open-sided auditorium where music can be heard by thousand sitting on well-kept lawns given decent weather – a project knowı to one and all as 'The Shed' – cost in 1938 a little short of $100,000 but since then it has become a place of pilgrimage to millions o concert-goers. Here one can hear some of the finest symphoni performances in very happy conditions. Close by, in the Berkshir Music Center, chamber music of the highest quality is a pre occupation. This was Koussevitsky's pride and joy, and to attrac students there are professors probably unequalled anywhere – conductors like Bernstein, Maazel, Mehta and Ozawa, composers like Copland and Gunther Schuller, and some of the finest sol instrumentalists the world can produce. There is very much a family feeling there. Speaking to Armando Gittala, the famou first trumpet player of the Boston Symphony, one can detect a deep pride in the work there. 'One of the warmest sights on a Sunday evening,' he says, 'is seeing the BSO players, who have already performed that afternoon, going back to Tanglewood iı the evening to hear the students play.' The orchestra feels, in fact that it serves the community; and certainly that community supports the orchestra. As one of these supporters says, 'It is a home team – and we're proud of it!'

The present conductor-in-chief of all this activity is Seiji Ozawa, and he enters into the manifold duties with conspicuous success. He has greatly expanded the repertoire, taken risks and won through. He is the thirteenth conductor to hold this post, has now survived fourteen years, since 1973, and seems to have an ongoing contract for any period he cares to name.

In all, the orchestra now presents 250 concerts annually, with audiences totalling one and a half million. The annual budget was more than £20 million in 1986/7, drawing upon federal and state government grants as well as sponsorship by many business foundations and generous individual supporters. It is certainly a fine and permanent orchestra, and can afford to shrug off any temporary setback such as the unexpected deficit in 1985 of $4.5 million; the hard work of many volunteers and staff plus large annual gifts and revenues from fund-raising projects more than covered this. The market value of endowment funds rose from $11 million in 1972 to $34.5 million in 1985, due to generous donor response and investment performance. They are, it must be said, not satisfied to let things stay like this – they are engaged in an ongoing campaign to find even greater sponsorship.

From conversations with several principal members there seems to be no doubt that the Boston Symphony is a remarkably happy orchestra. This is reflected in the exceptionally small turnover in personnel, which shows an average of only 3.3 per year over the past six years, and almost all of this due to age or ill-health. The Boston Symphony directors certainly know how to run an orchestra, and the bare bones of the work schedule is an indicator to the background of their success. Here are a few facts: eight appearances per week, with a fifty-two-week salary year and a mandatory free day in each week; eight weeks of vacation during the year, on full pay. Solo appearances are allowed during these weeks, but other orchestral or casual work is forbidden; additional leave of absence of four weeks per year as an entitlement, by arrangement, without pay. Extra services may be offered to players by the orchestra at special rates, but never involving more than five consecutive evening performances. 'Mileage' money is paid for any distance over ten miles, at $1 for every four miles (one way). Touring is on a different scale, with only five services per week; after five such consecutive days of service, there must be two consecutive free days. The annual salary is $45,760 minimum, with a bonus for Tanglewood concerts totalling $4,375 in 1985/6, and a seniority recognition of $10 per week for each five years of service.

One delightful agreement, seen from London, is that which stipulates the free days mandatory at the end of a tour. For a nineteen-day tour this is three days; for a twenty-six-day tour, four days. It contrasts nicely with the experience of the LSO, who returned very early one morning from an Italian tour in 1984 and were in the recording studios in London from 2 pm until 10 pm. Then, because some of them refused to play another session finishing after midnight, there was some quite bad blood (ironically, with the Boston Pops' own conductor). A simple guaranteed arrangement such as is to be found in Boston would have saved all this. Sadly, because they need such work for survival, the LSO could never afford one.

The Boston Symphony is obviously very much a going concern, and going in the right direction. It has many interested helpers hard at work, in addition to its numerous sponsors, both corporate and private. The Board of Trustees numbers twenty-five, with an additional eleven as emeriti. There are eighty-seven 'overseers' with such exotic posts as financial analyst and print production coordinator with a total administration staff of twenty. Their president's quoted epigram is 'In a world of economic uncertainty we need courage to insist upon the highest artistic ideals'. I think they live up to it.

The Berlin Philharmonic Orchestra is an organization which most people approach with awe; and rightly so, with its ancient and admirable record of achievement. Possibly nowadays there are other feelings mixed with this: of sympathy, possibly a touch of envy and just a hint of both perplexity and frustration. This mixture arises from the fact that the whole situation in Berlin is complex and even confused, now that it is only half a city pretending to be a complete entity. The fact is that most other orchestras as old as this one (it is over 100 years old) have a long and continuous line of development and history. This could not be so in Berlin, because everything there is split into prewar and postwar, and the orchestra is no exception. In the band-room of their concert hall, the splendid new Philharmonie, the players can see pictures and read about the orchestra as it was in the great days of Joachim or Nikisch, and feel a connection between what was and what is. But they are now in a different band-room in a different hall, and somewhere along the line the thread was broken.

The Philharmonie is certainly among the world's finest concert halls, and has been copied in scaled-down or modified form in the creation of many excellent halls including those in Toronto and Cardiff. You know as soon as you enter it that everything is in the right place and has a purpose. You find yourself in your correct seat without confusion or effort. When you have done so, you are quite near to the platform, wherever you have booked. You may be behind the basses when you would prefer to be watching the pianist's fingers, or facing the conductor when you want to check upon the leader's use of the fifth position, but that is the worst that can happen. You can always hear, and the sound comes to you in surprisingly good balance and perspective in spite of your rather odd angle of eavesdropping; even a full blast of eight horns pointing straight at you is somehow pinned to the floor instead of smiting your eardrums, by a subtle elevation of the seats which face their rear-pointing bells.

The band-room, flanked by many sumptuous dressing rooms with the bathrooms *en suite*, is approached from the spacious and magnificently carpeted lounge-corridor bar behind the platform, but isolated and soundproofed from it. There are so many advantages that they are difficult to list – fresh air and daylight, with a multiplicity of shelves for the storage of instrument-cases, instead of the usual clutter-up of chairs, which can therefore never be put to their proper use. There are also quite a few tables for drinks, and several of them are cloth-covered for card-players, which acknowledges that there may be some periods of leisure for this very favoured orchestra. The room is adorned with many pictures, some of them photographs of the past glories of the Berlin Philharmonic, from the days of Joachim, Nikisch and Furt-wängler, who held the post of principal conductor during the transition from the old Berlin to the new, and was with them almost continuously from 1932 until he died in 1954.

The orchestra was, from the start, a self-governing organiz-ation. It began in 1882, but as early as 1868 there had been a collection of players called Bilse's Orchestra, headed by Benjamin Bilse, a despot but a fine musician. These players started the Berlin Philharmonic. In 1882, after a disagreement, all fifty-four members left Bilse's employ, and started Germany's first self-governing orchestra. Like the LSO a score of years later, they founded a limited liability company, became shareholders, and engaged their own conductors. They did well, choosing Joachim, Wiellner and Klendworth, who shaped them well and spread their fame abroad; but it was Nikisch, in 1895, who proved to be the real genius of their development, and with Hans von Bulow as an occasional visitor he brought them inspiration, training and discipline, so that when he died in 1922 he left one of the world's great orchestras. There followed ten years without a permanent director, after which came Furtwängler's long reign, from 1932 until his death in 1954. So this fine orchestra had only a handful of conductors, most of them of the very highest quality, right from 1882 to 1954.

There are those who raise an eyebrow at the mention of Furtwängler's name because he was in control of Germany's finest orchestra during the long period of Nazi rule. This is unfair to his memory, because although he never set himself up as an active anti-Nazi, and suffered very little at their hands in comparison with so many others, there is no evidence that he was ever one of their number. Dr Berta Geissmar, in her book *The Baton and the Jackboot*,* is emphatic in her support for him. She was his administrative assistant at the time, before herself suffering exile, when she took up a similar post in London with Beecham. She recounts how in 1934 he resigned in protest at the political pressure applied to the orchestra, and was thereafter forbidden to leave Germany for two years, during which time he worked little. It was a sad period for the Berlin Philharmonic. Later he had what seems to have been a stand-up shouting interview with Hitler on their behalf, after which he was more or less unmolested and able to sustain the work of the orchestra through the difficult years which followed. There was compulsory 'Aryanization' of the orchestra, but according to Dr Geissmar it remained one of the few which had no Nazi 'cell' and one unwary member who turned up in party uniform was ejected. At the same time it was obvious that

* Hamish Hamilton, 1944

financial support could only come from the ruling clique, and the Berlin Philharmonic was part of the propaganda machine. I remember the feeling in 1934 when they came to London with Furtwängler, with a police cordon around Queen's Hall lending an incongruous note to the visit. The London audience felt this, but warmed instantly to their superb music-making. All this political pressure was difficult for the orchestra as well as their conductor, and the visit was never to be repeated. In 1939 they planned to come to London again, but events by that time forced an inevitable cancellation. It was only in 1946 that we in London became aware again of their activities, by which time the entire set-up was changed, and the modern period of the Berlin Philharmonic began, to be brought to a climax by their residence in their brand-new Philharmonie in 1963.

Playing in Berlin now, in their superb hall, one is constantly reminded of these historical facts. It is quite close to the Berlin Wall, and the ghosts of that old orchestra cannot be felt in the Philharmonie. As a result, there is something disappointing about the experience at a personal level, and one wonders if maybe their own players feel this too. Certainly their attitude is markedly different from those who went before. Even in 1936 the visit of the London Philharmonic Orchestra to Berlin made their old hall into a festival focus for a while. The whole Berlin orchestra turned out to hear the rehearsal, and this was anything but a Nazi gesture, as was proven after the concert, when they had a typical German *bier-abend* at the hall, and only musicians could attend. The proceedings lasted well into the night, and the climax was a Beecham tap dance on the table-top following a song by the maestro himself and a few of his inimitable stories. Now it is different. Although there is nothing else of this magnitude in Berlin, and the Philharmonie is the musical centre of the city, it is no longer a social centre in the way it was. During all the visits I have made, I have never once met a member of the Berlin Philharmonic at the Philharmonie. I know many of them, and meet them with delight, both abroad and in other parts of Berlin – but they are now the *world's* musicians, not those of the Philharmonie. Their working conditions are wonderfully comfortable, superbly efficient, intensely attractive, but vaguely hectic. Salaries, pensions and vacation arrangements compare with anything to be found in the USA, but they are not the Berlin

Philharmonic of the old days, nor do they wish they were.

This is not to say that what they are doing is less prestigious or less important. During the past thirty-three years Karajan has been principal conductor, and he and Celibidache, the resident conductor, have taken advantage of the rich subsidy provided by the West Berlin Senate and produced adventurous programmes of a well-prepared and carefully nurtured character. The sweet smell of success is everywhere, the talent prodigious, and the luxury inescapable; but under it there is a current of discontent which has made international news in even the serious papers. There was an incident in 1984 in which Karajan insisted upon the engagement of a player who was rejected by the orchestra, causing a serious rift between conductor and orchestra. Later, in 1986, exactly the reverse was the case, when the players voted 74 to 25 to get rid of the first horn player, because of his bad behaviour and even violence. He took them all, including the West Berlin Senate, to court, and he won. The amazing fact is that although relations between conductor, intendant and orchestra are at a very low ebb, they all want to get rid of the erring Seifert. He is staying – and playing, it seems, better than ever in 1987 which is what makes his position impregnable.

This is indeed a sad state of affairs, but it does sum up rather well the atmosphere in which music is made in West Berlin today. The Philharmonie is a wonderful hall, but it is of the present, not the past, and even their famous Dahlem Church, which is the delight of all recording engineers and the joy of those who buy the compact discs which are produced there, is a disappointment. It is on the fringe of the city, red-brick built, light and airy, spanking-new and smart as new paint – but entirely without atmosphere. It is the exact opposite of that other superbly acoustic venue in Paris, the dirty and disreputable ex-skating-rink, the Salle Wagram. They both just happen to *work*, in a technological age. I wonder if perhaps a mixture of the methods of Parisian and Berliner music-making could not be something rather special? Orchestras are all different, and not only different because of people. Places also have their effects, and Berlin shows that very clearly. The orchestra, with its ancient roots now merely in history books, is very much of today, and of the new Berlin.

The Vienna Philharmonic, one of Europe's most distinguished, was really born in 1842, when the orchestral personnel of the Imperial Court Opera Theatre gave their first symphony concert under the direction of the opera conductor Otto Nicolai. This connection with opera is interesting, because to this day the musicians are engaged by the Vienna State Opera which governs their salaries, contracts and pensions. They arrived in a city already catered for in concert halls, with the old *Konzerthaus* and its smaller *Mozartsaal* attached giving a flexible range of seating capacity. It was in 1870 that they moved to their new and permanent home, the *Musikverein* in the main hall of the building of the *Gesellschaft der Musikfreunde* (Society of the Friends of Music), with regular 'Philharmonic Subscription Concerts'. This is a breathtakingly fine hall, acoustically perfect and comfortable in every way – except possibly the strain of seeing all those human figures with arms raised permanently, supporting the balcony which is attached to side and back walls, an unusual feature of the design of the hall but not really its best.

The Vienna Philharmonic are certainly extremely lucky to play there, and they know it. Certainly in recent years we visitors seemed to have played in the *Musikverein* rather less than in the *Konzerthaus*, but possibly that is because the Vienna orchestras are using the *Musikverein* not only for rehearsals and concerts, but also for the considerable number of recording sessions they now enjoy. It is a hall which is certainly the equal of the Symphony Hall in Boston for acoustics, and certainly its superior in looks, which puts it right at the top of the world class. It is also a hall full of ghosts and famous associations. The first of these was unquestionably Hans Richter, the permanent conductor from 1875 to 1898, who had been a horn player in the orchestra. He was followed from 1898 to 1908 by the even more celebrated Gustav Mahler. Oddly, Mahler was at the time merely a well-known but rather irascible conductor: his compositions, now bestsellers the world over, were tolerated because he was there, but seemed to impress very few of his contemporaries. It was also at this time that the young Richard Strauss conducted the orchestra. Sibelius, then a student in Berlin, where Strauss also conducted, described him as 'the shy young Strauss' and I often wonder what his conducting was like at the time. Certainly in 1947, the last year of his life (which was the only time, I believe, that anyone still alive in Britain worked with him), I found his beat remarkably diminutive but decidedly firm.

Needless to say, he got every ounce of energy from us all in the Philharmonia Orchestra because of our tremendous admiration for him. But back to the Vienna Philharmonic. The next permanent conductor, from 1908 to 1927, was Felix Weingartner. He was reputedly amazingly popular and endeared himself to the orchestra by his unfussy and elegant style. He also displayed another feature which endeared him to his orchestra one morning at rehearsal, which was being taken for him by one of his pupils. The young man was becoming very expansive and giving all the secrets of his interpretation of Brahms' Symphony full reign in a long dissertation when he was cut short by 'Uncle Felix'. 'Do not talk at rehearsal,' was all he said. The orchestra applauded, because they had been as bored as he.

Weingartner was not alone in his directorship. Because he was a generous man, all the current great conductors conducted the Vienna Philharmonic in his day, including Bruno Walter, Toscanini, de Sabata and Otto Klemperer, who was at that time purely operatic in his repertoire. After the Second World War there was some delay in finding an operatic home, because the old opera house had been destroyed. Luckily the other halls all survived. It says much for the Viennese character that the opera house was one of the priorities of rebuilding, and when reconstructed in the same shape as the old house it was improved in many ways, especially in the magnificence of the orchestra pit. It is true that backstage it has possibly more the atmosphere of a luxurious town hall than the usual dusty ambience of a theatre, but it is comfortable, airy and convenient – or so it seems to a visitor. No doubt the inhabitants have their grouses, but I must say I have never heard any.

The orchestra also has a summer home at the Salzburg Festival, where it has been the leading orchestra since the start, in 1920. To meet them there is to feel links with the past that somehow make it most fitting that they should be the orchestra to play for the Mozart operas in his home town. They are charming and dignified hosts, most ready to discuss their self-governing status and compare it with those we know at home. They are proud, and rightly so, of the fact that they managed to retain their democratic constitution during the dark days when democracy in Austria was suppressed. Theirs is not a big administrative staff, or was not when I last inquired; ten people was all that were required, including librarian and financial director. It is notable that while they may have principal conductors, they do not have a musical director *or* a manager. All decisions are made by the general assembly – and in particular this includes choice of conductor. They also have a remarkable equity of financial reward, because revenue from all activities is distributed among all the players: for example, if you are required to play at the opera while the rest of the orchestra is recording, you share the spoils – the only case I can recall of this sort of democratic unity. Entry into the orchestra is difficult, and may be slow. Normally the young musician plays at the opera for three years before he can apply to be a member of the Philharmonic. The orchestra has, however, greatly increased in size since its birth. In 1842 it had sixty-four members. Now it has 140, and thus can undertake an opera and a concert at the same time, or play at Mass in St Thomas's in the morning without disturbing the rehearsal for that day's concert at the *Musikverein*. This is an admirable set-up, and one which allows the members to take part in solo and chamber-music activities, for which the demands are considerable. There are several well-known ensembles within this orchestra, including the famous octet. Such ensembles, happily, have always been a feature of our orchestral life, but are by no means ubiquitous the world over.

It is quite difficult to elicit from the officials of the Vienna Philharmonic the sort of financial details given readily by many other orchestras. The Austrians have a certain etiquette in these matters, a reticence which seems quite natural with their dignified and quite formal attitude to their fellows. The whole structure of their organization is founded upon the principles of social partnership which is the keystone of the fiscal management of their country. This is, it seems, not a political issue at all. There is no pushing or pulling over this plan, a fact which seems strange to anyone with the British background in mind. It is not a Socialist, Tory, or Liberal credo, they will tell you, but just a sensible way to run the economy of either a business, an orchestra or a country. Certainly the members of the orchestra seem to be prosperous, and if they have any quibbles they are about peripheral issues of control and management. It seems that they assume that Vienna remains the centre of the musical world as it was in the days of Mozart, Schubert and Haydn. This is probably not so, but it is a view which has certainly lasted until well into the present century.

The contrast between Berlin and Vienna is illustrated by Dr Berta Geissmar in her book.* The Vienna Philharmonic was most anxious to have Furtwängler's services in the 1930s, and he conducted them frequently, with success. Of them, Dr Geissmar says,

> The Vienna Philharmonic had a splendid etiquette for all they did. This was particularly felt when they were on tour. I learnt it on a short English visit in 1930, while Furtwängler was their conductor as well as the Berlin Philharmonic's. The superb self-assurance of every member of the orchestra and their ostentatious pride in belonging to this famous body of players was quite unique. As a matter of fact, every member of the Vienna Philharmonic feels himself to be a god, and expects to be treated like one, be it in London, Vienna or anywhere else.

This is strong stuff, and certainly not the impression most of us now have of our Viennese friends. It may have been due to the fact that Dr Geissmar suffered as a result of her employer, Furtwängler, failing to take up a post in Vienna in 1936, when he was in trouble with Hitler. As a result his assistant, being Jewish, was exiled, left Berlin and settled in London. She was also upset by the fact that the Vienna Philharmonic was one of the few orchestras which at that time failed to appreciate the genius of Beecham, her new employer. It is true that they had always displayed a rather insular attitude in this sort of matter, having always favoured Austrian and German conductors. There is only a remnant of this insularity now remaining. They are a friendly, articulate and hospitable orchestra, if still extremely dignified and proud of their achievements. Wherever they play, they demonstrate that even today music and everything connected with it plays a special role in their city – one feels that the Viennese taxi-driver is as likely to appreciate their work as is an aristocrat or, for that matter, his servant. Music is natural to the very air of Vienna. Their orchestra is what the Berlin Philharmonic would also be now if that city had not been divided in 1946. The line of development has never been severed in Vienna, and with their roots in the classical past and their musical present very rosy, they can look to the future with hope and confidence.

* *The Baton and the Jackboot*

The New York Philharmonic Orchestra is older than the Boston Symphony by almost forty years, being founded in 1842, the same year as the Vienna Philharmonic. It is thus the oldest in the USA and older than all but a handful of European orchestras. It can be said to have grown up with the nation, and to have played a most important role in its musical history. It must also be equated in its early days with the music of its time – and in 1842 Beethoven, Schubert and Weber were modern composers, while Brahms and Dvořák were mere toddlers. So the music it brought to the USA was both new and great. The first conductor of the new orchestra was a gentleman with the delightful name Ureli Corelli Hill, from 1842 to 1852. His is a forgotten name now, but he was a man of great influence. The Philharmonic was really waiting for a European influence, and this was not long in coming because the times were unhappy in Germany in the mid-nineteenth century, with the inevitable host of refugees finding new homes in America; and among these were some superb musicians. One of these was the conductor Carl Bergmann, and for twenty-six years, from 1856 to 1882, he was principal conductor of the orchestra, bringing with him a strong German influence, several superb players, and a new appreciation of Liszt, Wagner, Brahms and (perhaps surprisingly) Berlioz, a French composer. In the following years there were almost as many conductors as there were seasons, except for the long reign of Theodore Thomas from 1882 to 1891. Thomas brought the orchestra to a virtuoso level of performance before handing over to Anton Seidl, who was adored by public and orchestra alike. His premature death in 1898 at the age of forty-seven was such a blow that for many years there was no settled holder of the post. The turn of the century brought a succession of conductors, including Damrosch and Paur, and guests like Weingartner, Richard Strauss and Mengelberg. Even Mahler had his turn and stayed for two years, 1909–11. He was as always a controversial figure, but his years with them seem to have broadened the scope of the orchestra and done wonders for the establishment of guaranteed salaries and greater length of season. By this time the orchestra was firmly established in the magnificent Carnegie Hall for many of its concerts. This fine hall had been opened in 1891 by the New York Symphony Orchestra (a newer rival from 1878), at a notable concert in which Tchaikovsky conducted two of his symphonies.

The two orchestras existed side by side until 1928, when they amalgamated to become the New York Philharmonic Symphony. This title seems to have lasted for several years, but gradually ceased to be used – although during the important years of the reign of Arturo Toscanini, from 1929 until 1936, it was the official title. This was the period during which the orchestra gained true international fame and attained a style which set it apart. Those who played for it during those days admit that it was an unforgettable and truly remarkable experience. Not all of them were wholeheartedly enthusiastic about the sort of life working for such a maestro involved (nor did at least one member share my own enthusiasm for Toscanini's deputy Artur Rodzinski, begging me to give that worthy his regards, while bloodcurdlingly drawing his finger across his throat), but there is no doubt that this was a time of excitement and some glory for the orchestra. John Barbirolli, who followed Toscanini in 1936, and stayed until 1943, was a great change, and in some ways hardly less exciting. Wartime conductors, from 1943 to 1947, included Koussevitsky, Walter and Reiner as well as Monteux, Szell and Milhaud. It was in 1947 that a remarkable young assistant conductor, Leonard Bernstein, first appeared as a last-minute deputy, at a concert in which Bartók and his wife were the soloists. It was some years before Bernstein was to become the principal conductor, but when he did so, in 1957, for eleven years, as the first American to hold the position, a bright new chapter began. Television was now making musical history, and 'Lennie' and his orchestra were the spearhead, with the superb series of Young People's Concerts creating the audiences of the future. It was in 1962 that the orchestra moved to its new and permanent home, in the Lincoln Center. I was at one of the first rehearsals, as a listener, and found it sad and somewhat chilly acoustically after the wonderful ambience of the Carnegie Hall. The orchestra felt much the same about it, as did the public, which must have had an effect, as financial help had to be called for and luckily was received. In 1976 the hall was renamed Avery Fisher Hall in recognition of the principal donor, a complete reconstruction having transformed the hall to its present acoustic and physical delight.

In common with most of the world's orchestras, since that date there has been a period of great expansion in the work of the NYPO. Concerts have been extended into the spring and summer. There have been series of promenade concerts of a popular nature under André Kostelanetz, who first conducted them in 1952, and did so for twenty-seven seasons until he died. There are now symposia and discussions, with the composers present, following festival series of their works. Another new venture, Park Concerts, started in 1964 in open spaces in New York City, Long Island and in Westchester, has pulled in audiences for single concerts of up to 100,000, and at the opening concert of the series it is reported in the orchestral brochure that 225,000 people somehow heard some of it. A most unlikely follow-up to Bernstein's tenure of office, when he became Laureate in 1969, was the appointment of Pierre Boulez in 1971, as principal conductor. It was a tenure of six years, during which the orchestra's repertoire, like that of the BBC Symphony just previously, underwent startling changes not always to the delight of the players or the audience. Next came Zubin Mehta, a young conductor who had been music director in Los Angeles for sixteen years. With his directorship we come to the present exciting chapter in the history of this remarkable orchestra. He came in 1978, and as his contract has now been extended until 1990, he will be the longest-standing conductor in the NYPO's history. The present position of the orchestra seems to be comfortable, successful and artistically rewarding from every angle, and there is no doubt that the administration is to be congratulated upon its work. Although the orchestra now appears and is advertised as the New York Philharmonic, they are managed by the Philharmonic Symphony Society of New York, Inc – an organization of mind-boggling proportions and almost unlimited possibilities. There are no fewer than forty-four directors, fifteen administrators and separate staffs for advertising, audience services, development, educational activities and finance. The annual operating budget is well over £11 million, and of this about thirty per cent is provided by sponsorship, either corporate or individual. There are thousands of individual sponsors, proving that tax advantage is possibly the most important factor in keeping a great orchestra alive. Nobody expects the orchestra to pay for itself, as is so often suggested should be the case in Britain. Government help is a mere six per cent of the total, and ticket sales are expected to produce no more than fifty-two per cent. The remaining twelve per cent is provided by endowment income: the orchestra has been going for a long time, and investment has been wise and successful. All this is not to pretend that things necessarily run themselves more easily in the USA than here in Britain. Several of their finest orchestras have found themselves with deficits in recent years, but sponsors have always been found to cover these without the sort of delay which piles up interest costs and makes for a desperate situation. Quite often it is necessary only to transfer money into the system from a trustee-designated fund, kept for this very purpose. The NYPO is an excellent example of this skilful financial management.

As a result of this prosperity and steady achievement, turnover of orchestral personnel is very small. Resignations are rare. There were only three replacements in 1981, two in 1982, and in 1983, apart from retirements, only one resignation. Nobody left in 1984, and only one member did so in 1985. As might be expected, the members are true New Yorkers in every way, and to know them is to realize how very much they are part of the city's life. It is a tough, vibrant city, and any conductor will tell you that meeting such an orchestra on its home ground can be, to put it mildly, a challenge. Any hint of inefficiency can be greeted not with quiet reserved amusement, but with a resounding Bronx Cheer – or 'raspberry' as most of us know it. The sheer muscularity of this orchestra is evident in the playing at times, and certainly they are at home in every sort of music. There is an attached broadcasting corporation called Exxon, which relays nationwide broadcasts fifty-two weeks in every year. Being the nation it is, this means in Alaska, Hawaii, Puerto Rico and Samoa, as well as Canada. Programmes are often very unusual and exploratory, with a total of almost 200 world premieres since the Second World War. The estimated TV audience for their concerts is fifteen million annually, and the present live audience for their 200 concerts each year is over one million. The present season (1986/7) is their 145th. They carry 106 players, and rarely indeed split into two units, so that usually there is plenty of leisure for about a quarter of the orchestra. Zubin Mehta, their present conductor, is the twenty-second in their history, and shows signs of being one of the most popular. In addition to orchestral duties, many of the principal players are encouraged as concert performers with their own orchestra, and several important works have been com-missioned by the Philharmonic Symphony Society for this purpose. Chamber-music groups are also encouraged within the membership, and a whole series of Sunday afternoon concerts planned around them. These concerts involve combinations of all sizes from sonatas to works for ten or more, and bring great distinction to those involved. It is a very busy, very organized and well-thought-out pattern. As one experienced player put it to me, when asked about forms of management, 'Self-governing? Why should we – those guys can do it better than we can'. He was almost certainly right. At about £40 per hour for playing his instrument, he would be a fool to try to find out where the money comes from. Others know, and make sure it continues to do so.

The City of Birmingham Symphony Orchestra lives right in the heart of Britain, and is not to be confused with anything which happens in that other Birmingham, in Alabama, USA. The local people are proud to be living in the second city in Britain, but musically are not willing to admit to that secondary role. This was not always so, because Birmingham was a slow starter orchestrally and had no full-time professional orchestra until 1943. There had been many musical organizations before this, some of them worthy of note. The Harmonic Association, a largely amateur affair, was established in 1855 and gave four concerts each winter at the Town Hall, a very useful but somewhat over-resonant venue dating from 1834 which is still in use. This seems to have been an orchestra of considerable talent, with Edward Elgar himself playing in the first violins from 1881 to 1888, and taking part in concerts at which several of his early works (including the inevitable *Salut d'Amour*) were performed. There followed a long series of concerts conducted by George Halford, 1897–1907, and from then on the orchestra was fully professional, if not permanent. Henry Wood was their conductor 1901–10, and Julian Clifford from 1910 to 1920, when the first permanent orchestra, but not by any means full-time, called the Birmingham Symphony, was launched in a concert of Elgar's music conducted by the composer.

Their first conductor was Charles Matthews, until 1924, when the young Adrian Boult took over with conspicuous success. He was to go far later as the principal conductor of the BBC Symphony Orchestra from 1929 to 1950, and after that, having been retired by the BBC at the ludicrously early age (for a conductor) of sixty, as a conductor of international repute. He was with the Birmingham Symphony for only five years, from 1924 to 1929, but in that time he established an enviable reputation both for the orchestra and himself. It was still not a full-time job, being merely an orchestra created from the best players in the Midland area. During the tenure of office of the next conductor, Leslie Heward, there was some help forthcoming, because the BBC used thirty-five members of the Symphony as the BBC Midland Light Orchestra from 1935 on, and these became the nucleus of the full-time Birmingham Symphony when it was established in 1944.

Leslie Heward, who conducted them from 1929 to his early death in 1943 at the tragically early age of forty-six, was a conductor many of us felt sure would become world famous before long, and he did much to build solidly upon the foundation Boult had laid, but on a much bigger scale, with more players and more concerts. His successor, George Weldon, was another tragically short-lived maestro who died in 1951 in his early fifties. He was a pupil of Malcolm Sargent's, with much of his teacher's brightness and not a few of his mannerisms; but he had a quiet charm which we used to enjoy when he came to London to conduct the RPO, and his loss to Birmingham was serious. Rudolf Schwarz was next in the post of principal conductor, from 1951 to 1957, and he was a very different sort of musician. A soft and gentle man, who suffered terribly in a Nazi concentration camp during the war, he has brought to his conducting of this and other orchestras a tenderness which always makes for enjoyment. He, too, had his effect upon the orchestra, but it was not yet really of world-class as it now is, and it is interesting to follow the long crescendo which has brought it to its present enviable position. The excellent composer-conductor Andrzej Panufnik did something to further refine the playing from 1957 to 1960, and he was followed from 1960 to 1968 by Hugo Rignold, a very versatile conductor who had once been a remarkable violinist in jazz orchestras of the highest quality, but had established himself later as a serious conductor of no mean talent. Next came Louis Fremaux, from 1968 to 1978, and in my opinion his period was the turning point in the artistic development of the orchestra. By then it was the City of Birmingham Symphony Orchestra, having taken that name in 1948 following four years of generous grants-in-aid from the city council, and was for the first time in an international class. It was after a short gap, in 1980, that their present conductor, the young Simon Rattle, took over, and from that moment orchestra and conductor seem to have really captured the imagination of the public. He arrived as principal conductor and artistic advisor at the astonishingly early age of twenty-five. It wasn't even his first post; he had been associate conductor of the Liverpool Philharmonic and the BBC Scottish Symphony Orchestra for three years before that, and was in demand also from the London Sinfonietta and Glyndebourne Opera, with both of which he is still associated. In addition he was principal guest conductor with the Los Angeles Philharmonic, and he is a familiar figure to the orchestras in Chicago, San Francisco, Toronto, Cleveland and Boston. Certainly since he became the Birmingham maestro audiences have multiplied in a most satisfactory way, and a new series of Wednesday Subscription Concerts, as well as concerts in London and in Paris, prove that the orchestra is very much on the upgrade. Nor does Rattle do it with 'pot-boiling' programmes: Janáček, Britten, Weill, Nielsen and Messiaen, as well as the now familiar but none the less stunning Second Symphony of Mahler are all part of the scene. There have also been first performances of important works, notably the premiere in 1986/7 of Debussy's *Pelléas et Mélisande Symphony* – a realization by the French composer Marius Constant from the beautiful opera of that name.

All this looks and certainly feels like success, and I am sure the members are very happy to be on the crest of a wave. However, a glance at the annual reports over the past few years indicates it is all being done on a shoestring, without the sort of financial advantage that such work deserves, and certainly without the sort of prosperity which guarantees long-term loyalty from even the most devoted members. There is a reasonably long list of commercial sponsors – about twenty organizations help in this way – but the grants from the Arts Council of Great Britain, the West Midlands County Council and the City of Birmingham, totalling under £900,000, even with an average ninety-seven per cent attendance in the old Town Hall, still left them with £30,000 in debt in 1985 – a deficit happily defrayed by an Arts Council special guarantee in that year. Their hall is an old one, and all eyes are on the future, when a splendid new 2,200-seater will be available for them. This may well be a turning point, but such plans do not always work out, and it remains to be seen whether the bodies necessary to fill the seats will be forthcoming. Meanwhile a staff of 102 – eighty-six orchestra and sixteen office and management – share a salary bill of £1,112,000. An average of £10,900 per annum is a level which is hardly likely to attract and keep the sort of musician necessary for an orchestra of international repute.

All this is becoming increasingly important just now, when there is a very strong searchlight on the CBSO. The reason for this is the oft-repeated opinion of some members of the establishment that London is overcrowded orchestrally, and should be deprived of some of its riches so that the rest of Britain should profit. There was much talk in the 1970s in the London press of a '£1 million super-orchestra' – a figure which is so ludicrously low, as we can see from the Birmingham budget, that nobody took it seriously. The Arts Council then suggested that one of the London orchestras should move to the Midlands, although how this simple transposition was to be achieved, orchestras being people with homes and families, was never explained. Finally, none of the London orchestras being willing to quietly die or go away, but in fact all showing remarkable resource and skill in survival techniques, Sir William Rees-Mogg began to think of finding his super-orchestra *in situ*. Somewhere, he was sure, he could find a great international orchestra like those of Chicago or Vienna. The non-contract orchestras could not possibly be considered, as they were too concerned with filling schedules with TV, film and commercial work in an effort to survive (isn't there possibly just a touch of the Catch-22 syndrome somewhere there?). So, what about the sparkling Birmingham orchestra with their excellent young conductor? One must say that there have been moments of rather grim amusement in all this, because those of us involved – all the musicians in all the orchestras, in London and elsewhere – are very much the same in talent, industry and ambition. The very fact that the Arts Council thinks it can make a super-orchestra out of any section of our profession is an admission that it can only be done by money. We all know this to be true, because we know the players and set-ups in Chicago, Vienna, New York and Berlin, and they underline that very fact. So, if Sir William really means what he says, the CBSO is as likely a candidate for his plan as any; but not a £1 million orchestra, please. With budgets in Boston at £20 million, New York at £11 million, and the salary level of both at just about four times the Birmingham or London level, he will have to dig pretty deeply into the public purse. I am sure we all wish him a lot of luck in this – it is a great encouragement for Birmingham to continue its efforts.

The Sydney Symphony Orchestra, The Melbourne Symphony *et al* demonstrate the essential feature of the Australian orchestras which must be taken into account when comparing them with others – that there is really no single Australian 'scene'. In Chapter 3 we took a cursory glance at their activities, and I think this made it obvious that although all the big orchestras are under the banner of the ABC, to whom one must give due credit for their creation and sustenance over the past forty years or so, geographical and even cultural differences, together with the immense separation in mileage between them, makes it essential that their different orchestras should have different activities and even different treatment. They obviously have different aims and aspirations, and so should have different administrations. It is now being suggested that the ABC, having done excellent work in establishing its orchestras, is not the ideal institution for their continued success and well-being. That at least is the firm conclusion reached by what everyone now calls the Tribe Report. The full name of this 273-page document is *Study in the Future Development of Orchestras in Australia* (March 1985), and it makes fascinating reading, covering everything from 'Major recommendations as to the future ownership of management of the ABC orchestras as well as the Elizabethan Trust orchestras', to plans for a National Training Association for players, and even a discussion of dissenting opinions. The familiar 'Tribe Report' title springs from the fact that the chairman of the study group panel was Ken Tribe, and with him he had nine specialists from all the Australian states, including one, Tom Molomby, a Commonwealth representative, who was the dissentient voice and came down strongly on the side of the ABC.

Their terms of reference were wide and far-reaching, but boiled down to examining the status quo with a view to seeing how it could be improved, what future potential there was and what the cost of such changes would be. A further requirement was that of improving present artistic standards. While they decided quite firmly that the ABC dominance should end, and went into great detail as to how this should be achieved (and certainly most people now believe this will happen), they were not lacking in appreciation of the foundations laid by the broadcasting corporation. We shall see soon how they plan to alter orchestral life in Australia; but before that I think we should look at the start of it all.

Sydney's first symphony concert was given in 1901 by a group of amateurs called the Sydney Amateur Orchestral Society under an Italian conductor called Roberto Hazon. It was a short-lived enterprise, and nothing further seems to have been heard of it. Then, in 1908, there was a small professional group, organized by one George Plummer, and registered by him as the Sydney Symphony Orchestra. Forming this orchestra was not such a difficult task as it could have been, because at that time there were many immigrants from Central Europe, including some excellent musicians looking for just this sort of opportunity. It was not by any means a permanent orchestra, but appeared from time to time in the years which followed with varying degrees of success. The title was finally bought for £10 from Plummer in 1948 for the ABC by their general manager Charles Moses, but much water had meanwhile flowed under the bridges in all six states of the Australian continent. Between 1908 and 1948 the real mainstay of Australian music had been Bernard Heinz, a violinist who had studied in London, and returned with a burning ambition to recreate in his own land the musical activities he had heard there. He had conducting ambitions, and felt strongly that to start his project on a firm basis the place to begin was in the schools. He established a series of schools' concerts in 1924, with considerable success, and continued to present these for many years. In these concerts the ABC (created in 1932 as the sole broadcasting authority) found something they could use, and in 1937 they employed Sir Malcolm Sargent to continue them in all six states, with a total of half a million pupils as audience. This, however, was before the ABC orchestras had been properly established, and the orchestras were on an *ad hoc* basis.

Meanwhile, as soon as it was created in 1932 the ABC had started two small studio combinations of about a dozen players each, in Sydney and Melbourne, but nothing of a symphonic nature. They had invited Sargent to come and set up a symphony orchestra at this time, but arrangements broke down, and it was only in 1937 that he came. There was a lot of resistance from

Heinz, who by then was the boss at ABC. He was determined to have not one orchestra, but six, one for each state – his reason being that he was sure that each state had its own sound, making each orchestra a fascinatingly different musical entity. (How this could be is difficult to understand, as some of the players were not from the states they now graced, and many were from Budapest and Leningrad, to say nothing of Peckham and Versailles.) In any case Heinz did not enjoy the thought of Sargent and his single super-orchestra, saying, 'Have your visiting conductors by all means, but keep them as visitors. We are in danger of becoming the dumping-ground for the unemployed of the Old World.'* (This was hardly fair to Sargent, who at the time was very much in demand in several parts of the world, Old and New.)

It was Charles Moses, appointed by Heinz to look after ABC music (although originally a sports commentator) who finally succeeded in establishing the six orchestras, in 1936. These were the 'core' orchestras of the ABC, and geared to their different requirements as to size. Sydney had a playing strength of forty-five, Melbourne thirty-five, and the other states, Queensland, South Australia and Western Australia, seventeen each, while Tasmania had just eleven. It was a start, and over the years the ABC has steadily augmented these totals, so that the six orchestras now number ninety-seven, eighty-eight, seventy-one, fifty-seven, fifty-one and forty-two, totals which presumably reflect the amount of money available from the states involved in each case.

The years of the Second World War were among the most important in the development of the ABC orchestras, because of the American influence. Brisbane became 'Little America' because of the establishment of General MacArthur's head-quarters there, and one of their first imports was conductor Eugene Ormandy, the young successor in 1936 to Stokowski with the Philadelphia orchestra, and very much a rising international star. For him the ABC were willing to transport players all over Australia; and they had to, because he was promised 100 players wherever he went, and there certainly wasn't an orchestra of that size anywhere in Australia. This was all good for the enlargements of horizons and the extending of repertoire, whatever it cost in

* Charles Buttrose, *Playing for Australia*, Griffin Press, 1982

terms of broadcast cancellations of other than musical projects. The impact on audience and orchestras was electrifying, and if some of the cellos may not have sounded like their Philadelphia counterparts, as Joseph Post, their friend and conductor put it, 'Don't be hard on the poor bastards – most of them are playing on butter-boxes, and at least one of them has just finished a milk-round!'* I don't think Ormandy ever played again in Australia after the war, but his influence was certainly very important as a creator of foundations.

The next important step in the development of ABC music and probably the most important of any was the engagement in 1948 of Sir Eugene Goossens as conductor of the Sydney Symphony. To attract him it was necessary to find a salary far in excess of that paid to the Prime Minister or the chief judge of the Supreme Court. This was achieved by making him Director of the Conservatorium and paying much of his salary as a tax-free expense allowance, a total of about £8,000 per annum, which was a fortune in those days. In accepting he made a famous speech, pledging that he would make the orchestra one of the six best in the world, and with such a widely admired conductor the morale of the players was so raised that he certainly succeeded in making them internationally competitive. He had a successful eight-year reign, and he himself became a much more highly rated artist. It all began to become less sweet in about 1954, however, because his players began to think he was too flamboyant and remote, and in 1956, when he had trouble with the customs authorities over some 'undesirable literature' he was carrying, he left Australia without saying goodbye; his players confirm that few tears were shed for him. He had, none the less, been exactly what Australia needed at the time. I recall recording with him that year in London, when one of the RPO players suggested (in jest) that after his customs débâcle the obvious work would be *Pictures from an Exhibition*. Incredibly, that was exactly what we *did* record. But, back to the Australian orchestra.

By 1956, all the ABC orchestras were well-established, and in the years which followed there were many excellent and even famous conductors to brighten the scene. Unhappily Nicolai Malko, from pre-Soviet Russia, who followed Goossens in Sydney

* Buttrose, *Playing for Australia*.

in 1957 was not one of these. His powers were already waning when he took over and the critics, especially one Lindsey Browne, made the point in the *Sydney Times* very strongly. It was one of the few occasions when the usually gentle Malko spoke out – 'L.B.', he said, 'I think maybe that just means Lousy Bastard'. Malko was seventy-three when he was appointed, and he stayed until he died at the age of seventy-eight. Perhaps his appointment was too late in his career. He bored the orchestra, as I remember he had bored the RPO in London just previously, by constant nagging at rehearsal, albeit in a quiet and restrained voice. He also made the mistake of trying to replace one or two of the players. Again, upon his departure there were few tears.

Happily, in the years which followed the Australian orchestras had a succession of conductors, either permanent or visiting, who were more to the taste of both public and players. John Hopkins, who had been conducting in Britain as a young man; Klemperer, who liked the orchestras but thought there were too many women in them, to the great surprise of the Australians, who had never noticed it; and Georg Szell, one of the best so far as the audience went, but hated by most of the players. He is quoted as saying at the time, 'I'm a bastard and I don't care if everyone in the world knows it!' He flatly refused to conduct in Adelaide, saying that the playing was beneath contempt. Barbirolli and Beecham also appeared as guests; and Joseph Post, one of the best indigenous conductors, was heard to say after a Beecham rehearsal in Melbourne of the Schubert C Major Symphony, 'They can't play that well. It's hypnotism, bloody hypnotism. I've been with them all this week – and they *can't* play like that!'* They could, though, with Beecham.

Others who contributed to the development of the six ABC orchestras in the years which followed include Karel Ancerl, conductor of the Czech Philharmonic, who conducted in 1961 but could not get his two sons out of Prague and therefore could not accept the permanent post; André Cluytens from Paris, who entranced the orchestra in Perth; Henry Krips, brother of Joe Krips of LSO fame, but a much more light-weight character – and Dean Dixon, an American who conducted well, but insisted upon lengthy dissertations using the longest words he could find, few of

* Buttrose, *Playing for Australia*

which were comprehensible. (My own favourite of his was 'architectonics'. I knew what he meant, but cannot recall anyone else using it.) Later maestros have been Peter Eros, an easygoing and pleasant musician; the ex-principal second fiddle of the LSO David Measham, a popular figure with audiences in Perth who made the proms there very much his own; the celebrated Australian horn player Barry Tuckwell, conducting in Tasmania; and of course Sir Charles Mackerras, originally a principal oboeist both in Australia and at Sadlers Wells in London, and a man who did much to spread the reputation of Australian orchestras and music-making abroad. Another conductor I very much enjoyed playing with in Adelaide was Hiroyuki Iwaki, a young Japanese of considerable talent who has done a fine job there; and if Van Otterloo, who was in Sydney when I played there in 1978, was somewhat remote and occasionally seemed to lack humour, he did get excellent results. He died tragically in a car smash a few years ago and was succeeded by Louis Fremaux, who had done so much to improve the standard of our own City of Birmingham Symphony. All in all it has been almost forty years of expansion since the days of Goossens, and a period of which the ABC can be proud. The latest information, in 1987, is that they will be left in charge for the next three years on condition that they prove themselves able to reorganize the general approach to concert-giving; so the situation is both cliff-hanging and intensely interesting as seen from a distance, though possibly not so comfortable at close quarters. It will be interesting to see how the Sydney Symphony, in particular, develops during this period. Their present chief conductor, Zdenck Macel, of whose work I have no personal experience, seems to be bringing a new intensity to their activities. He will certainly have an interesting and important period ahead of him, if he stays. Unfortunately he suddenly left the country one Friday in August 1986 during rehearsals for a Saturday concert, and has failed to return. He was replaced by Vladimir Yampolski immediately, with success. It is all fairly hectic and exciting, but Macel's future must now be regarded as uncertain.

How does all this seem to those who are involved? None of the players has any illusions about becoming rich, except possibly the owner of a stud farm or a winery. A rank-and-file member can expect to make a salary about equal to a police constable or a clerk in the ABC, and for this to work a thirty-two hour week, which probably means that he/she hasn't a lot of time for the winery or the stud farm – although many of them certainly manage to find it. Most of them want to do nothing else but music, because they are fascinated by their work, and even seem to encourage their children to follow them in the profession rather than pushing them into a more secure job. A factor which is never taken into account is that thirty-two hours isn't the total work required to be a successful orchestral practitioner – preparation and practice certainly add another twenty hours or so to this total. I think that in Antipodean terms one can honestly *not* say that 'they have much more, there'.

We must not merely look at Sydney and Melbourne, with possibly Adelaide as a third contender, to make any judgement. Canberra has been a most active centre since 1946, and by 1960 it had over 2,000 subscribers to its concert series, as well as a prominent series of youth concerts and summer concerts. In later years this has been surpassed, and in Perth, which seems so far-flung that it can be regarded as an outpost, the new concert hall built in 1973 for A\$4.5 million has resulted in a growth in interest in concerts.

Queries as to satisfaction with conditions meet with varied responses from the players. One Sydney principal emphatically is very definitely not satisfied with the management, but is hopeful of the future because of recent changes, including the election of an orchestral committee which seems to have a voice in the organiz-ation. There is a feeling with others that perhaps self-government might be a solution, but there is no real experience to go on. Salary is regarded as fairly satisfactory by most, and rehearsal halls, canteens, travel facilities and general convenience are compared favourably with those in Britain by some players who have experienced both. Pensions are looked after by the state, and most people find them satisfactory. Security of tenure is not so good as it used to be, and turnover of personnel is becoming more frequent. General camaraderie and morale do seem to be high, and there seems to be a commendable pride in performance standards.

So far we have considered only the ABC orchestras, but the Elizabethan Theatre Trust orchestras in Sydney and Melbourne are of almost equal importance, and are very permanent organiz-ations, with a turnover of personnel of less than ten per cent per annum. The formation of these orchestras was an interesting offshoot of the ABC, because the establishment of a national opera company in 1953 would not have been possible without the use, free of charge, of the ABC orchestras. This meant that the ABC had a finger in the pie as to the dates and productions involved, as well as the right to broadcast any performance. It was, none the less, very generous of the Commission, who were obviously getting less value from their own orchestras as a result of the arrangement. There was also the objection from the Musicians' Union that one orchestra was really doing the job of two; so in 1967 two new opera orchestras were created for the Trust, with the same salaries and conditions as the ABC. The Commission had therefore supported the Trust for a full thirteen years, and credit is due to them for helping to start opera in Australia.

The general opinion of players in the Trust orchestras is the usual one of orchestras in pits: they feel secondary in importance, and complain that anything on-stage is regarded by the management as of primary interest. There is also widespread dissatisfaction with Sydney Opera House as a place to actually present opera, as my own experience bears out. A poor pit, very low and noisy, bad sight of the conductor, and generally cramped conditions make the bulk of the orchestra unhappy, as do the many 'split-call' days when a player has to concentrate upon more than one opera at a time. There is also dissatisfaction at not having a long-term musical director but instead a series of conductors, good and bad, making a settled style impossible. Such complaints are interesting for any opera-orchestral player to hear, because they are common throughout the world, except possibly in Vienna.

The Trust orchestral strength in Sydney is sixty-nine, with sixty-seven in Melbourne, and both are used by an opera company and a ballet company, which means that they feel a certain loss of identity, especially as they have very few opportunities to give concerts. In Melbourne, recent years have involved twenty weeks of opera and twenty-four weeks of ballet (twelve of them on tour); and in Sydney, thirty-six weeks of opera and only twelve of ballet. Retirement is at sixty-five, with a quite good superannuation scheme. The Trust is still looking for more funds to improve salary levels and the size of the orchestras. They expect that in 1987 the Melbourne orchestra will be transferred to the Victorian Arts

Centre Trust, as recommended by the Tribe Report.

Certainly, as seen from an orchestral seat in London, the nine or so calls per week which appear on their weekly schedule seem to provide leisure a-plenty, as do their settled venues and short journeys to work; but the wider interest of concerts and recordings, films and TV sessions is not for them, and the sense of frustration they suffer comes over strongly in any conversation. Australian players do, in spite of all this, retain a sense of humour about their work. One of them, Kevin Murphy, when I asked him what was his greatest moment in the orchestra, told me of a Goossens rehearsal he once suffered. Eugene was not noted for his short rehearsals, but on one occasion he stopped at 12.55, just five minutes from the end, saying, 'Thank you, ladies and gentlemen, that will be all!' and the clock chose that moment to fall from the wall. Then there was the Australian trombone player who said of Dean Dixon, 'You don't mind a man giving you a downbeat with his chin, but it's confusing when he has a double chin. You don't know which one to follow!'

Yes, I'm glad I have met so many of the Australians over the years. They may not have more, there – but they certainly seem to make the best of it. As to the future, if the Tribe Report is implemented, it will certainly be different. The study group recommends without reservation (and I quote) that:

(a) all ABC orchestras should be divested to independent local ownership by the end of 1988, with all funds now being apportioned to them to be taken from the ABC and given to each orchestra to support itself; and

(b) the orchestras must provide a designated number of hours to the ABC each year for broadcasting purposes, the frequency of which should be as it is at present. Benefits expected from this change will be, as mentioned in the report,

(i) better use of public funds, which will add forty-four musicians to the total employed, and increase the number of concerts by twenty-five per cent;

(ii) better programmes because of more money for soloists and conductors;

(iii) increased touring by orchestras;

(iv) improved working conditions; and

(v) reduced administration costs.

In the opinion of the study group this will lead to the development in the orchestras of 'standards of international excellence' (where have we heard this before?) which can be achieved in no other way.

Further recommendations are that the Elizabethan Trust Orchestras shall also be transferred: that in Sydney to the Australian Opera and the Melbourne orchestra to the Victorian Arts Centre Trust. This is in progress at present in 1987 and seems to meet with the approval of the players. Probably because touring will be limited to four weeks per year, concert appearances will be increased (including some chamber concerts), and orchestral sizes will be expanded so that rotation of string players becomes possible.

It is all an exciting new deal for Australian musicians, and the rest of us certainly wish them luck with it. The report is far too detailed and voluminous for discussion here. One can only say that it seems to be thoroughly well-thought-through and steady in its conclusions, and to give much food for thought. I hope its recommendations are adopted, and that they will succeed in improving orchestral life in Australia. The players there deserve this.

The Cleveland Orchestra (Ohio) is another organization which gives much encouragement to those in Britain who see no reason why orchestral excellence must be located in the capital city. Cleveland is a large industrial city on the south shore of Lake Erie, important for timber and corn, fresh fish and a variety of manufactures – automobiles, agricultural implements, screws, nuts and bolts – and an orchestra which has for possibly the past twenty years had a very plausible claim to be the premier American contender for the title 'The Greatest'. True, the population, at almost one million, is well able to support such an organization, but the reasons for it doing so are fairly obscure and make interesting reading. The orchestra came into being in 1918, and was soon the primary concern of the local Musical Arts Association, which still has a board of trustees governing its activities. For a long time the activities of the orchestra were fairly obscure; but in 1931 it moved into a new and permanent home, Severance Hall, a delightful and wonderfully ambient venue. (I often wondered when I played there what sort of 'severance' had had such happy results. In fact it was the gift of the well-known philanthropist John Long [*sic!*] Severance.) In 1933 our old friend Artur Rodzinski took over, as conductor for a full ten-year span, and anyone who has played for him knows that this must have been a period of great foundation-laying, training and discipline. Then in 1943 Erich Leinsdorf took over for three years, and possibly a new warmth began to emerge. It was, however, in 1946, when Georg Szell became the permanent conductor for twenty-four years, until his death, that the truly great period in the life of the Cleveland Orchestra began. To a London player, as well as one in Sydney, this seems incomprehensible, because he was without doubt the most universally-hated conductor in the world. Of his ability there can never have been any doubt; but as I've mentioned he always said he intended to prove he was a bastard.* A fine example of this was when he spent a week in London during 1968 recording Tchaikovsky's Fourth Symphony with the LSO. The orchestra were quite thrilled with the sort of results they got (or so I hear, since I was in the BBC Symphony Orchestra at the time). At the end they thanked him warmly and he graciously deigned to reply, 'Gentlemen,' he said, 'you have been more than generous. I asked you for only one pitch. Throughout the week you have given me two or three.' He walked out, never to be seen by those players again in this life; but he insisted for the remainder of his days that the recording should not be issued. It was not by his own orchestra I suppose. Some years later, as a BBC presenter of record programmes, I unearthed it. It is the finest recording of the work I know.

In spite of Szell's personal failings, he was perfect for the Cleveland Orchestra. Bob Marcellus, their excellent principal clarinetist, worshipped him, even though Szell gave him such little freedom as a soloist that the only recording I know of Bob's is a wonderful Mozart concerto. Szell insisted upon expanding the orchestra to 104 players, and the season from thirty to fifty-two weeks. Incredibly, he also started successful family and children's concerts, and was the inspiration for the opening of the Blossom Music Center in 1963, situated in 800 acres of open country at Cuyatoga Falls, a summer venue which has become world famous, and was later used most effectively by Szell's successor in 1970, Pierre Boulez, a very different sort of man and conductor. The

* Buttrose, *Playing for Australia*

next conductor in Cleveland was Loren Maazel, a remarkably
efficient and most exciting conductor who had once been ar
excellent violinist, and brought the knowledge he gained in tha
pursuit to illuminate his work. Playing with Maazel is a pleasure
as he wastes no time at all and gets excellent results by trusting hi:
players. He was in Cleveland for ten years, 1974–84, and ther
departed for Vienna, where his talent and personality seem tc
have been less keenly appreciated. The present music director
who followed Maazel in 1984, is Christoph von Dohnanyi
grandson of the well-known composer, and his work has so fa:
been greatly acclaimed. During his first season, in 1984/5
attendances ran at 99.9 per cent of capacity, and as a result hi:
contract has been extended to nine years' duration.

All this may sound like the crest of a wave, so it is somewha
surprising to learn that the season in question resulted in a ne
deficit of $111,009. No reason is given for this in the president':
report for the year, nor does it seem to give cause for concern. A
solid volunteer staff are at work on the Sustaining Fund, which ir
1984 reached a total of over $2.5 million, and another group is a
work on the Fund for the Future, which aims at raising $12 millior
as a buffer against such future difficulties. The president main
tains that the Association is in sound financial condition, and the
orchestra, who are never bothered by such details, are withou
doubt in excellent artistic heart. The financial stability of the
Association is, as in all American organizations, the result of wide
and well-organized sponsorship, both corporate and individual
There are several thousand of these sponsors, all honoured to be
supporters of one of the world's great orchestras.

The players, it is hardly necessary to say, are very happy indeec
to be in such demand throughout the world, and recordings, TV
appearances and much-appreciated foreign tours are very mucl
to the fore. The orchestra made ten international tours betweer
1973 and 1982, as far apart as Japan, Mexico and Australia, Latir
America, South America and Europe. In spite of such remarkable
busy-ness, services per week are a mere seven and a half or eight o
two and a half hours each. The *minimum* weekly salary is £580, witl
extra pay for each five years' service of £11 per week, and extra
payment for records, TV and touring. Holidays on full salary
amount to eight weeks per year, and each week must have a
completely free day. Extra rehearsals above the eight-service cal

are paid at £50 each. Sick leave for a player of ten years' service is thirteen weeks per year on full salary, and thirteen weeks on half salary. In the event that a player becomes totally disabled, he receives fifty per cent of his salary up to the retirement age of sixty-five. 'Rest days' after a tour vary from one, after a four- to ten-day tour, to four after a twenty-five- to twenty-eight-day tour, in spite of the fact that on tour there is an average of one and a half free days per week. Eighty per cent of medical bills or hospital bills are covered. The annual budget is at present just under $13 million – and for a city of one million inhabitants it is one of which they can be proud. They certainly have more, there.

L'Orchestre de Paris. Regular radio listeners who have persisted over the years (and by that I mean over twenty years and more) may have been puzzled at the disappearance of a very familiar French name in the orchestral world, 'l'Orchestre de la Société des Concerts du Conservatoire de Paris'.

It used to be a superbly sonorous prelude to many a sparkling broadcast from Paris, as well as a delightful tongue-twister to those of us who had to announce it from time to time on the air from BBC studios. There seems to be no explanation as to why this title should have faded out, or why one suddenly became aware of the much simpler 'Orchestre de Paris'. Those in charge of the newer orchestra simply state without preamble or amplification that the new title took the place of the older, while pointing out with some pride that the Society Orchestra, which dated from 1828, was the oldest professional orchestra in the world. They have every right to this pride, because it was the Orchestre de la Société, etc, which brought many hitherto unknown works by Beethoven, Weber, Schubert and Mendelssohn to Paris, to say nothing of its intimate association with Berlioz. It was also a favourite orchestra of Richard Wagner, and in the later period between the wars it presented new works by Debussy, Dukas, Chausson and Richard Strauss. Stravinsky was also inspired by its typically French sound, and I sometimes feel that several of his works were orchestrated with just that sound in mind. Those were the days when orchestras had very much more individuality than one can find nowadays, and Parisian woodwind and brass both had qualities not to be easily mistaken.

From 1938 to 1945, directed by Charles Munch, the orchestra

had a really magnificent period of expansion; but after that, in spite of the heroic efforts of André Cluytens, it began to succumb to the financial difficulties being felt by many Parisian artistic enterprises; and after a life of 139 years, in 1967 it virtually ceased to exist. It was then that André Malraux and Marcel Landowski decided to create l'Orchestre de Paris, founding it upon the spirit of the venerable institution, but giving it a new breath of life. The mission was stated to be 'to play the leading role in Parisian and French musical life, and to carry the prestige of French music abroad'. To this end, financial support was obtained both from the state and the city, but possibly the most important involvement was that of a large number of French companies called the *Cercle de l'orchestre de Paris*. The rules of the new orchestra were quite simple, but certainly firmer than those which governed the society's orchestra, whose players came and went much more freely than was good for continuity of standards or style. The new orchestra insisted upon first call upon the services of the players, who were recruited by competition (and usually heard behind screens by the audition panel) and had to serve a whole year on trial before acceptance. One hundred and fifteen players were engaged, and Charles Munch, who had been such a success with the society's orchestra, was re-engaged as music director. He was not merely their conductor, but in charge of the complete musical policy. This was in 1967, but by 1968 Munch was dead, after collapsing on a tour of the USA with his orchestra. He had been known to us as a superb visiting conductor, and we recognized how serious his loss was to the Paris orchestra.

They had, however, made such an impression under Munch that they had no difficulty in continuing, and from 1969 to 1972 they were fortunate in having Herbert von Karajan as their director. This was a period during which they established a most worthy reputation, and since then, with Sir Georg Solti from 1973 to 1975, followed by Daniel Barenboim, from 1975 to the present, they have gone from strength to strength. The orchestra has been the main preoccupation of that remarkable young musician, who was barely thirty-two years of age when he took over, and is among the greatest pianists of his time, as well as an excellent conductor.

Another creation of the *Cercle* has been the Paris Choir of 200 amateurs under the direction of Arthur Oldham, who used to be chorus-master to the LSO chorus. They join the orchestra in many large-scale works which happily the Salle Pleyel, the home of the orchestra, can easily accommodate. This hall, now one of the best in Europe, was completely renovated in 1981 by the Crédit Lyonnais, and is used also for the many chamber-music activities which are part of the orchestra's activities. These smaller concerts started in 1975, and have become so much a part of the Paris musical scene that since 1984 they have simply been handed over to the players, who choose and submit their own programmes.

The regular pattern of a working week in Paris is: Monday, two rehearsals; Tuesday, two rehearsals; Wednesday, rehearsal and concert; Thursday, repeat concert; Friday (sometimes), concert; Saturday and Sunday free. This is not out of line with what one expects in the USA or elsewhere – seven or eight appearances; the number of concerts per year is, however, quite small in Paris – about seventy – which means that touring accounts for quite a lot of the orchestra's activities. October and November 1968 found them giving thirty-one concerts in twenty-four towns in Canada and the USA. October 1976 was given over to twenty concerts in the USA, and there have been many other similar tours over the years. They estimate an annual audience for their Paris concerts of 150,000 and have attracted such conductors as Abbado, Boulez, Giulini, Haitink, Kubelik, Mehta and Ozawa. In addition they have children's concerts which draw audiences totalling 50,000 per annum, and they have been happy to invite several celebrated foreign orchestras to take part in their concert series, including the New York Philharmonic, the Amsterdam Concertgebouw, the LSO and the Chicago Symphony.

In addition to their prestigious concerts in Paris, the orchestra does not neglect the French provincial musical market. Each year they settle for several weeks in an outpost where they can establish a mini-festival: Lille in 1983, Marseilles in 1984 and Bordeaux the following year – places the old society orchestra would never have considered visiting. There is also a fine French Youth Orchestra under the same banner as l'Orchestre de Paris, and it is expected that this will form the nucleus of the players required for the future.

A worthwhile aspect of the policy of the orchestra is the inclusion in their programmes of new works by living composers, many of them French, but several, like Xennakis and George

Crumb, Lutoslawski and Berio, from other countries. These new works appear several times each season, and prove that if they are introduced with tact and care – that is to say in a properly balanced programme – they need not empty the hall as they have sometimes done in London and elsewhere.

The musicians, when asked, are all very happy and optimistic. They seem to be doing what they want, and doing it as they wish. They are certainly not as well-off as their American friends, but they are prosperous enough, and do not feel things should be radically changed. They work on a year-to-year contract, which they seem to like, and have a good pension scheme. Being French, they wish to have a certain freedom of action as well as a certain stability of employment, and most of them think the set-up is a good one. I am inclined to agree.

The Royal Liverpool Philharmonic Orchestra is a surprising phenomenon which reveals some remarkable facets when one starts to look into its history, achievements and activities. It is the oldest orchestra in Britain, and pre-dates most of the proud names in foreign climes, including the Vienna Philharmonic, which is two years younger. Since 1840, when the Liverpool Philharmonic Society was founded, there has been an almost unbroken series of concerts up to the present day, and since 1849 the orchestra has had its own hall, used for concerts with choir if need be, and latterly for broadcasts and recordings. This settled home is a very restful and satisfactory aspect of the work. There was a homeless period of six years between 1933 and 1939 while the old hall, destroyed by fire, was being replaced by the magnificent one which now exists, a forward-looking design by Herbert Rouse. Hardly any of us saw this hall in its early days, due to the outbreak of war, and I still recall the delightful surprise with which I first saw it in 1944, on leave from the RAF. It was at the time far better than anything else in the country, especially since London's Queen's Hall had disappeared in the Blitz. To this day it still retains quite a lot of its original magic, and it still has one added advantage found in very few others: the back of the stalls and the balcony can be shut off when desired, leaving a superb chamber-music hall holding about 500, and still sounding good.

There have been some famous names associated with the RLPO. Max Bruch was musical director from 1880 to 1883, and

Sir Charles Hallé, in spite of his Manchester orchestra founded in 1857, was the holder of the Liverpool post from 1883 to 1913. He was the forerunner of the modern jet-set conductor, although it must be said that the railway service between the two cities was then superb, and the distance is only thirty-five miles. There followed Sir Henry Wood and Sir Thomas Beecham as the main conductors, and in the interwar period up to the destruction of the old hall in 1933 such names as Ansermet, Koussevitsky, Monteux, Furtwängler and Weingartner were frequently to be seen in their programmes. The orchestra suffered in the early days of the Second World War, because such was the damage to the city that concerts were unthinkable. But the new hall was luckily un-damaged, and in 1942 the orchestra was reformed with many of the old London 'stars' and a few of the disbanded BBC Salon Orchestra under the direction of Sir Malcolm Sargent. I remember this as one of the high spots of the Liverpool orchestra's life, especially a great performance of Dvořák's Cello Concerto in 1944 which brought Pablo Casals to the country for the last time. He never returned after the war because he felt we in Britain should not have recognized the Franco government in his beloved Spain. The performance was unforgettable for the incredible personality of the little man who was its centre. I suppose Sargent *did* conduct, but he seemed to be invisible; and the orchestra was quite incredibly good, by any standard.

After the war, predictably, there was a drift away from Liverpool by many of the best players, back to London: violinist David Wise, viola player Frederick Riddle, clarinetist Reg Kell and several others left the orchestra, so there were gaps to fill. Gwydion Brooke, returning from the desert tank he had occupied in the war, got out his bassoon again and was a leading light for the first year; but he succumbed to the Beecham magnet in 1947 and joined the new RPO. None the less, excellent replacements were soon found, and before long the Liverpool orchestra was of international standard once more, conducted from 1948 to 1955 by Hugo Rignold. As I've mentioned, the Polish tour I did with them in 1970 was most memorable, and Sir Charles Groves, who was their principal conductor from 1963 to 1977, was as always a joy to be with. Before him there had been a period of excellent development with Sir John Pritchard, from 1957 to 1963; and it was at this time, in 1957, that the title 'Royal' was bestowed on the orchestra, by Her Majesty the Queen.

Their history since 1977 has been most distinguished, with three years under Walter Weller, three more with David Atherton, and a further three, to the present, conducted by Marek Lanowski. Contemporary music has always featured strongly in their programmes, with Musica Viva Concerts as their focal point. They also have a composer-in-residence – currently Edward Cowie – and have given first performances of many new works by him and other living composers. One of their happiest associations is with the Friends of the Phil, fundraisers and moral supporters over 2,000 strong, and belonging not only to Liverpool but also to the other towns in which they regularly play – Preston, Blackburn and Warrington regularly, as well as Southport, St Helen's and the Wirral. It is primarily a concert-giving orchestra, in spite of its recording successes, with a very strong community responsibility. There has never been any doubt as to the value of the work they do, the standard of performance, or the industry and enthusiasm of those who perform. Yet of late there have been great worries and dangers, and at one time in 1985/6 things looked very black for the continued existence of this 150-year-old organization. The Conservative government decided to abolish the Metropolitan Councils, among them Liverpool, which simply meant that the RLPO would lose their magnificent hall. Upon such far-away events do our artistic endeavours depend for their existence. Happily, 100,000 local voices were raised in protest, and somehow disaster has so far been averted, but nobody in the orchestra can feel entirely secure with such a threat still somewhere off-stage.

The RLPO is, however, an orchestra of very buoyant morale; very much a family affair, and the husbands, wives and children of the players meet each other much more frequently than is the case in many another orchestra. There is general satisfaction with the way the orchestra is managed and the sort of schedule worked, not least because distances from home to work are not so great as in some cities, and there is a regular and pleasant venue for rehearsals and concerts. There are some criticisms of backstage conditions, which I must say I find less than satisfactory, especially if one has to change clothes or eat; but there is a corporate feeling of pride in the work which helps to sustain the remarkably poorly-paid rank-and-file members, and I think they all feel privileged to be one of the 'high-spots' in a very depressed area. There is also a slight feeling at times of envy for the few better-paid members, which is not surprising (though nobody is making a fortune in the RLPO). The cost of living in Liverpool is not as high as in some major cities, which certainly helps, but with such an orchestra and such a need, financial aid is essential, both quickly and in quantity. Security of tenure, as in the Hallé Orchestra, is good, and dismissals are rare. Departures are not quite so rare, because players of the standard of these are in demand. It says much for the ambience which surrounds the title RLPO that so many of them show such loyalty, and says much for the loyalty of the Liverpudlians that their Special Activities Fund, in addition to support by almost 300 commercial institutions, can boast donations big and small by 250 private individuals – money on which they have already paid tax. As their principal bassoonist, Edward Warren, says, 'One has to generate one's own enthusiasm with not-too-many "shots in the arm" by way of prestige dates. The orchestra's mission is to supply the standard classics to a regular circuit of northern towns, who otherwise would never hear them; but there is less hassle here than in London, and a feeling of being wanted. That helps.' It would also help if salaries could be remotely comparable with those enjoyed by orchestras of this standard abroad – but as we have seen this is a familiar phenomenon in Britain, even with an orchestra whose recording of such works as Elgar's *Gerontius* and Handel's *Messiah* are regarded as classics, and who were chosen by Sir William Walton when he wished in 1975 to record and conduct his own *Belshazzar's Feast*.

The Los Angeles Philharmonic Orchestra. If any orchestra might be expected to have 'much more' (with the possible exception of one domiciled in Texas), it would be the Los Angeles Philharmonic; and so it turns out when their situation is examined. They are rich, and they make use of their wealth. The surprising fact remains that they do provide a tremendous service to their community while they are at it. It is the nearest thing to getting a quart out of a pint pot that one can find in the world of music, in my opinion. To start with, they all work all the year round, from the beginning of the concert season in the Dorothy Chandler Pavilion in the Los Angeles Music Center in October to the end of the summer season at the Hollywood Bowl in mid-

September, a total of more than 200 concerts. With all the rehearsals involved, this adds up to a great deal of work; yet they work only eight services per week, and have eight weeks of paid vacation. The secret is good organization. They carry 105 players including quadruple winds in all departments, and a string section of sufficient strength to 'rotate' quite comfortably.

It obviously wasn't always like that. The orchestra was founded in 1919 by an amateur musician and art patron, William Clark, and a conductor called Walter Rothwell. Concerts were given from that date until 1963 in the Philharmonic Auditorium, and during that period there was remarkable expansion and a very marked improvement in artistic standards, especially from 1930 onwards, when Artur Rodzinski took over as conductor and worked his usual training magic for three seasons, to be followed by a man who could well use a properly trained orchestra – Otto Klemperer. He carried on until 1939, when illness forced him to take his leave. He was followed by Alfred Wallenstein, who conducted a season at Glyndebourne during his tenure of office, which ended in 1959. The RPO found him secure but uninspiring in the Stravinsky work we were playing; but we appreciated his obvious knowledge. He had been Toscanini's principal cellist, and told us of his farewell to that maestro in 1935. The volatile Italian had wished him luck in his rather frigid way, but expressed the firm hope that *his* principal cellist would be as awkward to deal with as he had found Wallenstein!

From 1959 there have been four very celebrated conductors, all of whom have left their stamp upon what has become a very fine orchestra: Eduard van Beinum (1956–9), Zubin Mehta (1962–78), Carlo Maria Giulini (1978–84) and André Previn to the present. The gaps, due to Klemperer's illness in 1939 and the death of van Beinum in 1959, were filled by a succession of guest conductors.

Certainly theirs is a job which requires stamina, especially in the Hollywood Bowl season each summer, where audiences of about 15,000 can sit in their little 'corrals', each family a private party, and a good many of them turning over the beefsteaks in their barbecues to the accompaniment of Beethoven's Ninth or Brahms' Fourth. Here on Friday one plays a Marathon – a concert which starts with marches and waltzes in the first half, from 6 until 9 pm, and usually tucks in a choral item, Sibelius' Violin Concerto and one of the bigger Tchaikovsky symphonies in the second half to end at midnight. It's not so bad for the winds, who can work separate halves of the concert; but for the bulk of the strings it can be quite a trying experience, and when the LSO did it without quadruple winds we all wondered how life could be supported in those circumstances.

During the winter subscription season things are very different and much more rewarding. Working conditions are remarkably good, and almost all eventualities are covered in one of the most comprehensive orchestral agreements ever printed. Programmes are varied and quite adventurous, with a special ensemble of thirty-five of the orchestra's members performing as the 'new music group'. In addition there is a wide range of contemporary music played by the whole orchestra, and during one week of subscription concerts a living composer is invited to conduct a complete programme of his or her works – including Boulez, Lutoslawski, Berio, and most recently Penderecki.

As a result of its interesting activities as much as anything else, the orchestra continues to attract and retain the loyalties of its members over long periods. The average years of service at any time amount to over fifteen. Salaries are excellent, with a basic minimum of about £35,000 per annum, severance pay after ten years of over £10,000 and many extra payments for recording, TV, chamber music and solo appearances. Earned income from ticket sales and so forth pays for eighty per cent of the orchestra's budget, which is £16 million, and thirty-four per cent of this is paid out in salaries. Support from the city is £35,000, from the county £195,000, from the state £207,000, with a national grant of £517,000. These are generous indeed, but it is the endowment fund which is the mainstay of the whole enterprise, bringing in no less than £5.5 million annually.

With this sort of wealth it is easily possible to take care of the players. Medical benefits exist 365 days per year, sick leave on full pay stands at 182 days per annum, and the players contribute just twenty per cent towards the premium which produces a very generous pension. Touring is limited to twenty-one days per year, and the normal tour length is limited to eleven days. It is a system which has established itself slowly over the years, but there is no doubt that the shape is to some extent the work of the executive director, Ernest Fleischmann – a name we have come across earlier in this book as the manager who took the new LSO to the top of the league table in the 1950s.

Fleischmann, who went from London to the Los Angeles orchestra in 1969, is also general director of the Hollywood Bowl, and in the past sixteen years has greatly extended the orchestra's activities in many directions, including concerts at the Bowl, in southern Californian communities and in youth projects. He has also promoted a great deal of contemporary music. He was born in Germany, has lived in South Africa, and his range of talents is wide: he is a chartered accountant and a Bachelor of Music. As a result he has tried his hand at both conducting and administration, as director of the Johannesburg Festival in 1956. Obviously, with so many people able to do the conducting side of the job reasonably well, he chose to be a superb organizer and planner, with the results we now see. He is certainly at the head of one of the world's most successful musical enterprises, and one his players are happy to belong to. There are just one or two of these who, when asked, suggest that in such a flexible organization they are sometimes made to feel rather like a moveable chess piece or a small and sometimes over-lubricated gear-wheel – but you can't have everything, and they certainly seem to have most of the essentials of a happy orchestral life.

The Hallé Orchestra (Manchester) is among the oldest in Europe, and certainly much older than any of the London orchestras. I recall as a small boy hearing the BBC Symphony and other smaller combinations in broadcasts almost daily, and the occasional and dramatic appearances in programmes of the Hallé Orchestra were special treats, always seeming to have something just a little different about them. The difference of course was that of a live concert after hearing so many studio broadcasts – but it was a long time before I realized that this orchestra, with an obviously French name and usually conducted by some guest conductor or another from abroad with a name like Ansermet, was in fact simply an old-fashioned northern English combination, and the pride of Manchester.

Charles Hallé, a conductor, founded the orchestra in 1858, and gave the first concert in the Free Trade Hall at an exhibition of art treasures. He continued to conduct frequently until his death in 1895, by which time the pattern for the future was established with the Hallé Concerts Society, an organization which still exists to this day. After Hallé's day there were several important permanent conductors, the best-known being Richter (1899–1911) and Hamilton Harty (1920–33) and a number of celebrated guest conductors, the most prominent being Beecham. There was something of a slack period in the 1930s, when thirty-five of the principal members of the orchestra were also the BBC Northern Orchestra; but all this changed dramatically when Barbirolli returned from the USA in 1943 to reform the Hallé Orchestra, and auditioned everyone in sight, including at least one bass player who swore he had never been up in that part of the 'G' string before. The new orchestra was a revelation to everyone who heard it, and gave performances of Berlioz's *Symphonie Fantastique* which had rarely been equalled up to that time. The orchestra now receives grants from the Manchester Corporation and the Arts Council, but has had serious financial troubles in recent years. It is a quite essential feature of music-making in the north, serving as it does Bradford, Sheffield and Leeds as well as the Greater Manchester area, Hanley, Nottingham and Wolverhampton. Later conductors have been George Weldon (1951), Maurice Handford (1953–70), James Loughran (1971–83) and, since 1984, Stanislaw Skrowazewski, who still holds the post of principal conductor.

A glance at their itinerary shows that although they are based in Manchester, with the Free Trade Hall as their home, they are usually 'on the road' most of the time. (The Free Trade Hall, incidentally, is a new one. The original was accidentally destroyed by fire towards the end of the Second World War. This begins to look like a northern habit, as the same thing happened in Liverpool in the thirties.)

There are hardly two Hallé concerts on successive days in the same place, which must make the job extremely tiring and difficult to organize. It says much for the resilience of the players that the standard of playing is usually very high. Concerts amount to almost 150 annually, of which one-third may be in Manchester, and about a dozen abroad in Europe on what must be one of their very welcome breaks from routine. It is obviously also very hard work for any conductor, so in any month there may be two or three involved, usually the resident conductor and a couple of guests like James Loughran and the young Welshman Owain Arwel Hughes.

The conditions of employment are interesting, as are the details of administration. In direct contrast with their London colleagues, neither the players nor their administration are represented on the board of the Hallé Concert Society, which is twenty-five strong (fifteen elected by the Society, six by the local authorities and four from selected sections of the community according to the need of the moment). However, the board seems to be content to allow the general manager, Clive Smart, to settle all matters of budget and policy. He has been with the organization since 1958, as has the orchestra's leader, Martin Milner, with whom he has been able to discuss decisions for many years. However, it seems that in 1987 Martin is to take early retirement (possibly as a result of a slight fracas hinted at in Chapter 12). His post will then be taken over by Michael Davis, the leader until then of the LSO, but a Hallé player for many years before that.

The general Hallé contract is subject to thirteen weeks' notice of termination on either side, but this is rarely required. In fact twenty-five members of the 100 or so total are not on the standard contract but prefer to be paid on a fee-per-concert basis, which gives them a minimum level of earnings similar to that to be found in London. Having discussed these fees earlier one can say that this may be acceptable, but only just. As to the rest, the standard contract, when equated with the amount of work involved and the hours of travel required, gives a remarkably poor return for artists of the standard of the personnel of the orchestra. It must be remembered that this is an orchestra whose work is compared daily with the best to be found anywhere, and the rewards are certainly not comparable. The rank-and-file players, on entry, have a salary of £7,395 per annum. There are increments for the first eleven years of service, taking them up to £9,207, at which point they stop. Principals start at £8,319, and rise similarly to £10,353. There are certain extra fees to be paid for meals away from home and bonuses for arrival back in Manchester after midnight – neither of them significant. Retirement is at sixty-five and there is a pension scheme giving 1/60 of the final salary for each year of service, so that a whole playing-life of forty or so years will give a pension of 2/3 salary, say £6,000. This is certainly an improvement upon many British orchestral schemes.

The funding of the orchestra, which is a great problem, resulted in a deficit of £110,336 in 1984/5, which was helped out to some extent by £50,000 from the Hallé Endowment and Trust Fund, but left an accumulated deficit of £152,000 to be carried forward. This was in spite of the fact that this season was regarded as a considerable artistic triumph, and that the income from concerts in Manchester was seventeen per cent up on the previous year. Grants and guarantees from the Arts Council, the Greater Manchester Council and City Council, as well as Lancashire and Cheshire, came to £892,000. Sponsorship brought in just over £56,000. In view of the deficit, and the fact that the Greater Manchester Council was abolished by the government in April 1986, there is grave doubt as to where the next year's support will come from. The government has promised to provide 'the greater part' of this loss, whatever that means, but says it is looking to the metropolitan districts to make good the shortfall. Many members of the Hallé Society have serious doubts on this score. Meanwhile, the Society pays VAT on its activities, and the total in 1985 was £184,000 – certainly enough to cover the deficit and leave a profit on the year. It is all a very sad state of affairs, and quite a national disgrace when one considers the huge population of the large area in which the Hallé Orchestra is the only musical organization of any symphonic stature. Meanwhile the hundred players and the handful of staff who support them carry on bravely, doing what they believe in and hoping for the best.

Music in the Low Countries is dominated by one great major orchestra, the Concertgebouw of Amsterdam, which is certainly among the world's finest; but if one takes into account also the Benelux group of countries, thereby adding Belgium and Luxembourg, it is the sheer size of the orchestral picture which is impressive. I was most surprised in 1975, when invited to tour as soloist with an orchestra I had never heard of, the Over-Ijsell Philharmonic, from Enschede in the west of Belgium, to find that the standard was so high, the cultural spread so wide, and the number of people involved so great. This orchestra was formed by simply adding together two community orchestras, that of the small town of Enschede and the orchestra resident in Arnhem. The arrangement is not a permanent one but happens several times each year when programme demands make it expedient. When it does so, two orchestras of fifty-plus make an excellent full-size symphony orchestra, and their performances of Mahler symphonies can be most impressive. I learned at that time that Belgium may well be the only country in the world with a symphony orchestra for every million of the population, with several left over. The sort of amalgamation they practise in Enschede is by no means unique. Possibly the best-known example of this was the collaboration in 1984 of the Amsterdam Philharmonic (not the Concertgebouw), the Utrecht Symphony Orchestra and the Netherlands Chamber Orchestra, to become the Netherlands Philharmonic. That all this seems to have been done without job losses and consequent industrial action is amazing, and shows careful and tactful planning. It is too early to judge the artistic success of the amalgamation, but this could be considerable.

State aid for music in the Low Countries depends upon a network of organizations founded by the Ministry of Culture, the two chief names being Gaudeamus and Donemus. One of their avowed aims is the encouragement of the music of today, and without doubt their activities make the contemporary British investment in such projects quite derisory by comparison. The climate is good for contemporary music, and the plain fact is that they believe in and encourage Dutch music. In conjunction with the promoters Nederland Impresariaat, they organize 2,000 concerts each year, using government subsidies to offer reduced fees to the promoters. More than eighty per cent of the chamber concerts in the Netherlands are handled by NI and although it has been criticized as a government-aided monopoly there is no doubt that it brings great riches to the scene. As a result their many orchestras, while not occupied in earthshaking activities, are working steadily, profitably and on the whole happily, providing a wealth of music for the people who pay the taxes, which after all could be spent on much less worthy pursuits, and so often is, elsewhere.

There is one exception to the comparative anonymity of the Benelux scene – the fabulous Concertgebouw Orchestra of Amsterdam, which is one I have always loved hearing. It is named after the superb concert hall which is its home, dating from 1893. The word just means concert building, and there is something of a paradox here, because the orchestra was founded five years earlier, as the Amsterdam Orchestra, and assumed the name which it has made famous only at the time it came to occupy the hall. Perhaps its most important years were 1894–1945, when Willem Mengelberg held office as conductor. They were years of intense growth, development and increased international prominence, and may well be a record for length of office in such a post. He was succeeded by Eduard van Beinum until his death in 1959, and since then by Bernard Haitink – a fine succession of conductors who have well maintained the standard of excellence expected of such a combination of artists. They are supported by generous subsidies from the Dutch government and the City of Amsterdam, and have ninety-eight players on a very comfortable full-time contract which gives them leisure, prestige and also the freedom to play adventurous programmes in ideal conditions. Amsterdam has been described as being in the 'fast-lane' of European culture, with over 70,000 performances of all sorts in the city every year. The rule seems to be well-mixed programmes, possibly with Schoenberg and Berio in the first half and Wagner and Mozart in the second – a sure recipe for disaster in London, but successful in Amsterdam. There is also always in the background the booming giant electric and electronic concern Philips, a farsighted enterprise which once proved to me that planning can be the most important of human activities. I was having coffee on the terrace overlooking a huge lake adjacent to the lawn of the house of their president Mr Trompe, a delightful man who spoke excellent English. I commented on the happy choice of site. 'Surprising,' he said, 'when I built the house five years ago this was a stretch of open country. They told me the water would rise and make a lake. It did, last summer.' For me, the surprising thing is where it stopped – exactly at the fence at the end of the lawn. Sometimes I feel that the musical activities of the Low Countries have just that sort of superb planning.

The Bournemouth Symphony Orchestra is without doubt among the most important in the British Isles in the size of the area of its activities and the responsibility it has for bringing music to places which would otherwise be a desert. The whole of the West Country is its bailiwick, because there is not a single orchestra along the whole of the south coast, and whereas such towns as Brighton and Eastbourne can legitimately be expected to be served by London, Portsmouth, Southampton, Plymouth and Bristol are all orchestra-less, and while Cardiff, Swansea and

Gloucester are within range of the excellent BBC Welsh Orchestra, which does exist very much as a concert-giving entity, more is required than it can provide. Incredibly, the future of this vital Bournemouth orchestra is very much in the balance because of a tug-of-war between the management, the Arts Council and the local councils of Bournemouth and Poole for the necessary funding. Thereby hangs a tale. Why, for instance, is Poole involved; and why does it seem possible even now in 1987 that the orchestra may move lock, stock and barrel to Bristol, of all places, a full sixty miles distant?

The orchestra, which was formerly the Bournemouth Municipal Orchestra, is a very old one – older than any of London's. It started in 1893 to play on the pier and in the old Winter Gardens Pavilion, with the celebrated Dan Godfrey as conductor. He started Thursday Symphony Concerts in 1895, increasing his thirty players to forty-five for the purpose, and carried on doing so in a steady crescendo for thirty-nine years. During this time he not only entertained and even educated his audiences by a regular repertoire of the works of great and established composers; but he was also responsible for the presentation of new works by ninety-six British composers – 184 works in all. His retirement in 1934 left an orchestra in good heart and high esteem, and Richard Austin, who succeeded him, carried on the good work. With the war the orchestra did not cease operations, but was reduced in size to twenty-four players only until 1947, when Rudolf Schwarz took over, and it was once again increased to sixty-five. Charles Groves conducted from 1951, since when there have been several conductors who have brought the orchestra to a very high standard of performance. The title was changed to Bournemouth Symphony in 1951, and in recent years the same management has also been in charge of the Bournemouth Sinfonietta, a quite excellent chamber orchestra which tours widely and with success.

So much for the thumbnail history of the orchestra. The reasons for the present difficulties are not quite so straightforward, and seem to be many-sided. Bournemouth, wishing to make use of its orchestra, can see little justification for supporting it alone if it is so obviously benefiting others too. This resulted, in 1985, in the removal of the centre of operations to Poole, much to Bournemouth's chagrin (audience as well as council), so the famous Winter Garden lost its symphony concert series and Bournemouth audiences had to travel to Poole Arts centre, ten miles away. There was such antipathy that when Bristol came up with an offer to put on concerts at their fine Colston Hall if the orchestra would move there, the management were quite ready to accept. The orchestra thought otherwise, and eighty-five per cent of them voted against the move. The decision was not theirs anyway – Bristol finally decided against it – but there is as yet no firmly established plan either way. The orchestra is therefore on tenterhooks, in 1987, just waiting for their fate to emerge. As Raymond Carpenter, their principal clarinetist of thirty-eight years' standing, commented, there seems to be a complete lack of loyalty to what the name *Bournemouth* Symphony Orchestra stands for.

The general feeling of the players is, however, against self-government, of which they have little experience. Salaries are not regarded as satisfactory, and hours of work are said to be ridiculously high because of unpaid travel time. There is also a lack of satisfaction as to comfort in coaches, rehearsals and in concert halls generally. The pension scheme is reasonable, but has some critics because it is salary-related instead of index-linked. Security of tenure seems to be good, and resignations and replacements are few. There is also excellent morale within the orchestra, who appoint their own conductor and have excellent relations with him. He is regarded as a fellow-sufferer, and having shared dressing rooms with one or two of the maestros in question, I can vouch for the fact.

Here is an orchestra which deserves to do well, a good orchestra and one with great self-respect. It would be a thousand pities if it ceased to exist after the best part of a century. Funding simply must be found, if the West Country is not to become a musical desert. It is shameful that an established orchestra that has brought symphonic music of a very high standard to a wide area of southern England, should find itself in danger of extinction.

The Chicago Symphony Orchestra, widely regarded as one of the very best in the world, is old in comparison with most of our British orchestras.

Chicago got its new orchestra in 1891 when the conductor Theador Thomas brought it together and polished it until his death in 1905. Just a year before that unhappy event the new Orchestra Hall was opened. It remains one of the world's finest, well able to resist the perishing cold of the Illinois winter, with sub-zero gales blowing straight across the Great Lakes, as well as the remarkably hot summers which are enjoyed there, although usually at that time one plays at Ravinia Park, several miles out of town, and with an unlimited audience. The reason for this is the open-sided auditorium, seating over 2,000, but giving line-of-sight to about 3,000 more and well-managed amplification to the 10,000 or so picnickers who are present, if unseen, within a mile or so. (It is the only place I have ever seen thunderous rain actually travelling horizontally across a concert-hall – but that was luckily at rehearsal!)

Thomas' successors were all remarkably fine conductors. The first was Frederick Stock (1905–42). I never saw him at work, but those who did found him impressive. Then came Desiré Defauw (1943–7), who left less of a mark on the orchestra. Artur Rodzinski, who was also short-lived in the post (1947–8), possibly had more impact. Certainly by 1950, when Rafael Kubelik took over for three years, it was a remarkably fine orchestra already with its own sound, especially in the brass section, led then as now by the incredible first trumpet player Adolph Herseth. There are some people, possibly with shorter memories than mine, who attribute the splendid standard of playing to the later conductors Fritz Reiner (1953–69) and Sir Georg Solti (1969 to the present). I do not agree, in spite of the talents of them both. In 1950 the sound and discipline were exactly as they are now, and I feel sure that one of the secrets of this orchestra is continuity of style, personnel and tradition.

One hardly needs to add that it is a prosperous orchestra, a prestigious one and a much coveted post for any orchestral player. Turnover of players has been slow over the years as a result of this. Soon it will speed up, because although the retirement age is seventy (late for any great orchestra) a number of fine players have stayed well beyond that age – and in time even these must leave. The facts of life are much the same as in other major orchestras in the USA: a fifty-two-week year with eight weeks of paid holiday and a regular 7.5 services per week for a minimum salary of £32,000 per year, a sum which could well become £50,000 for many of the players, with extras for TV, radio and recordings, as well as seniority pay and special rates for principals. The maximum pension for 1987 reaches £17,000.

In such conditions one would expect few complaints from the players, and this is so. Some think the pension could be better, one considers there are too many personnel in the office, but all seem happy with salary, management, conductor, security of tenure, and the hall, canteens, travel arrangements and the general camaraderie. Nobody wants to try self-government – why should they? A glance at the programmes shows the works played to be middle of the road for the most part, especially at Ravinia Park, but works like Perle's *A Short Symphony*, Takemitsu's *Riverrun* and Ives' *Holiday Symphony* can hardly be regarded as 'pot-boilers', and in the Orchestra Hall series there are several names which would be guaranteed to empty most South Bank seats – Schwanter, Lutoslawski, Griffes, Stenhammar and Hindemith jostle for position with Beethoven, Mozart and Liszt.

It is all a saddening spectacle as seen from an orchestral seat in London, because it is so exactly what we have all been aiming at for so long. A further glance at the same programme explains why they have succeeded – sponsorship, most of it private generosity. There are eighty-five trustees requiring an executive committee of eleven to organize their activities; 355 governing members; five gifts of over $25,000; twenty-two of between $10,000 and $25,000; sixty-two of between $5,000 and $10,000; 500 between $1,000 and $5,000 – and about 200 who gave what help they could without it hurting too much, up to $1,000. All this in one year, with the promise that the next will be even better, because already the top-paying patrons have more than doubled, and this is a January programme, a half-way house in the season. It is perhaps slightly ironic that Claudio Abbado, musical director of the LSO, should have been simultaneously, during 1982–5, the principal guest conductor to the Chicago Symphony. I have never discussed differences in funding with him, out of courtesy for both orchestras. I personally think he got very much the same sort of *performances* from both – concerts at the very top of the world class. There is one deficiency in their plans in Chicago, which I find disappointing. They do not seem to make use of several world-class soloists they have within the orchestra. Could it be that some prophets are now without honour except at Orchestra Hall? In every other respect they seem to honour and treasure their favourite local artists, a shining example of what makes an orchestra world-famous.

The Toronto Symphony. I feel certain that while we have been looking at the world's orchestras you will have gained the impression that in my opinion there are overwhelming similarities between them in a personal sense. The Toronto Symphony is the prime example of this familiarity in all my experience. To see them playing at one of their Summer Pops in a park out of town called Ontario Place, giving alternately serious and riotously comic interpretations of works great and small, is to cast one's mind back to the open roof of the Barbican and their early seasons of just that sort of concert, given by the LSO and now given indoors because of the notoriously uncertain London weather. What is more, to actually meet and work with them is an even more familiar experience. In 1986 I was asked to join them for a concert they were giving in Cardiff, on a big European tour, and at times I could hardly believe I was not in one of our British orchestras – and it wasn't merely the language, or the fact that their conductor for the past twelve years had been one of our own young stars, Andrew Davis. There was something in their approach to the whole business of orchestral playing which was familiar, comfortable and satisfactory. This is the case of course with most of the world's orchestras, but particularly with them.

Most people now regard the Toronto Symphony as Canada's leading orchestra, and it certainly has made great strides in recent years. It is a fairly young organization, founded in 1922 as the New Symphony, at first as a part-time orchestra conducted by Luigi von Kunits. Most of the players were theatre or cinema-pit musicians who welcomed the opportunity to play symphonic music and were willing to give their spare time to rehearsing it. Gradually the emphasis changed, so that by 1926 it was officially the Toronto Symphony Orchestra, a title it continued to use until 1964, when it became simply the Toronto Symphony.

Conductors since 1922 have included some famous names, and involved only two permanent homes – the Massey Hall for the first sixty years, and since 1982 the excellent new Roy Thomson Hall, one of the most airy and dramatically-lit in the world. There is a thirty-seven week season there of thrice-weekly concerts, as well as about twenty schools' concerts and a liaison with the educational services which takes many of the principal players into the schools themselves for master classes. Touring internationally is a regular feature of the orchestra's activities, and has made them many friends. Possibly the most powerful influence was the twenty-five-year reign of Sir Ernest MacMillan as chief conductor from 1931 to 1956. He was a man of considerable force in the music world, and attracted some excellent soloists and conductors, including Heifetz, Stravinsky, Beecham, Sargent and Boult. He was followed by Walter Susskind, from 1956 to 1965, a conductor · whom I always felt was underrated. A fine pianist who came to London in the 1930s as part of the Czech Trio, he was an elegant conductor and a man of great charm, and expanded the activities of the Toronto Symphony greatly during his nine-year stay. The next conductor was one who certainly brought a dazzling intensity to the post from 1965, the young Seiji Ozawa, but he stayed for only four years, and his effect upon the orchestra was transient. The next four years, from 1969 to 1973, probably did more to establish a settled style in the orchestra, being the last in the life of the superb Czech conductor Karel Ancerl, the creator of the Czech Philharmonic. It was in 1974 that Andrew Davis took over, and his period of office has been most successful and happy. He was just thirty when he was appointed, and has in fact developed along with his orchestra in a most satisfactory way, while finding time and energy to leave them from time to time and experience most of the world's best orchestras.

The Toronto Symphony now enjoys a reputation as one of Canada's most financially sound organizations. It is contracted for forty-eight weeks per year, and busy but not oppressively so during that time. It has an overall budget of about £9.25 million and payments to the orchestra of 105 members, conductor and soloists total £5.5 million annually, making the earnings of the average player very much in the American range. The money is raised in many different ways, and kept well under control. Only forty per cent of it is accounted for by earnings (ticket sales, radio and TV, recording etc); the remainder comes from grants from the Canadian Council, the Ontario Arts Council and the Metropolitan Council, totalling £2.5 million, and donations totalling £1.5 million. It is the raising of this last sum which, as in most other successful orchestras, is the turning point. The organization is headed by a board of directors comprising sixty-nine members representing practically all the facets of the professional and artistic life of Toronto, and in addition there is a women's committee almost 400 strong, whose avowed aim, in addition to fund-raising, is to stimulate musical appreciation in young people. They recently published the Toronto Symphony Cookbook, sponsored five CBS recordings of the orchestra, have acted as a business sponsor, endowing several of the most important chairs in the orchestra, presented a Steinway concert grand piano and furnished a splendid Green Room. They have published a book on orchestral activities, and liaised with the board of directors, upon which they have three representatives. They have a junior department, equally dedicated, who perform the more mundane tasks like Christmas teas and fashion shows, all fund-raising and vital in their way. There is a huge list of associates – professional and business people who act as sponsors and find new audiences whenever they can bring their influence to bear.

The foundation, in spite of all this, is not satisfied with its achievements. With assets of £2.5 million, they feel that other North American orchestras are better placed, and regard a target of £12 million as desirable and achievable. They stress that this sum must not be at the expense of the annual donations which keep the orchestra afloat. They expect, and are getting, bequests and special deeds of gift to create this fund. There is one further enviable factor in the lives of this very familiar-feeling orchestra – the splendour of their concert hall. I don't know who Roy Thomson is or was, but the hall which bears his name, designed by the architect Arthur Erickson and completed in 1982, is a masterpiece. From outside it is a multi-faceted glass shell right in the centre of the city. Inside there are sweeping staircases, soft-carpeted lobbies and walls of mirror and glass, all surrounding an auditorium which seats almost 3,000 (just the right limit for hearing a concert properly). The visual perspective is quite remarkable, and has some of the admirable features to be found in the Berlin Philharmonic Hall and St David's Hall in Cardiff: no seat is more than 107 feet from the stage, creating a sense of intimacy and allowing for different aspects of the performance which can keep interest alive. The hall has variable acoustics, with thirty movable reflective discs suspended above the stage and woven woollen banners which can be lowered to deaden things a little, as for instance in projecting the human voice. (This is an important aspect of concert-hall creation, but can be dangerous, as it does let someone fiddle with the sounds produced. I recall the 'goldfish bowls' at the Barbican, the roof sound-relays at the Royal

Festival Hall which took a long time to settle in, and the disastrous experiments at Glyndebourne with sound-delay equipment which made it sound rather like a sluggish Albert Hall.) But, back to the Toronto Symphony, an orchestra which is 'going places', and seems to know where it is going. Their artistic policy is admirable, their funding most securely organized, and the morale of all concerned extremely high.

With them we must leave our survey of a few of the world's orchestras I have personally met. There are many more even in this category, and a greater number I do not know so intimately and therefore will not review. I have been able merely to touch upon life in the BBC Symphony, an orchestra I have admired for a lifetime and played in for nine years in the sixties. No details of their current salaries are available to me, but I do know these are not princely. Conditions of work, including the hours involved, are better than those found in the freelance world, but it is a job which fails to excite, and is therefore less attractive to most players I know than a post in the LSO or LPO. It is in any case financially much less rewarding than anything to be found in the USA, and compares badly with most European contract orchestras in this respect. There is also an excellent book about the history and activities of the BBC Symphony Orchestra which makes any further discussion here unnecessary.*

The orchestra of the Royal Opera House, Covent Garden, I know only as an infrequent guest player, when I have enjoyed playing in it. Their total calls per week average seven and a half, and the rank-and-file salary is as low as £11,000 per annum. Some players are lucky enough to be able to participate in the freelance activities in London in their spare time, and with these additions they have a profitable, varied and stimulating professional life. The remainder, in my experience, tend to become introverted, unhappy and dispirited.

No review of this sort would be complete without mention of the Northern Sinfonia of Newcastle-upon-Tyne, a smallish combination which has for twenty years or so brought excellent music to the dark places of my own Tyneside homeland. Again I have met

* *The BBC Symphony Orchestra 1930 – 1980*, Nicholas Kenyon, BBC Publications

them only as a soloist at odd concerts, but I admire them greatly, and am delighted to know that they are now expanding to enable them to perform much bigger works, and also seem to have some bright ideas up their collective sleeve. In 1987, for instance, they have appointed an artist-in-residence – a young sculptor and painter whose job it is to illustrate the music they perform, and who works in such unusual media as cracked porcelain, stainless steel and polished teak, and can illustrate anything from a Shostakovich Symphony to the *Carnival of the Animals* in vivid shapes. The Northern Sinfonia seem to be facing a future full of interest and possibilities.

Finally, an orchestra I have scarcely mentioned except *en passant*, but which is one of the most important – the Scottish National. There are several reasons for this omission. First, though I have quite a few friends in their midst, I have played with them only as a soloist, and scarcely know the sort of life they lead. More important is the fact that Glasgow, their home town, is due to receive so much artistic attention in the coming years that anything I could say here would be pale in comparison.

During 1990 Glasgow will become the European City of Culture, which will be the climax of that city's efforts during the past five years to clean up its image and foster an interest in the arts. Their excellent St Andrew's Hall was destroyed by fire in 1962. In 1987 a start is being made on a £14 million concert hall, designed by Sir Leslie Martin. One hears that this should be the best in Britain, and as it is within a stone's throw of the new Royal Scottish Academy of Music and the Theatre Royal, home of Scottish Opera, it could well be the finest arts complex in the country.

Much of the credit for this must go to the conductor of the SNO from 1959 to 1984, Sir Alexander Gibson, a man who made adventurous additions to the repertoire of the orchestra, inspired the establishment of Scottish Opera, and started an annual festival of contemporary music, called at first Musica Viva, and now continuing as Musica Nova. These are exciting on-going activities, and I am sure they will be in the news during the next two years.

The SNO undoubtably has a bright future, and with Stephen Carpenter as their general administrator and Neeme Järvi as their music director things will certainly not stand still. The orchestra is not only involved in a huge quantity of work, but the quality is being maintained at a very high level, and I hope and believe that it will become an orchestra able to offer very happy and increasingly profitable employment.

There are other important orchestras I have not even been able to mention. The characteristic of them all, here and elsewhere, is, as the French say, 'Plus ça change, plus c'est a même chose!' They are in fact all made up of very much the same sort of people, doing the same job – but *not* in quite the same way. If one can draw a reasonable conclusion, does it not seem that we may be guilty, in Britain, of shortsightedness in the support we give our orchestras? It could be the shopkeeper attitude we proudly boast about. (If it doesn't pay, don't stock it.) Could we not possibly change our use of current English speech, whereby we *spend* money on museums, art galleries, garbage collection and parks, as well as of course upon unemployment – but we *lose* money on concerts! Just a change in that one word may bring a new attitude, and it is one that many of us think could have considerable returns to make. Our orchestras are excellent exports, and fine ambassadors. Let us keep them safe, as others certainly do theirs.

PART FOUR

FINALE
Sempre Pomposo
('Our Conductor's the End!')

12

Batuto Non Sempre Giusto
('At Times You Can't Trust That Beat')

After the usual topics of wine, women and just the occasional excursion into song I find that the orchestral player's favourite, or at least ubiquitous, topic of conversation is conductors. The rather surprising question is often asked, 'Is your maestro really necessary?'; and to this I have to say 'Yes', but with just a touch of qualification. That such a question is asked at all tends to demonstrate that the issue is not so clear-cut as it might seem to audiences who are accustomed to the phenomenon of the Man in the Middle. One must remember that there are still people who are not converted to this phenomenon of a silent but powerful musician and are puzzled by it when they first encounter it.

I once met one of these Philistines at Newark, New Jersey, about a hundred miles south of New York, and a place notorious for the race riots which occurred only a few weeks after I was there in 1970. It was a strange choice of venue, at that time, for the sort of concert the LSO were about to give: a concert for schools, in a town where the whole atmosphere seemed to crackle with the static of suppressed violence, and where one might have supposed the main function of a teacher was to hope to keep the peace. In spite of this the complete orchestra and their most distinguished conductor Gennadi Rozhdestvensky had travelled down specially for the event, to play quite an advanced programme which presumably had been chosen by the local authority. There was no plan to have an interlocutor, so we expected that the spadework would have been done in the schools, and the programme explained to the pupils. No such luck.

Instead of the long queues of thousands of schoolchildren we expected at 11am, a dribble of about fifty children of all ages and several hues wandered into the huge super-cinema, herded by a single teacher, just before the conductor entered. The silence was hardly deafening, because they were not a silent community by nature; but of recognition or applause there was none, apart from sarcastic tapping of bows and scraping of feet from the orchestra. I was with the teacher in charge, as was my wife Joan, trying to get at least some of them seated, when the fatal question came from the educator herself, who seemed puzzled at the arrival of Rozhdestvensky and the orchestral silence which followed. 'What's that guy for?' she asked. It took just a couple of seconds for me to realize that she wasn't joking. She didn't know.

Assuming that she wanted to instruct her young charges, I gave a fairly rudimentary explanation of the function of a conductor with his orchestra. She was unimpressed. Obviously if the guy made no sound, he had no place at a concert. 'Where's he from?' was her next query. 'New York', I replied, 'like the rest of us – but we are usually in London – England' I added hurriedly, because I'd been caught on that one before: there are quite a lot of Londons around. 'As for the conductor,' I added, 'he's very famous, and usually conducts in Moscow.'

'Gee,' she almost shouted. 'You don't mean to say the guy's a Ruskie?' Saying which, she gathered together her charges like a mother hen her chicks, and as Berlioz's overture *Les Francs Juges* ran its thrilling course, they made noisily for the exit. It just shows that by no means everyone knows what a conductor is for, nor even if his presence is necessary, let alone essential.

I agree that this may well be an extreme case, but the doubt has obviously also been expressed in Britain, because the LSO did a TV show in 1972 with André Previn which had that very title, *Is Your Conductor Really Necessary?* This time we put it to the test, with interesting results, and very little rehearsal. It was some well-known Dvořák with which we started, and the plan was that André should start us on it, then walk off and leave us playing on our own. It had, of course, been carefully selected, and upon his exit there was no serious difference, so after about a minute he scrambled back on to the podium, muttering something about 'not letting these fellows give our secrets away like that'. It was a clever ruse, because he chipped in just before a change of tempo which would have made it pretty obvious that we *did* need a conductor. I can't remember how this was demonstrated in the remainder of the show, but I know it was. (This was of course a 'fun' concert, so no real conclusion was attempted.)

One would like to be able to say 'Yes, the conductor *is* essential', but one cannot be quite as definite as that. I think perhaps one can say that there can be no great performance without a great conductor, and that most performances are safer and happier with a conductor than without. On the other hand, it is possible to have excellent performances with a small orchestra *without* a conductor, although in this case the leader is really doing the maestro's job as well as his own. Many of us, incidentally, are now saving impressarios large parcels of money by playing classical concertos in this manner, with a tight liaison between soloist and leader. It works quite remarkably well, and is enjoyable. It saves the conductor's fee, and everyone is happy, except him. I suppose it might even be possible to extend this sort of activity to a larger orchestra; but the choice of work would be crucial, and would need a lot of concentration. It could also be disastrous.

Finally I think it must be said that although all conductors have tremendous influence over performances, that influence is not necessarily always to the good. There have been, in my experience, a handful of conductors whose influence is, or has been, bad in a *positive* sense. They do not give *poor* performances, but make an orchestra which normally plays naturally musically play really *badly* and unmusically. Some of these have been rich and famous. Wild horses will not drag their names from me, because I bear them no ill will. I have never had a personal dislike for any of them, but rather a deep sadness in their presence. They are unlucky to be bad musicians. We are unlucky to have to play for them.

There is another factor which makes conductors and their work a constant topic of discussion. Not only do they influence performances: they affect every aspect of the life of an orchestra, and even the individual lives of its members. Every orchestra is looking for its dream conductor, unless they have had the incredible luck to find him already. If they have, life is sweet, until he leaves or is absent for long stretches. If they have not, the conductor they do have is in trouble, because everything he does will be compared with the dream, and found wanting. This is unfair, because of course he is only a man, and is certainly doing his best; but it may not be so unfair as all that, because his critics can quickly point out that he is not supposed to be just a musician like them. He may quite recently have put down his bow or left his piano stool, but it was with the certain knowledge that from that moment on the people who employ him consider that he is now worth more than the whole orchestra in financial terms, and regarded in addition as knowing more about every player's job than the player himself. As a result of this all conductors become deeply philosophical, and some players slightly cynical, although it may be a case of sour grapes with most of them. It is a circumstance which has no possible solution, because unless a conductor does become the complete master of the situation he is certainly not doing his job, and in that event he is likely to please his orchestra even less. He does need the cooperation of the players, however, and occasionally the good will which is essential for peaceful relations between conductor and players (and especially the orchestra leader) breaks down momentarily. Such occasions are sometimes sad, sometimes amusing, and almost always unintended by either party. Usually they are covered up nicely by displays of somewhat frigid good manners, but on occasions even this aid to the maintenance of the status quo is missing. An example of this sort of slip happened in 1986, and involved the principal conductor and leader of one of our most famous British orchestras in the north. They were holding auditions for a vacant seat in the first violins, and it was a very searching affair, involving many important orchestral passages which the maestro conducted with a multiplicity of flourishes and frequent tempo changes, to say nothing of a wealth of *rubato*. Finally he gave his verdict of the playing of one violinist who had impressed the leader. 'He's not bad,' he said, 'a good sound and technique. I just wonder how he'd get along with a really bad conductor!' For a moment the leader was off his guard. 'I don't know about that,' he retorted. 'He seemed to do pretty well in the things we heard him tackle this morning!' Relations in 1987 are reported to be seriously strained . . .

In a personal sense I must honestly say that I have not suffered at all from bullying conductors – but I can vouch for the fact that there have been such people, and they are not a pretty sight. It is a breed that has largely died out now, happily, because of the jet-age and the fluid situation, with quite a small number of top-line conductors holding multiple conducting posts with the main orchestras in the world. Such marriages do not now usually last long, nor are they expected to. The well-known book published in the USA about forty years ago called *Dictators of the Baton** wasn't

* David Ewen, Alliance, 1943

really supposed to be insulting to those included. The concert-goers expected their conductors to be dictators, and paid for them to be so. I don't think one could honestly compile such a book now with any justice; now, like actors, conductors have ceased to be a race apart with an accent and an ambience of their own. They are now *people*, and do not expect to be treated as super-beings, as did their predecessors.

The famous cellist Gregor Piatigorsky is most amusing about his conducting experiences in his autobiography, called simply *Cellist*.* A giant of a man, he was a concert artist from the age of nine, and at fourteen was principal cellist of the Imperial Theatre in Moscow. That was in 1917, a fairly critical time in the history of his country. Leaving home, as so many others did at the time, he became principal of the Berlin Philharmonic in 1921 until 1928 and thereafter devoted himself to solo playing in Europe and America. In Britain he is remembered especially for his commiss-ioning and first performing William Walton's Cello Concerto in 1956. Obviously he is the best possible example of a great orchestral player who became a great international soloist. But he did also have one or two conducting opportunities more or less thrust upon him, and the results were surprising, especially to him. The first thing he noticed was that he now had the best room in the backstage area of the concert hall, and usually the one with the best piano, in spite of the fact that he now needed one rather less. What really surprised him, however, was that he was immediately taken quite seriously as a conductor, even though his experience of this aspect of his art was nonexistent, and he was relying heavily upon the skill of the orchestra to unravel the mysteries of the works involved. Further surprises awaited him after the first half of the concert, which he thought he conducted rather badly, and the audience seemed to find very impressive. He is probably being unduly modest in this description of his conducting debut. He was that sort of man – although just a little later in the book he tends to counter this impression, by saying that he was extremely disappointed at the reception he got for his Dvořák Concerto in the second half of the concert which he thought he had played really well, and the audience greeted with remarkable coolness. As he says, 'The little baton won such an

* Da Capo Press, New York

easy victory over my Stradivari, but it was a bitter victory rather than sweet, and when offers to conduct began to come from all over the country, I swore never to touch the baton again. I never did.' He is, however, very appreciative of the advantage of being a guest conductor, saying,

> There are three reason why a guest has advantages over a permanent conductor. He really knows his one programme, the orchestra does not really know him, and everyone knows he will go away. He differs from his players in almost everything. He dwells at the top of the heap, and one never hears of a conductor working his way up to become a bassoonist. I have played with all kinds of conductors – with young and old, famous, unknown; with groaning ones, stamping ones, with masters and mediocrities. But, healthy or sick, there was never one who suffered from an inferiority complex.

Piatigorsky's experience is one we can all echo.

There is another fact about important conductors which I find puzzling. Some of them, who make just a few appearances, are vividly recalled and stored away in the memory. Others – and some of them more famous in the end – pass unnoticed when they first appear, and only later begin to assume importance. In several cases I have looked back on old programmes and found names which are now among the most celebrated, which I had missed at the time. Possibly this is because they emerged in circumstances which did not allow them to blossom, or they had been involved with works in which they were not really at their most inspired. In 1950 we had Ferenc Fricsay to conduct nine performances of *Figaro* at the Edinburgh Festival. For us it was a non-event, and all we can recall is his sadness at not being able to get the very special *pianissimo* he wanted because of the shallowness of the pit. Others seemed able to do so, but Fricsay really failed, and the orchestra found him less than impressive; yet within a year or two he was achieving great success with the Berlin Philharmonic Orchestra, and hearing him perform made one wonder how we had somehow missed one of the good ones. This lack of recognition of talent has happened quite frequently, and I always feel it is more likely to be noticeable with conductors than with instrumentalists. Perhaps Fricsay's trouble was that in the 1950s he was overshadowed by a most magnificent *Ariadne auf Naxos*, the first version of Strauss' opera, with Molière's *Bourgeois Gentilhomme* (the play) as the first half, complete with Strauss' splendid incidental music. The stage production was by Miles Malleson, and the opera version in the second half was conducted by Beecham and produced by Karl Ebert. There are some things one should not have to compete against, and possibly Fricsay knew it.

Perhaps more surprising was the appearance, a little later, of Georg Solti, at Glyndebourne in 1954. Again the opposition was quite formidable, with Gluck's *Alceste* given a rare and wondrous series of performances by Gui, and Paul Sacher rising to great heights in Stravinsky's *Rake's Progress*. Solti was in charge in nine performances of *Giovanni*, and at the time nobody seemed to feel that a great new maestro had arrived. There was no great frisson so far as audiences went, either, judging by their applause at his appearance; yet history has since shown that such first impressions, or lack of impression, can be very misleading. The bubble of fame sometimes takes its own time to inflate. There is something else any player will be wise to know about conductors, especially if he himself intends to stay long in the profession. He must know not only who is who, but who is *going* to be. It isn't easy to come to terms with the fact that the very young second fiddle in the Martin String Quartet in London, with whom one did a very early broadcast – 1948 I think – of a Mozart Quintet for the BBC (which was far from epoch-making on anyone's part), is now Sir Neville Marriner. (We get along very nicely, in spite of the fact.) Then there's the rather interesting chat I had with one of my oldest associates, Wilfred Hambleton, sometime bass clarinettist of the Philharmonia. We were at the time trying to recall the 1950s, and the year 1951 came up for scrutiny. It had been a memorable year for the Brymers, full of doubts, illnesses and the birth of my son Tim to bring it to a dramatic conclusion, but that wasn't the sort of thing we were discussing. It was a year in which Beecham had done one of his Inland-Revenue-inspired disappearances to the USA, leaving the RPO at a loose end; von Karajan had just had his final row with Walter Legge and gone off to Berlin, leaving Philharmonia similarly unemployed. Brymer and Hambleton, full of resource, took a little job at the Haymarket Theatre (now demolished) in a tiny orchestra of eight, four strings and four woodwind in a deep, narrow pit, directed by a musical director in the middle at a mini-piano. 'You remember,' said Wilf. 'It was the Jean-Lous Barraud show, something about Amphytrion and his wife, with Jupiter dressed up as Amphytrion, barging in on her and pretending to be just back from the wars. The small dark chap in the middle, who didn't speak much English. You've seen him since. Do you remember who he is? Pierre Boulez!' Suddenly I did remember – and it stirred another memory, too. I was at that time a professor at the Royal Academy of Music, and on the way to the Haymarket Theatre (you could actually park cars in those days) it was my custom to stop for a meal in South Audley St at the remarkable International Music Club. It was a place of many advantages, including not only sumptuous lounges and bars (with Malcolm Arnold usually in close attendance) but a dining room where you could get a meal equal to anything at the Ritz for a sixth of the proper price. The deficit, it seems, came at six old pence in the pound from the taxation of a friendly wealthy American lady who happened to like British music and musicians. It was a short-lived benefaction. Before long the tax man declared it an operation obviously aimed at loss rather than balance of books, and it ceased to exist; but while it was going its merry way, if you ascended the deeply carpeted stairs to the sumptuous lounge, you could often find William Glock – a friendly soul who seemed to have a lot to do with the organization of this remarkable club. I had met him before, in 1948, as an excellent pianist at some chamber concerts at Glyndebourne. I was to meet him again as Sir William, controller of music at the BBC, while I was a humble employee there, and a man who did more for contemporary music, both British and foreign, than anyone before or since. I related all this to Wilfred. 'Ah yes,' he said, 'but when you left the club and came down to the theatre, do you remember the name of the deputy second clarinet if I wasn't there? Colin Davis . . .' (another of my favourite friendly conductors, I'm happy to say). Where, I wonder, did Hambleton and Brymer go wrong in the years which followed?

It must not be thought that all this discussion of the magic of the baton is purely theoretical, because almost every decent musician has a go from time to time at waving a stick about. Some find it easy, some discover quite a few hidden reefs they had never suspected. Very few indeed are deluded into thinking that world fame is just around the corner, because being a great conductor is second only in difficulty to being a great composer, and that, as we all know, is completely impossible now that all the good tunes have been used up. There is one aspect, however, which I think should be cleared up before launching into a survey of some of the most distinguished maestros encountered in a long career – that of the so-called Magic Memory. Some conductors have made a tremendous reputation out of this – the ability to recall the details of a complicated score, bringing in the essential instruments at the right moment and arranging the climaxes at just the correct points in a given movement, all without reference to the written notes. It is certainly very impressive, and in many cases quite remarkable. It is, however, not by any means as difficult as it looks.

As Piatigorsky says,

> Once the conductor has disposed of his instrument, his gifts reach undreamed-of heights. His feeble memory for music develops phenomenally – instead of peering prosaically at his second violin part, he will with ease conduct the entire score from memory. His health improves beyond recognition. There are but few octogenarian virtuosi; when they exist they are freaks of nature. You do not see such a monument in any orchestra.*

This is an opinion most players share. Those of us who try to conduct may well find it possible to get through the whole of Tchaikovsky's Fourth Symphony without opening the score, yet on trying to play it from memory may fail after a few lines in spite of decades spent in performing it. Suddenly, with the baton, it is all in C major, and merely a series of graceful shapes to recall with delight without bothering about technicalities. It isn't too difficult to dispense with the score. What *is* difficult is to reveal first to the players and then to the audience what the composer has put in it – and many of the conductors we will now be looking at have had, or *do* have, that supreme gift – with or without the score.

The Magic Memory really hardly matters, except that with no score to gaze at, the conductor's eyes can communicate to his players his desires and intentions, and with no music-stand in front of him he can move freely and expressively.

It is quite impossible in a book of this size to attempt to describe more than a fraction of the number of conductors who can claim to be worthy of inclusion. We have already met some of them, because their work has been so bound up with the development of the various orchestras we have looked at that their personalities have had to be revealed. I have talked about only those I have

* *Cellist*

played with and met, because it seems to me to be the only way to reveal anything of real value. I can honestly say that in the case of almost every conductor I have first encountered as a member of the audience and have later worked with, the true personality has been something of a surprise. There have been one or two exceptions, but certainly no more. So I make no apology for the shortness of this list of conductors. I have played for many more, and enjoyed most of them. Here are just a few who have made a lasting impression, and whose personalities may be of interest to you.

First, let us dispense with the composer-conductors. They are the ones who should have the gift of communication, but it is rarely found to be the case, and many of them would be wiser to allow the more talented conductors to reveal their works. There are a few exceptions. Benjamin Britten always seemed to get details from his works that no other conductor could. Stravinsky had a unique ability to convey his complicated rhythmic patterns. As he used to say, 'You have five fingers, five toes. Why do you not *think* in fives?' (He was right – but it is slightly unnatural to the rest of us mortals.) Aaron Copland also presents his own music very ably, even though I did have to perform his clarinet concerto with only ten minutes' rehearsal at his Eightieth Birthday Concert in 1980 at the Royal Festival Hall in London. Hindemith was a borderline case; his is quite romantic music which he conducted very dryly, for no reason one could easily find; in his speech he was a man full of humour and warmth. Khatchaturian was a staunch champion of his music, and brought great strength to it. Richard Strauss had an excellent reputation for conducting his works, though at the end of his life in 1947, I found his beat rather undramatic for such full-blooded music. Others, like Sibelius, Bax and Debussy, seem to have had mixed fortunes as conductors, but some of my older colleagues of the LSO in the thirties remember Elgar as conducting excellently, other composers' works as well as his own.

Coming to the non-composing conductors, Beecham has been so often discussed that he needs no further attention from me. We have also met Sir Eugene Goossens and Sir Charles Mackerras in Australia, seen Arturo Toscanini and Herbert von Karajan briefly at work (which is all I ever did), been slightly appalled by Georg Szell, admired Rudolph Kempe, been impressed by the majesty of

Klemperer, and told tales of Cantelli, Rodzinski and Krips. We turn now to some of the other important conductors who have left an impression on my consciousness over the years – unlike the gentleman who conducted the Philharmonia in 1949 at a less-than-inspiring concert at the Albert Hall, when Alec Whittaker was the principal oboeist. Asked in the pub later who had conducted, he hardly broke his drinking rhythm. 'Don't know,' he said, 'I didn't look!' My own list contains none of these faceless friends, and is roughly alphabetical for ease of reference (*roughly* because whereas Ozawa and Previn make excellent contrasts in juxtaposition, others contrast better slightly out of sequence).

13

Senza Malizia, Ma Non Sempre Con Ardore
('Not Intentionally Rude, But Sometimes Slightly Critical')

Ernest Ansermet (1883–1969) was certainly one of the best of all Swiss conductors, yet to work with him was somehow a very French experience. He was an expert in French music, and brought the Parisian touch of Stravinsky, Debussy and Ravel with him in a most natural way. His conducting of Ravel's *L'Enfant et les Sortilèges* in particular was a delight; he even knew the exact tone of voice the speakers needed, to give it a particular childlike sophistication which is essential to its success. Many people found Ansermet sad as a person, but his music never drooped, whatever his shoulders may have done. He was a gentle-voiced man, and incredibly fastidious in his music-making. I sometimes felt he should have settled outside Switzerland, because in his time the orchestra he conducted there, the Suisse-Romande, was not among the world's greatest; but he did get some excellent results from them, and was certainly a local hero. I once heard him greet Beecham with the words, 'Unfortunately, Sir Thomas, you will not have a full hall. I am here tomorrow with my orchestra, and we are sold out. They will not come twice.' Oddly enough, they did, and Sir Tom winked broadly at Ernest, who was sitting in a prominent place, as he walked on. Ansermet had a long life, and was also a successful composer in his day. He had something quite special. He had the privilege of restarting the Glyndebourne Opera after the war, in 1946, with the world première of Britten's *The Rape of Lucretia* (fourteen performances in the draughty and damp place it was at that season). He did not appear there again, which is a pity because I am sure he had the sort of musical integrity which would have been impressive in those later years when his own favourite repertoire of French opera was explored at Glyndebourne.

Claudio Abbado (1933–) is undoubtedly among the great

conductors of today. He combines in some ways the three essential factors: first the image of the famous maestros of the past, with their excitement and personal attraction; second, a capacity to go into details which are missed by many; and third, the most important of all, the ability to give first-class concerts every time. He was born in Milan, of a musical family. His brother is director of music at the Verdi Conservatoire, and Claudio was taught conducting by, among others, Carlo Maria Giulini, a maestro for whom he retains a very high regard, as do we all. As a very young conductor, Claudio won many awards including those in New York, Tanglewood and Vienna, and he has been principal conductor at La Scala, Milan, with the London Symphony Orchestra, and the Vienna State Opera. He is quite vocal in his appreciation of music-making in London, which is now his true home, calling it the Classical Capital of the World, but strongly deploring the unadventurous programmes made essential by financial circumstances. He is quite choosy in his selection of orchestras, and has been known to refuse some famous engagements if he felt that the time and place were not appropriate (the Berlin Philharmonic for instance have succeeded in getting him for no more than about one in five of their requests). He can also be very demanding of rehearsal time and conditions, and several famous singers have been excluded from productions on this score. The LSO experience has been somewhat similar, in that they would prefer to do less rehearsal, and are certain they would get the same excellent results. Claudio thinks otherwise, and rehearses in great detail and at length. But that he gets superb results there is in no doubt whatsoever. He also has personal charm and social grace which carries with it an air of kindness which is essential to the sort of relationship he has with orchestras. He is quite outspoken about them: 'Vienna, Berlin and Chicago are great for the German romantics – Schubert and Brahms; but for Stravinsky, Bartók and the rest you need the London Symphony, the greatest in the world for this repertoire.' I may add that some of Claudio's Mahler, with any orchestra, is in that very class.

Sir John Barbirolli (1890–1970) was one of that rare breed, an orchestral cellist, and a good one, who became one of the world's finest conductors. He didn't start as a cellist, but his habit of wandering about while playing the violin upset his family, so with the cello he became 'anchored'. At the Royal Academy of Music in London one soon gets used to seeing lists of past prizewinners with the name Giovanni Batiste Barbirolli prominent. He was a prodigy, a recitalist at the age of eleven at the Queen's Hall. After eighteen months' service in the Army in World War I, he returned to orchestral and chamber music and solo playing, but from the age of twenty-seven he became a conductor, and quickly made a name for himself in both opera and symphony. In 1936, to everyone's surprise, he succeeded Toscanini as conductor of the New York Philharmonic. I knew his work only from 1944 onwards, but by then he was certainly among the most inspiring of conductors, with something of the Toscanini drive, much of Beecham's magic and an intimate knowledge of stringed instruments which he put to good use at rehearsal. We wind players used to enjoy the long stretches he set aside for this purpose – almost as much as John enjoyed the short gaps he himself used to make in the proceedings for a 'wee dram' of this or that potion. Barbirolli was certainly one of the most memorable and important of all our British conductors, one of the few who could come and 'shake things up' without destroying them. He gave many thrilling performances, and quite a number of very tender interpretations. He was one of the best of British!

Leonard Bernstein (1918–) is a man of so many talents that to classify him simply as a conductor is an understatement. He has appeared briefly in these pages as the young assistant conductor of the New York Philharmonic Orchestra who in 1957 became their principal conductor, and carried them to new heights of TV stardom and prestige that possibly no orchestra had before scaled. It says much for the integrity of this remarkable musician that it was several years before his conducting became known to other orchestras. He stayed in New York, although we all made sure of making contact with his rehearsals there on every possible occasion, and found them both intensive and revealing. This was hardly surprising, because in addition to his talent as a pianist which was possibly his earliest asset, he studied conducting with Reiner and Koussevitsky, and was assistant conductor to the latter at the Berkshire Music Centre while still in his early twenties. He also took a great interest in the development of the Israeli Philharmonic Orchestra from 1948. As if this were not enough, he composed copiously the while, including sonatas, a symphony, song cycles, an opera called *Trouble in Tahiti*, and of course later the scores for some notable musicals including *Candide* and the quite unequalled *West Side Story*. Few of us in London will forget the impact of this last opus upon the West End in 1958 from the point of view of the pit-orchestra involved. It was so very different from the *entr'acte* type of music usually to be found there. For one thing, it involved jazz players, who had to have real style. They also had to read with great accuracy, and this isn't easy music. Then again, the woodwinds were expected to double on all sorts of instruments from bassoon to piccolo and saxophone to cor anglais – and play them all up to a solo standard of performance. In London this was easy, and even the American trumpet player who was imported to sit in and advise the brass section proved to be unnecessary after the dress rehearsal. In Paris a year later it wasn't quite so simple. In the second act, finding the whole brass section had become unhinged, he chose a point in the score which could be recognized as a landmark because of the instruction *Con sordini*, and shouted 'Mutes!' The response was immediate. All eight players inserted their mutes, and then gazed at the music again – still lost.

Bernstein may possibly have gained less prestige than is his due because of this extremely wide range of musical vision. 'A gifted technician, he combines classical and popular styles in a clever, racy manner which has won him considerable success' is the most *The Concise Encyclopedia of Music & Musicians** can say about him; but to be in the orchestra when he conducts the opening of Mahler's *Resurrection* is to realize the deep passion of the man, and this opening frenzy is sustained for the whole great length of the work. At a post-concert reception in London in 1986 someone asked me, 'Who do you think will follow Lennie?' Perhaps it was an indiscreet question, as the mid-sixties is young for such a musician, but it seemed to demand an answer. 'It's simple enough,' I said. 'Just find someone who can write another *West Side Story* or the *Prelude Cadenza and Riffs* we heard tonight. Then get him to write a really intense Mass, and follow it with a performance of Mahler like the one we had yesterday. After that, see if he can play the Ravel Piano Concerto while conducting the

* Hutchinson, 1958

Vienna Philharmonic, and turn the TV lights on. If you have someone who can do all this, you have another Leonard Bernstein.' There really may be such a person, but if so he has not yet come my way, and if he did so he would be phenomenal, as is Lennie himself. He has accepted the post of president of the LSO in 1987, and will be a most welcome visitor whenever he comes to London.

Pierre Boulez (1925–) was, as mentioned earlier, director of music to Jean-Louis Barraud at the age of only twenty-two. That is by no means his only claim to fame, because he is without doubt among the most celebrated *avant-garde* composers of this century. That he is not regarded as a composer-conductor is perhaps surprising, but his extreme professionalism and his intense interest in other people's music have meant that he can be regarded as a conductor *and* as a composer, which is a rare coupling. In his compositions, of which I, like my BBC Symphony colleagues (he was our principal conductor from 1971 to 1978), have had a very wide experience, Pierre Boulez is abstract, unemotional and Euclidian. The sounds are always pleasant and unstrident, but the rhythms are of a complexity which few have equalled, and Boulez is entirely capable of conducting these with security and style. To see him at work in Moscow in 1976, where such music was unknown when we played it, was a remarkable experience – and the young Moskovites loved it. With his Schubert, Mozart and Brahms I myself felt much less satisfied, and sometimes wondered if he should conduct the sort of music he has obviously rejected in his own writing. Recent years, however, have shown a pleasing change in his attitude, and most players now feel a secure warmth in his conducting which he did not have as a young man. It will be interesting to see what the next stage turns out to be, as he enters his sixties.

Sir Adrian Boult (1889–1983) was among the most English of conductors which may not be regarded as a great compliment by some people but is certainly intended to be one. He was a great champion of the music of Elgar, which he felt deeply and conducted superbly. I once played *Falstaff* with him, in 1950, and was delighted to find that one section, which had always disappointed me in his recording, played at too fast a pace, was now smooth, even and leisurely. I asked him about this, and was rewarded with one of his gracious smiles as he said, 'Ah, my boy, you've got to remember that we all had to live with the tyranny of the four-and-a-half-minute disc' (it was before the days of LPs). 'Even Elgar couldn't do anything about that!' It didn't seem to bother him at all, any more than when Terence MacDonagh asked him what he was beating at letter D. 'Not much,' said Sir Adrian, 'as usual.' He was not always so flippant, and there were occasions when his face became flushed in a most dramatic and even alarming way, with flashing eyes that boded ill for someone; but these were rare occurrences, and for the most part Sir Adrian was the perfect English gentleman. (He once heard me say this in a BBC broadcast, in 1968, and never forgot it.) His Brahms was also at the very top of a world class, having a breadth and a warmth few others could give it. He was one of the few conductors who really did improve with age. In his middle years he seemed somehow to lack drive, sparkle and 'sizzle'. In later life, without tremendous exertion (which was in any case against his nature; he once told a friend of mine, 'The afternoon's the time for *sleep* – right between the sheets!') he was able to inspire an orchestra to great climaxes. I was always amazed to hear that in his twenties he had conducted a season of Diaghilev ballet, and had been an early champion of English contemporary music, because in later years he was less adventurous. His was a long career, and one of a steady crescendo.

Fritz Busch (1890–1951) was one of my earliest memories of the Glyndebourne Opera, and by the time we met in 1949 he was already a legend there. In fact he was one of its founders in 1934, having left his native Germany as an anti-Nazi. He had been the director at the Stuttgart Opera, and brought with him a long experience of opera which we lacked at that time in Britain. It can be said that he was the true musical mainspring of prewar Glyndebourne, and to compare the programmes then with what they have since become is revealing. In 1934 he conducted both the Mozart operas (*Così* and *Figaro*), in 1935 he did the same but added two more (*Magic Flute* and *Seraglio*), and in 1936 he did all four and added *Giovanni*. This could not go on as an arithmetical progression, so in 1937 he did all five again, but made up for this by adding two operas in 1938 (*Macbeth* and *Don Pasquale*). Perhaps not surprisingly, in the last prewar season in 1939, there was simply a repeat of 1938, but a total of no less than thirty-eight performances in all.

The next chapter in his Glyndebourne history is less than happy, with a quarrel with John Christie over the possession of the production rights of *Macbeth*, and this resulted in Glyndebourne restarting in 1946 without Busch, a situation which lasted for four years after which Busch was persuaded by the new and brilliant young general administrator, Moran Caplat, to return and Glyndebourne became itself again. It was a wonderful year, with a warmth of feeling I can't recall in any other opera house, but the triumph was short-lived. During a performance of *Giovanni* in 1951, Busch was suddenly taken ill, and John Pritchard had to rush in from Eastbourne (his car burnt out on the way) to finish the show. In less than two months Busch was dead, and we had lost one of the most oustanding Mozart conductors of our time – a man of modesty, charm and unfailing good humour.

Antal Dorati (1906–), is an American of Hungarian birth, in spite of his adopted Italianate name. There is no doubt about the strength of his personality, nor about the tempestuousness of his demeanour, but that is by no means the complete man. He has an extremely wide-ranging talent not only in conducting but in music generally. When I first met him in 1962 as a frequent conductor of the LSO, particularly in recordings of rather exotic music, we all thought of him as something of a specialist in the music of Bartók, Kodály and other very colourful composers of that period. He is the last person I would have expected to appreciate the 'authentic performance' movement which has gained such impetus during the last ten years, yet I feel he was among those who largely inspired it. It is true that he seems not to have insisted upon, or even experimented with, the sound of instruments of bygone days; but possibly his most important contribution to music has been his painstaking and scholarly recordings of all 104 symphonies by Haydn with the Philharmonia Hungarica, a most flexible and nicely scaled-down orchestra with which Dorati always tried to follow the composer's original instructions to the letter, very much according to the researches of Robbins Landon. It is true 'period' Haydn, and was among the first in the field of 'authentic' performances which are now so fashionable.

Dorati is also a composer of considerable talent, his output including two symphonies. I have played only the second of these, and found it extremely well-crafted in the way Hindemith used to write, and also quite listenable in a way much twentieth-century music is not. We played it at Dorati's final performance as principal conductor of the BBC Symphony Orchestra in 1964 while I was a member, and I regret that this performance was never heard by the public then, because the recording was never finished. We were recording in No.1 studio at Maida Vale, with a very small invited audience (a setting hardly worthy of such an occasion, but the BBC can be like that, sometimes). It must be said that relations between Dorati and his orchestra had not always been of the sweetest, largely because his temper had such a short fuse, and he often said things he didn't really mean before walking out to cool off. On this occasion all went remarkably smoothly, and we all enjoyed the performance and wondered why we had never been asked to play this music until then. Unfortunately, about thirty bars before the end, all hell broke loose somewhere in the rear. A more than enthusiastic percussionist succeeded in dislodging the huge tam-tam (a gong of truly epic proportions such as is used at the start of most old black-and-white Korda films) from its stand, high up on the final 'rise' of the orchestral stage, upon which it rolled its deafening way right through the orchestra, from back to front. Maestro Dorati, this time, refused to walk out. He simply gritted his teeth, turned to the control-box, and shouted, 'From letter X'. The recording resumed. Sadly, at exactly the same spot, the tam-tam once again became dislodged, and made an even noisier descent through the second fiddles. This was too much. Throwing the score in the air the maestro departed, and the recording was abandoned; a pity, because it was a pleasant work, and would have been a revelation to quite a few listeners. It says much for the character of Dorati that only ten minutes later he was drinking a farewell glass of champagne, having bought a gaggle of bottles for the orchestra, with all his players, including the recalcitrant Jack Lees, the champion dislodger of tam-tams.

Sir Colin Davis (1927–) is the conductor who followed Dorati in the post of principal conductor of the BBC Symphony in 1964. He was still a young clarinetist in 1951, as I've mentioned, but at that time already an aspiring conductor with the Kalmar Orchestra and the Chelsea Opera Group. This brought him some local fame and was soon acknowledged by the BBC, who appointed him assistant conductor of the BBC Scottish Orchestra in 1957. He became principal conductor at Sadlers Wells Opera in London in 1958, and it was obvious to most musicians that something important must soon emerge for him. His great moment came in 1959, when at a moment's notice he took over a concert performance of *The Magic Flute* at the Royal Festival Hall in place of the ailing Klemperer. His success was immediate, and in a few months he was in great demand internationally. He successfully conducted the RPO at Glyndebourne the next year in place of Beecham, who was also ill, and from that time forward he has been a great conductor with almost every important orchestra worldwide. He has also had several important posts, including the principal conductorship of the BBC Symphony from 1964 to 1971 and Covent Garden Opera from 1971 to 1985, and is at present the maestro at the New York Met.

His ability to turn his talent to throw light upon many sorts of music has made him very popular and a conductor who is very much in demand. The London Symphony Orchestra have always held him in great esteem and affection, and I know from my conversations with members of the Boston Symphony that the same feelings exist there. One aspect of his work, which I always feel he inherited from Beecham, is his mastery of the music of the very French composer Berlioz. It is quite surprising, but two British conductors really do seem to have had an insight into this music which one would expect to be more noticeable across the Channel. I think it is possible that both of them have always brought to it an intensity as well as a tenderness which may not be so typically French as is the music of Debussy or Ravel. It could be the most important achievement of Sir Colin.

Norman Del Mar (1919–) has been mentioned earlier, as a member of that remarkable horn section of the RPO when we joined forces with the French Radio Orchestra at Haringey in 1947. From this it is obvious that he was a first-rate orchestral musician, and must have spent much time and energy in becoming one. It is therefore all the more surprising that only weeks after Haringey he should have been in front of us, in place of Beecham at a very prestigious concert, and with Richard Strauss in the audience listening to him conducting one of his (Strauss') big orchestral works, the symphonic poem *Macbeth*. (For many years I carried in my memory a picture of Norman conducting *Don Juan* on that day, but he insisted otherwise, and to my surprise I find he was right.) The amazing fact was that he so obviously knew the scores he conducted from cover to cover that he must have spent a great deal of time in preparation for his career, too. He was at the time only twenty-eight years old, and had spent five or six of those years in the RAF Symphony Orchestra, so obviously he had not wasted much of his time. He was a most impressive assistant to Beecham in the year which followed, but it was soon obvious that he was never going to be anyone's shadow (he is too big in *every* way for that) and in 1948 he became principal conductor of the English Opera Group, a post he held until 1956. During the last two years of his tenure, he was also principal conductor of the ill-fated Yorkshire Symphony Orchestra, bringing music to dark places in a most worthwhile way, but finally without sufficient support to have any future. In 1960 he became conductor of the BBC Scottish Orchestra, and for several years he greatly enlarged his repertoire, as well as becoming one of the most frequent guests of the BBC Symphony. He is now very much a roving conductor on the international scene, and notable for his extreme professionalism and his amazing knowledge of the most complicated scores. To most people, the sound of a single orchestral chord is just that. To Norman it may be from the *Adagio* of a Mahler symphony or from the third act of *Butterfly*, or maybe the first act of *Wozzeck*, according to the way it is laid out in the orchestra. He *knows* – and as he was in the orchestra himself, if not for very long, it all seems to be second nature to him. He is an excellent conductor who makes his intentions very clear.

Wilhelm Furtwängler (1886–1954) is one of two conductors I am including in this collection for whom I have never played, and I feel he is worth this exceptional treatment. To see him at rehearsal or at a concert, with his own Berlin Philharmonic or one of our London orchestras (he conducted several times on his visits in 1924, 1937 and 1948) was to realize that in him one was watching a conductor who could afford to dispense with all the usual assets a conductor is supposed to have. His movements were ungainly to the point of near-caricature, his beat a joke throughout the world of music, and his presence undistinguished. He just happened to have the gift of making superb music. When he stood in front of an orchestra, the sounds which emerged from it were recognizably smoother, richer or more exciting than they were with most other conductors, and how it happened was a mystery even to those who made them.

This was his unique gift. The remainder of his armoury was due to a very solid background of experience and study. He first conducted in Munich in 1906, but his first important post was as musical director at the opera house in Lübeck, when he was only twenty-five. Four years later he moved to the same post in Mannheim, where he stayed for five years, until 1920. We have looked at his career with the Berlin Philharmonic, where he followed Nickisch in 1922, and to which orchestra he devoted the rest of his life – though he was also a great favourite in Vienna as well as in London, and (before the Second World War) in New York. His direction of the 1937 (Coronation Year) opera at Covent Garden was masterly, and the two cycles of Wagner's *Ring* he conducted there in 1938 are still spoken of with awe.

Perhaps the saddest event in a life of ups and downs because of political pressures was his near-arrest in 1945 by the almost defeated Nazis in Berlin. He escaped to Switzerland, and emerged in 1946 to direct the Berlin Philharmonic once more; but his reputation had been tarnished by his supposed association with the Nazi hierarchy, and even his official de-Nazification in 1946 did not completely eradicate this. He was welcome in Europe for the rest of his days, but not, it seems, in the USA.

As I have said, to see him conduct was a remarkable experience, and in conversation with those who played for him I found that their experience was even more of an adventure, because his down beat was roughly in the shape of a quite slow shaft of forked lightning, and the trick was to know where the 'click' was supposed to be. If you weren't careful, you could interpret it as being at any one of the six or so bends in the many-convoluted stroke. Reginald Kell, the clarinetist, once told me that the trick was to wait as long as you dared, and then not play until you heard someone else come in. The Berlin Philharmonic knew this. Our London orchestras took time to discover the secret, and there's a story (possibly untrue) about an exchange of duties he once had with Sir Malcolm Sargent. Furtwängler, in London, gave his usual beat at the start of Strauss' *Don Juan*, and the orchestra came in sounding like a skyscraper collapsing. Sargent, in Berlin, priding himself as always upon his crisp down beat, did his unambiguous best with an immaculate karate chop in the same work. The orchestra let him do this, waited as they usually did for Furtwängler's, and they too came in like a ragged thunderclap. It seems you have to know your own conductor; and when you did know Furtwängler he was one of the finest of them all.

Vittorio Gui (1885–1975) seemed to us in the Royal Philharmonic to be quite an old man when we first met him in 1948. He was in fact only sixty-three, but he brought with him such a wealth of operatic and orchestral experience that his authority was immediate and undeniable. He was also a strangely complex person as far as mood was concerned. He was a friendly soul, but became immediately dejected-looking if intonation faults were found. He had been for many years a mainstay of opera in Italy, especially in Milan and Turin, but he had also done important work in Florence where he directed the annual Spring Festival for many years. His most savage rebuke, if ensemble was imperfect, was a sadly-intoned, 'You sound like an opera house in See-sal-ee'. For me, his greeting each year was the same – ' 'Ello Brymer, 'ow are you? The food 'ere is 'orrible!' In spite of this somewhat negative attitude, which was really nothing but a pose, Gui produced the most beautiful sound from an opera orchestra, even in the acoustically 'dry' pit we then had at Glyndebourne, for the fifteen seasons he was there. His Rossini was the finest in my experience, and I sometimes wonder why most other conductors have not realized the simple fact that most of his scoring requires a particular sort of staccato. Gui had this to perfection, and could even vary it if acoustics changed; he did so in *Cenerentola* when we recorded it for EMI during the 1959 season. His Debussy was especially fine, and his *Pelléas et Mélisande* in 1962 and 1963 most memorable, which for an Italian opera-conductor was not really to be expected. He always talked of his native city, Florence, as the only place to live, and I was delighted when visiting it during his lifetime to hear his name mentioned with extreme reverence. He was a most memorable character, a true lover of music, and a most worthy operatic guru.

Carlo Maria Giulini (1914–) is among the most exciting conductors of our day, and as with so many brilliant performers his first impact upon the Royal Philharmonic Orchestra was quite unexpected. It was a great moment. We were rehearsing in the (deserted) canteen of Glyndebourne Opera one morning in 1955 without benefit of soloists or chorus, and the work was Verdi's *Falstaff*. Many of us knew the music, and were on the lookout for the very opening bar, which starts with what can only be described as a *fortissimo* empty beat – in real terms, a solo for conductor. If he is good, it is secure. If not, the whole attack of the orchestra sounds like a pack of cards being dropped by a rather unsteady hand. Giulini strolled in, young, handsome and friendly, a delight to the ladies present but oddly enough not revolting to the (very) male members of the RPO. After saying a polite 'Good morning' he simply picked up the baton, looked suddenly stern and concentrated, and made his solo down beat. Before it had reached bottom, everyone present knew that we were in the presence of a great conductor, one who really knew this work in detail. So he proved in every rehearsal and at the many performances which followed both at Glyndebourne and the Edinburgh Festival a couple of weeks later. The whole series was of a tension and vitality which is so essential to this music. It was possible to play it with freedom from worrying about balance – loudly when necessary, without ever drowning the singers, and as light as thistledown at other times, as in the accompaniment to the gossip of the Merry Wives of Windsor, who are part of the story. All this made us look forward very much to our first concert appearance a month later with Giulini, in London.

The first item on the programme was the very gentle *Hebrides* Overture by Mendelssohn, entirely different from the intense Verdi we had played with him up to that time. It was a great occasion, and Giulini was given a most warm welcome by a large audience at the Royal Festival Hall. After smilingly acknowledging this, he turned to us, and the familiar look of intense concentration appeared on his quite classic features. It was *Falstaff* all over again, and for a split second we all felt he was about to start conducting the wrong work. He raised his arms dramatically, paused in concentration, and then began what was obviously a power-packed, sizzling down beat. Half-way down it suddenly changed into a relaxed, soft, gentle caress which the basses neatly caught and launched us into the smooth lines of the opening tune – because that's how Mendelssohn's *Hebrides* Overture has to be presented. It was a strange and somewhat disturbing moment, but the start of a truly magnificent concert, full of nuance and ecstasy. Since then, Giulini seems to have grown even finer as an interpreter of music of a wide spectrum. He is a conductor we have seen too rarely in recent years, possessing all the qualities one looks for in a conductor, but rarely finds.

Erich Kleiber (1890–1956) was, unfortunately for me, another conductor with whom I missed the pleasure of working. I believe the only British orchestra to enjoy this privilege was that of the Royal Opera House where, in 1952, at the height of his powers and at the age of sixty-two, he conducted an amazing series of performances of Berg's *Wozzeck*. Without exception, all the players of my acquaintance considered it the experience of a lifetime, and hoped for more like it. His had been a strange and disturbing life. Austrian by birth, he studied in Prague, after which he became very much a German conductor, at Darmstadt, Dusseldorf and finally, at the early age of thirty-three, director of the Berlin State Opera. There he was a great success until 1935, when he was expelled by the Nazis, fled abroad and took Argentinian nationality. He spent the war years there and in very prestigious tours of the USA, returning to Europe as soon as the war was over, often at international festivals. Those who worked with him were particularly impressed with his readings of Mozart, in whose works he insisted very firmly on adhering to the details in the score rather than adding personal touches, and the works of Richard Strauss in which he seems to have had real insight.

This aspect of his conducting was of particular interest to the LSO in 1984, when his son Carlos (born 1930) conducted them for the first time. We found his rehearsals fascinating and most instructive, and had no doubts about his supreme musicianship. His concerts, too, were most memorable and deeply musical. Unhappily, although the majority of the audiences were quite enthralled, some people seemed to miss the point, as he is certainly not a showman conductor in any way; sadly, some of these people were critics, and Carlos Kleiber has never returned, nor shown any sign that he intends to do so.

Rafael Kubelik (1914–) is another conductor who has briefly flitted through our orchestral review (he was the young wizard who was in charge of the Chicago Symphony Orchestra during our 1950 tour, and fell foul of the vitriolic critic there, much to the discontent of all who knew his true achievement). He became a friend to many of us in all the London orchestras in the years which followed, and right up to the present has remained a rare but most welcome visitor to these shores.

He is the son of the violinist Jan Kubelik, one of the greatest Czech musicians of his day. The younger Kubelik started his conducting career very early in life, becoming the principal conductor of the Czech Philharmonic at the age of twenty-two. Those of us who recall his concerts in London only two years after this, in 1938, were not at all surprised at the power he showed twelve years later in Chicago. But a lot had happened to him, and to the world, by that time. Rafael left Communist Czechoslovakia in 1945, settled in England for a while, moved to Chicago in 1950, and was back in Europe a couple of years later. He was musical director at Covent Garden Opera from 1955 to 1958, during which time we were delighted to have him for two seasons of summer opera at Glyndebourne. Either there or at Covent Garden he met and married the well-known soprano Elsie Morison. They have remained a most popular couple ever since, even though we have seen less of them in recent years, as they have lived in Switzerland since 1973 (although Rafael was chief conductor at the Met in New York during 1972–4). He is a very complete musician, a charming man, and an outstandingly good conductor.

Loren Maazel (1930–), a conductor of much later vintage, can be said to have had the opposite sort of experience to that which befell Kubelik: he was a success in America, and has had his difficulties only in Europe, particularly in Vienna. Perhaps this contrast is hardly surprising, as two more different characters could hardly exist, in spite of the fact that both are strikingly talented conductors. Kubelik is quiet, withdrawn and contemplative most of the time. Maazel is direct, extrovert, efficient and very much in command of himself and those around him. He was born in France, but somehow seems typically American in most ways. An excellent violinist, he is able to go into technicalities with an orchestra of any nationality, and he has held several important conducting posts with success. In 1972 he was chief conductor in Cleveland, having left a similar post at the West Berlin Opera with the Radio Orchestra there. He then settled at the Vienna State Opera, and for some reason failed to find favour there, so that he left in 1984 after a quite public disagreement. Perhaps Maazel is a conductor for short seasons. Certainly he is able to sustain interest and give great pleasure over a month or so, as most London players will agree. After a very successful season of concerts here with the LSO, he made a remarkably good impression on a quite difficult Spanish tour, and his handling of the 1986 Italian tour was quite dazzling at times in what could have been impossible conditions. As well as difficult and exhausting travel, some of the playing conditions themselves were very testing. It was wonderful to spend most of each day (or at any rate each morning) by a luxurious hotel swimming pool in Sorrento; but to give a concert each evening in the distant ruins of Pompeii, in the 2,000-year-old arena there, and with some of the lava dust from the ancient and disastrous eruption of Vesuvius still stirred by every footfall, could have been trying with a conductor who insisted upon a rehearsal each day. With Maazel it was easy, successful and even thrilling. Few conductors could have brought it off as he did.

Pierre Monteux (1875–1964) was a man of a very different type, and a conductor so individual that it is impossible to put him in any category. A tiny man, precise and neat, hardly anyone now alive can recall him as anything but old; yet he was full of vitality, wide awake and bright-eyed to the end. Naughty, too, in almost every possible way. He must have been seventy-five when first I knew him in 1950, but still had an eye for the ladies, and his much younger wife was always in attendance in the wings at every concert. I recall waiting in the wings for him to emerge after the overture to join me in a concerto performance in Cologne. All he required was a towel, a touch of pomade for his bushy jet-black hair, and a comb. No drink. We used to pull his leg a little over the colour of his hair, because his big and droopy moustache was snow-white. 'Ah,' he used to say, 'but you see, my moustache 'as 'ad much more experience than my 'air!' He used to excuse his late arrival at an afternoon session in typical fashion, too. 'Sorry,' he would say, '*force majeuré*. Madame is in town – I must do my duty!'

Monteux's wife Doris, in her book *It's All In The Music*, gives his 'Rules for Young Conductors', which reveal the sort of nature we all remember. Among these are (i) Stand straight, even if you are tall(!), (ii) Never bend in *pianissimo*. The effect is too obvious from behind, (iii) Never conduct for the audience, (iv) Don't practise or learn the score on the orchestra, and (v) Don't be disrespectful to your players (no swearing). Don't forget their individual rights as persons. Don't undervalue them simply because they are 'cogs in the wheel'.

I cannot remember seeing any conductor use his baton with greater economy. His *sforzato* attack was a stab of about one and a half inches, and got immediate response from any orchestra. There was always a standing joke with the LSO at every rehearsal. At each double bar which involved a repeat he would raise an eyebrow, and the orchestra, not wishing to make the repeat, would understand. Once he stopped and said testily, but with a sly wink, 'But how do you know I don't want the repeat?' A critic who was present marvelled in the press next day at the second-sight the orchestra obviously had, to be able to read his mind. What he did not know was that with any orchestra I have ever met you have to *force* them to make any repeat – it is such a waste of energy at rehearsal – and old Pierre knew this as well as we did!

Monteux was responsible for the first performances of many famous Diaghilev ballets in Paris between 1911 and 1917, including the occasion when the first showing of Stravinsky's *Sacre de Printemps* was greeted by boos and showers of fruit. But the second performance, a concert version at the Salle Pleyel, found him being carried in triumph from the hall on the shoulders of the crowd. 'You know,' he used to say, 'Diaghilev never forgave me for that!' He was also principal conductor at the New York Met for two years, and later with the Boston Symphony and the San Francisco Symphony. He founded the Orchéstre Symphonique de Paris, and spent his last years as principal conductor of the LSO.

Sir Yehudi Menuhin (1916–) and **David Oistrakh** (1908–

1974) are two conductors I find it difficult to contemplate separately, possibly because on several occasions, including the first at which I met them as conductors, they appeared at the same concert. I need hardly say that they are/were both great violinists; but each was at the time extending his activities to include the baton, and Menuhin is of course still continuing to conduct with great success. The occasions were those somewhat sensational concerts given on Sunday evenings at the Royal Albert Hall in London in the sixties. As a change from Tchaikovsky's *1812* Overture (with cannon and the band of one of the Brigade of Guards off-stage), someone had the bright idea of two violin concertos, one in each half, the first played by Menuhin and conducted by Oistrakh, and the other a mirror image of it, with roles reversed. It was a splendid idea, but one which can never be repeated, because David Oistrakh died in 1974 at the age of sixty-six. He was eight years older than Menuhin, although he probably became known to most of us much later than Menuhin, who was famous from the age of twelve.

Perhaps the most interesting thing about the conducting of these two world-beating violinists was that they both conducted exactly as they played, yet their personalities were in strong contrast. Oistrakh, while not exactly taciturn (he could be found in a corner during most intervals talking to violinists about fiddles), was a man of few words on the podium, and facially deadpan most of the time. Menuhin is sparkling, lively and excited by what he is doing, and not afraid of showing it, and this has always been the sort of contrast their playing has shown. They showed two sides of the coin in a most intriguing way, and I for one would welcome more concerts of the type they shared. It must have been a very interesting experience for them, because from quite similar starts in life their careers diverged in a most remarkable way. Menuhin was born in New York, and started his studies in San Francisco at the age of four, in spite of the fact that he was of Russian ancestry. Oistrakh was born in Odessa of a violinist father and an opera-singing mother, and virtually never left his native land except to tour as a virtuoso. Menuhin was known worldwide by the time he was in his teens. Oistrakh made his début as a soloist at the age of twenty and his name was hardly known to us in London until some of his remarkable recordings began to be heard in Europe and the USA in the late 1930s.

Menuhin's playing days have been something of a *diminuendo*, possibly because of his early start. Exactly the reverse was the case with Oistrakh, whose tours became better known in his later years. So to see them together in London, and to experience them both as soloists and conductors, was a rare privilege. It would have been good to see and experience more of Oistrakh. Unhappily it has not been possible. It *has* been good to see more of Yehudi – now Sir Yehudi – who happily still combines his two talents in his seventies.

Seiji Ozawa (1935–) is the prime example of a conductor who seems to give different impressions from time to time and place to place, as well as inducing in his players widely differing emotions. I can detect in my own fairly slight experience of his conducting something of this. I have never worked with him over a long period, so it is perhaps unfair to make such a statement. Those who have, and in particular the members of the Boston Symphony Orchestra, seem to have a deep understanding of and affection for him. None the less I feel he may have more to offer the American temperament than the European, so far as orchestras are concerned.

I first met him when he was quite young, certainly no older than his early twenties, at a recording session with the LSO. The impression at that time was of efficiency and little else. Later, perhaps around 1970, he conducted an LSO concert and produced a warmer response. Ten years later he conducted an important series of concerts at the Salzburg Festival, and by that time the American/European contrast was evident: he had all the efficiency and image of an American maestro without, for us, the humour and warmth of a European. There was a really amusing incident when the celebrated trumpet soloist Maurice André was rehearsing the Hummel Concerto with us at the *Festspielhaus* one morning in 1982. He got nicely warmed up and in tune, smiling around as the orchestra played the *ritornello* which leads up to his entry (which should sound like the arrival of Solomon in all his glory). He raised his beautifully polished trumpet to his lips and we waited with bated breath. Two beats before he was due to give voice, Ozawa stopped the orchestra, cut to the next *tutti* passage and continued to instruct the strings in their bowing and dynamics. As the next entry approached André again prepared to play – and exactly the same thing happened. What is more, it continued to happen right through to the end of the movement, and through the *Andante* and *Rondo* which followed. André stopped looking puzzled after a time, but never failed to be 'at the ready' whenever he should have made an entry. He was never allowed to play a note. As the final cadence rang out, to the sarcastic applause of the whole orchestra, he bowed, smiled, said, 'Zank you verra mooch', and quickly left the stage. The orchestra fell about laughing. Not Ozawa. He wasn't amused. He wasn't even annoyed at the sarcastic applause. Somehow this lack of mental empathy between conductor and orchestra did have its effect upon the performance. There was never a moment of unpleasantness during the whole series; not a wrong note or a fumbled beat. The performances were unquestionably good, but somehow un-memorable – so much so that although every concert was recorded, and cassettes of them all were available at very moderate prices to the players, very few indeed of the Ozawa records were ordered, while others by conductors of no greater claim to fame were in great demand. This indicates that in some cases conductors have different effects upon different orchestras, because it hasn't always been like this with Ozawa. It could be that in him there was then just a little too much involvement in the international orchestral scene, and possibly at that time he had not yet stayed in one place for long enough.

Born in Japan in 1935, he was a pupil of Herbert von Karajan in Berlin (which could have been an alarming if vivid experience), then musical director in Toronto for just two years, followed by San Francisco for six. In 1973 he became musical director of the Boston Symphony, and there, for the first time, put down roots. He has without doubt done wonderful things there, and met with universal acclaim. A glance at the bare facts alone establishes this quite firmly. He is now in his thirteenth year as director and there is no talk of a successor. He has taken his orchestra on tours all over the world, invariably with acclaim, and they have together made recordings which are regarded as exemplary. His repertoire has become wide, and has begun to include works by contemp-orary composers, many of whose names may not be known outside a fairly small circle of American enthusiasts, but seem to be very popular there, and also by a more generally accepted group of composers such as Roger Sessions and Andrzej Panufnik. Ozawa seems to be, in Boston, the sort of prestigious figure which has become rare in these days of kitchen-sink drama and the worship of the ordinary. One has only to read the quotations from the local press in the orchestra's brochure to get quite a 'purple' impression: 'His body conducts music's energy as if it were an electric charge'. 'He moves with extreme grace'. 'His hands clarify even the most shifting rhythms'. While in no way attempting to deny this himself, he is much more down-to-earth in his objectives, and gives one something of a surprise, after Salzburg. 'My job is to make a situation where the musicians can have fun and pleasure in making music.' It does seem that his players think so, too.

All this demonstrates a humble fact: one can be wrong part of the time at least. Fun is the last thing I would have expected of Ozawa; but I am glad to be wrong, because in his statement there is hope for us all. Music has to be fun, even the most serious music; if it is, it will be good.

André Previn (1929–) must be the most strongly contrasting character, in the world of conducting, from Seiji Ozawa. He still lives in Britain, perhaps surprisingly, although he is as well-known in the USA, or Europe, or anywhere else for that matter. An incident like the trumpet rehearsal in Salzburg just couldn't have happened with André. I could easily imagine him gently pulling the leg of a soloist in that way, but it would be with a complete awareness of the incongruity and a keen if deadpan sense of the ridiculous. His quickness of mind is apparent in all he does, and is a God-given talent. Probably the contrast with the Ozawa approach is due to differences of background, contrasted patterns of development and a much more keen awareness of the reactions of the people involved – if you like, the ability to get his head out of the score and see the world. It is certainly in no way attributable to a difference of objective, which for both men is serious music-making.

André Previn was born in Germany – a fact he rarely discusses. In a very few years it was obvious that his family could no longer stay there, and they moved to Los Angeles, where most of his upbringing and education took place. In 1943 he became a young citizen of the USA, and before long his quite remarkable musical talent was obvious. At the age of eighteen he made his début as a concert pianist with great success, and shortly thereafter became known as a composer. Soon he was to be found in the famous MGM studios in Hollywood, directing some of the finest of all American orchestral musicians – the tough bunch of slick and expert professional film-fitters, the West Coast 'Session Boys'. There is a rather nice little story about this début of 'The Kid' as Benny Goodman always used to describe André. It illustrates quite perfectly the surprising awareness he has always manifested, without the slightest sign that he is conscious of so doing. Like the apprentice on the building site who is usually sent to get 'chimney nails' or 'the long stand' (which simply involves having to stand in a corner for half an hour), young conductors can be subjected to certain ritual tests. On this occasion the whole orchestra of eighty or so were assembled, on time as usual, and ready to see what the young genius, who had composed the music he was about to conduct, had to offer. With thirty seconds to go before the first down beat was expected, and the conductor not yet on the podium, they took the tuning note from the first oboe – a nicely modulated B flat instead of the universally accepted A natural. It didn't take long – the string players are fairly adaptable in that part of the world, and soon the whole orchestra fell silent, prepared to play a semitone sharp. André entered, quite quietly and with due modesty. His greetings over, he elected to record first the title music for full orchestra, and raised his baton for attention. This was going to be good, because the whole orchestra were going to play a semitone sharp. He did not, however, give the down beat immediately, having heard that tuning note from a distance. Instead, just before he did so, he said, quite quietly, 'Of course I assume you'll all transpose this piece down a semitone. It might be better that way!' From then on it was quite obvious that here was a young man with a firm grasp of the situation, and for several years these studios were the focus of his musical life. This is without even considering the talent by which he was first known to most of us – his really superb jazz piano-playing, which put him among the big names in that category as a very young man, and introduced him to all the 'greats' on other instruments. Talking of Benny Goodman (which I was) brings to mind an incident of which André once reminded me. I had told him of my visit with Benny to the Half-Note Club – a favourite jazz venue in New York. André remembered it well, because for a short time he had led a trio there – I think with Ed Thigpen on drums and Ray Brown on bass.

Benny heard them, liked them, and not only got André to arrange a dozen numbers to include himself, making a splendid quartet, but engaged them to record these arrangements in a studio in his own garden, at Stamford on the Connecticut coast, and many miles from New York, at the unheard-of hour of 9.30 am. In spite of a 2.30 am finish at the Half-Note, they somehow got there, one dark November morning, and set up the drums ready to start. It was freezing cold, and when Benny arrived, all three of them said so, as politely as they could through chattering teeth. 'Yeah, I guess it is,' said the laconic Benny. He left – and came back quite soon wearing a heavy woollen sweater . . . But – back to André himself.

All this now seems a strange start for a man whose destiny was to take him up the ladder to the dizzy heights of symphonic conducting; but it is quite characteristic of André, who has a diversity of talent rarely found in any musician. While still in his thirties he decided that he would desert the lighter side of music, and as he was one of the finest Mozart pianists he had a foot already in the classical camp. Studying conducting seriously was his obvious next step, and he seems to have found this both fascinating and easy. In 1967 he became principal conductor at Houston, Texas, and before long some of the records he made there showed the sort of results he could achieve. In 1969 he came to London as the principal conductor of the LSO, and the rest is too well-known to need repetition. He stayed for eleven years, the longest tenure of any LSO conductor, and during that time he did a most important job in bringing their sort of music to the general public, especially in TV programmes of his special sort. He also did much to promote British music during that period, and showed himself to be an expert in the works of Walton in particular, and rather unexpectedly in the music of Vaughan Williams. In spite of his very popular image, André has never attempted to bring down the standard of dignity of his symphony concerts as some conductors have tried to do, and if his classical offerings of Beethoven, Brahms and some other composers have not been at the very pinnacle of world class, there is hardly anyone who produces Shostakovitch, Prokofiev or Rachmaninov to compare with him. It need hardly be said that in some American music he remains supreme, and his ability to perform and simultaneously conduct Gershwin's *Rhapsody in Blue* or one of several Mozart piano concertos is quite unequalled. It is this spectrum which has always been his forte, and no doubt he still displays this now that he combines, after a spell with the Pittsburg Symphony, the principal conductorships of the Royal Philharmonic in London and the Los Angeles Philharmonic. To us he showed it all in one tremendous season in 1973, while he was at his busiest and most seriously involved with the LSO. It was at the South Bank Summer Festival, and all chamber music. In just two weeks André played (i) quintets for piano and wind by Mozart and Beethoven; (ii) sonata recitals with violinist Chung-Wa Kyung; (iii) ditto with cellist Siegfried Palm; (iv) piano duos with Vladimir Ashkenazy, sometimes as second pianist, sometimes as first (the great Rachmaninov duos); (v) directed and played Scott Joplin rags in his own arrangement; and (vi) finally played duets or alternating solos with the tremendous jazz pianist Oscar Peterson. He told me he wasn't terribly fit at the time, which was perhaps less than surprising – but nobody would have guessed that he was having a spot of trouble with a damaged finger. All performances were dazzling. Incidentally, a key became detached from my clarinet during a rehearsal for some of this, and André was much amused. 'With Buster Bailey I might have expected it,' he said, 'even with Benny Goodman – but not with Brymer!' Yes, I enjoyed working with André. I wonder if he ever knew?

Sir John Pritchard (1921–) is another of the category I mentioned before, a colleague who rose from comparative obscurity to the very summit of music in quite a short time – but not so short that he arrived there in any way unprepared. There is probably no better training ground for an aspiring young conductor than the opera house. There you can start as a humble singing coach, become an important répétiteur, and then decide whether you are a Jani Strasser or a John Pritchard – you either stay backstage and shape the musical pattern which exists there, or get out into the pit and govern the whole bag of tricks from that vital spot with your back tight against the front row of the stalls and your front clearly visible (you hope) to soloist, chorus and orchestra alike. There is probably no better venue of that sort than Glyndebourne, and it was there that I first met young John – then in his mid or late twenties – as a répétiteur about to become assistant conductor. When he did begin to direct opera –

especially Mozart – it was obvious that he had the rare talent of combining the roles of continuo (usually playing harpsichord) and conductor in a quite remarkable way. He soon became a fully-fledged conductor, and his part in the production was always notable for its accuracy, freedom and spirit.

As a concert conductor he still had something to learn. In 1948 at some early Sunday concerts at Glyndebourne he merely showed promise in this sphere. Three years later it was obvious that this promise was more than being fulfilled, and that here was a young man with something to add to the store of knowledge on the musical scene. Thereafter his rise was not meteoric, but steady and sustained. He became principal conductor at Glyndebourne in 1952, as well as guest conductor at Covent Garden; he conducted at the Vienna Opera in 1952 and 1953, and at the Berlin Festival in 1954. He was at the Edinburgh Festival during 1951–5, and by then he was so much in demand abroad, in Cologne, Zurich, Brussels and Nuremburg, Oslo, Wintertur and Rome that his itinerary is impossible to list. He became principal conductor, as I have mentioned earlier, of the Royal Liverpool Philharmonic in 1957, and is at present principal conductor of the BBC Symphony Orchestra, to the delight of everyone there. I vividly remember one occasion when he flew out to Kiel, in Germany, to conduct that orchestra in the late 1960s. We were in the middle of a tour, and the main work of the evening was Schubert's great C Major Symphony – a work which can be among the most thrilling for any orchestra, but also in some conditions the most boring (the description of it as 'Schubert's Heavenly Length' has been quoted by many a weary fiddler, in many a band). John hardly rehearsed it at all, yet the performance was nothing short of masterly. Then there was the time on the Philharmonia Tour to Expo 70 in Osaka (obviously in 1970) when he conducted a Mahler symphony on the first night, flew back to London for a Glyndebourne Prom of *Così fan Tutte*, and two days later was back in Tokyo with us for Mussorgsky's *Pictures at an Exhibition*. Incredibly, he seemed quite wide awake at the reception in the foyer of the Bunka Kaikan Hall afterwards; but he did tell me a couple of months later that he had spent several days in bed after the tour ended; that sort of clock-cheating does catch up with you in the end. That sort of big occasion is just what Sir John has always risen to. He is a man of the moment, and when he

declares that his main hobbies are good food and wine, with the
theatre next on his list, he is being modest. He enjoys life, is always
ready for a challenge, and can become bored if things 'keep on
keeping on' for too long. Who can blame him? His greatest
performances are among the very finest anywhere.

Gennadi Rozhdestvensky (1926–) and **Mstislav Rostropovitch** (1927–) are two great Russian artists I can never
consider separately. This is almost certainly a subjective response,
and arises because for some years I (and quite a number of my
London colleagues) never met them apart. Rozhdestvensky was
always the conductor then, Rostropovitch simply the superb
cellist who seemed to have no human limitations. Now Rostropovitch spends as much time as a conductor as he does playing his
cello, but as recently as 1986 he showed us all, in the open-air pre-
Christian amphitheatre at Pompeii, that there is nobody quite like
him in his instrument. The first impact of these two artists was a
great surprise, at a time when we knew very little about Soviet
musicians other than David Oistrakh and his son Igor, or possibly
Emil Gilels and Sviatoslav Richter. The arrival in 1962 of these
two soberly-dressed men, very lively and full of fun, to conduct
and play with the Royal Philharmonic at the Royal Festival Hall
in London was a memorable event. For one thing, they looked
older than their years, which by hindsight we can now see was in
their thirties. For another, they were so much like the other
talented musicians we knew that working with them was the most
natural thing in the world. Shostakovitch had by this time reached
his Tenth Symphony. It is a work which shows his brilliant gifts to
the full and Rozhdestvensky, at this first performance in London,
revealed it all to us with hardly a word. Here was a conductor who
really *knew*. He could leave the score, the podium even, and
wander around the front of the orchestra, sometimes jabbing out
the odd accent, sometimes pulling up the tempo a fraction, but at
times doing nothing at all, simply letting the dramatic music make
its own points and find its own impetus. It was a new sort of
conducting, and most impressive. What is more, it did not tie up
all the loose ends or make a predictable performance. It was of no
use asking him to repeat a passage of which he approved but which
may have seemed a trifle 'chancy'. The answer was simple: 'No – it
will be good tonight!' It usually was – and there were other, new

things at the performance as well. The realization came to us all that in this thirty-six-year old conductor we were meeting one of the greatest of all time, and one who had no 'act' of any sort, but simply a down-to-earth excellence in the music he knew so well that revelation was inevitable. In the years which followed he has changed little, in spite of his geographical meanderings. The extreme difficulty in both writing and pronouncing his name does not seem to have been any disadvantage wherever he has been, and incidentally it should really have been quite unnecessary, as his father's name was Anosov, and he also was a conductor. But, using his mother's name, Rozhdestvensky became principal conductor of the Bolshoi Theatre in Moscow from 1965 to 1970, and since 1975 he has directed the Stockholm Philharmonic, apparently with the full approval of the Soviet authorities. Most people recall one of the last dual associations of 'the two Rs' with something like awed reverence. It was a series of cello concerto concerts, sometimes with one concerto, sometimes with two, and of course a full symphonic programme as well. The complete series was given twice with the LSO, in the late sixties, first in London at the Royal Festival Hall, and then in New York at Carnegie Hall. Rostropovitch played no less than thirty-six different concertos in the three weeks involved in each series, all of them from memory and all superbly. Many people had forgotten there were so many works for the medium, and the performances were a revelation to us all. The partnership between conductor and soloist was something to treasure; being so entirely familiar with each other's art, they were able to cooperate in a quite unique way, and as a result the whole series was simplicity itself for us. This could hardly have been so for Rostropovitch, but he showed little sign of strain. He did, however, have to work most of every night in preparation for the next day's performance, and this gave rise to a most amusing incident in New York. Twice in the course of the final week I was with Barry Tuckwell, at that time our first horn, crossing the road from the Carnegie Hall to the Sheraton Park Hotel where we lived in some splendour. On both occasions we took the opportunity of congratulating Rostropovitch upon his wonderful performances, and suggested a drink at the bar. Twice he gave the same answer – 'No, I'm sorry; but tomorrow is Walton (or Milhaud) and this I must learn before 10 o'clock tomorrow!' He then ascended to his penthouse apartment where special arrangements had been made for him so that he could play, undisturbed and undisturbing, until about 5 am. By 10 am he was on the platform and able to dictate the correct phrasing, if necessary, to the third trumpet or second flute. On the third road-crossing of the week, on the penultimate evening of the tour, Barry was alone (and I swear that until this moment it had never struck me that this could be the reason for what followed), and when Rostropovitch was invited this time the answer was different. 'Good,' he said, 'tomorrow is Dvořák. This I know. I can drink!' Barry was delighted, and said so, especially as it was his birthday. 'Your birthday?' shouted Rostropovitch. 'Come with me!'; and up they went to the penthouse, whereupon the cellist immediately began to empty several drawers upon the bed. Finally he chose a pair of socks, which he smelt with great care. 'New,' he said, 'You have as present!'

With such delightful characters as 'the two Rs' working together one could hardly fail to have not only success but fun too, and most of us are sorry that it is a partnership which is no longer in operation. Rozhdestvensky comes to us too rarely now, and Rostropovitch, although he now conducts frequently, is not seen often in Britain. We miss them both, because while they are certainly excellent apart, together they were incomparable.

Sir Malcolm Sargent (1895–1967) has had such a plethora of biographers that I do not feel that I need say much here. He was such a vivid person and presented so many aspects of his personality to the world at large that there have always been many and varied opinions about him, both as a man and as an artist. Speaking generally, choirs loved him, orchestras disliked him, and soloists were widely divergent in their views. For choirs he had a magnetic charm, good looks and the sort of voice which seemed to them to help the vocal quality of the rehearsal. Choirs also like to be gently bullied, and he had this art to perfection. Orchestras do not, and he was inclined to treat professionals with a lack of tact and sympathy which they found irksome. He once, in the 1930s, stated publicly* that no orchestral player was worth more than fifteen pounds per week, when that sum was the expected wage of a plumber's mate; and that went down badly, coming as it did from

* Charles Reed, *Malcolm Sargent*, Hamish Hamilton, 1968

a man who had spent some time in Switzerland recovering his health on a diet of champagne and sherry at the expense of a fund into which many of the people he was talking about had paid their hard-won earnings. I think maybe Malcolm was in some ways his own worst enemy, because knowing him as a private person, if briefly, was a different experience.

Certainly as a soloist one found him not only helpful, but deeply understanding. I recall playing the very first TV performance of Aaron Copland's concerto with him in about 1952 in the Maida Vale Studio at one of the series of Sunday afternoon concerts they always televised from there. He was most anxious not to over-tire me at the morning rehearsal, and insisted that we should 'mime' the interminable repetitions of the necessary camera-shots. He was equally kind at my various Prom concerto appearances — those terrifying lonely affairs, always in a heatwave and with people almost at the bell-end of the instrument, most of them loudly turning the pages of the score and side-glancing each other with any slightest departure from the printed phrasing. Yet Sargent could sometimes dig in his heels with his soloists, and at times he came unstuck in so doing. One such occasion was during a recording of the policeman's song from *The Pirates of Penzance* with Owen Brannigan. Owen had sung the part often and had his own very 'broad' version of the character, including one line which grated upon Sargent's ears as not being worthy of the many Savoy Opera performances he had directed: 'the po–liceman's lot is not a nappy one' was how Brannie thought it should go. Sargent insisted upon a much more refined and standard BBC/Oxford version, to Owen's obvious displeasure. He got it, of course, as conductors always do; but the broad version had already been recorded, and on the final record you can heard them *both* as verses one and two.

The disappointing feature of Sargent's career is that for such a dynamic and purposeful musician he left a remarkably poor recording legacy. Some of his choral works have survived, but all have since been surpassed. Even the years he spent with the BBC Symphony Orchestra, 1950–7, have left only a few works of note on record. One of these, certainly, is Holst's *The Planets* which I feel is a work he found perfectly suited to his musical style, and which he certainly understood as few others did. He was an excellent musician in most ways, although orchestral players did not find him a good conductor – and they are usually pretty good judges. He, for his part, had a healthy contempt for the sort of ability they possessed, and even more for their morale. He once said to a spokesman of the LSO 'If one gives musicians too much security they'll not be on their mettle. They'll sit back and you'll not get the best out of them.' When it was pointed out to him that he too was a musician, and that he had spent a great deal of energy in raising sponsorship for his own enterprises from Courtaulds and others, just to give *him* security, he seemed quite puzzled. He also, in 1936, spoke to a *Daily Telegraph* reporter* about the suggestion that pension schemes should be instituted for orchestras, saying, 'There is a snag. As soon as a man [*sic!*] thinks he is in his orchestral job for life, with a pension waiting for him at the end of it, he loses something of his supreme fire. He ought to give his life's blood with every bar he plays. It sounds cruel, but it is for the good of the orchestra.' This outspoken attitude brought him a great deal of criticism from most of the eminent musicians of the day, Sir Hugh Allen of the RCM, Sir John McEwen from the RAM and Sir Dan Godfrey of the Bournemouth orchestra among them. It moved Sargent to say, when criticized by Dan Godfrey soon afterwards, 'It's one of the things I wish I had never said', but he added that he hadn't changed his mind a bit. In so saying he became, in 1936, the least popular of all conductors among British orchestral players. This changed a little, but only very much later, in his very last and more mellow years. Sargent was a strange mixture of characters, but he had an important place in the scheme of things musical. He gave a lot of pleasure to many people.

Hans Schmidt-Isserstedt (1900–1973) is a name from the past now, and a conductor who was known in Britain for only a short time, but he was a man of strong personality who is certainly not forgotten by those who played for him. I cannot recall hearing of him before the Second World War, which may not be surprising since he was still in his thirties and did not appear to leave Germany for any significant periods. It was in 1945 that I became conscious of his work, when Europe began to open out once more, and an orchestra known as the Nord-West Deutsche Rundfunk, or

* Charles Reed, *Malcolm Sargent*

the Hamburg Radio Orchestra, began to make an excellent impression with its broadcasts on the BBC, relayed direct from Germany. It somehow linked the two recent enemies in a way little else could, and as it was an orchestra founded by Isserstedt only in 1945, Britain was among the first countries to appreciate the work of this very sensitive and friendly musician, who was a composer as well as their conductor. It was a most interesting experience when he first came to conduct the Royal Philharmonic a few years later, because those of us who remembered the war recognized in him a prototype we had seen so often on screens and in photographs – the bright blue eyes, the blond hair, the rugged features, the interesting limp, all made an obvious Panzer commander – and of course he was anything but! We soon found that he was not only *not* the archetype of a wartime German, he was very much a post-war European and something of an Anglophile, so much so that his son was educated in Britain, became completely English as Erik Smith, and is now a very famous producer of classical recordings. Hans, however, remained very much a mainstay of music in Hamburg for many years. He was their principal conductor until 1971, and by then the orchestra he had founded had a fine international reputation. Meanwhile, he travelled widely, and in 1955 and 1958 he came to Glyndebourne for the summer and fitted into the scene as if he had been born there. His first appearance with us was a miniature occasion, at the Edinburgh Festival in 1954, when he directed Stravinsky's *Histoire du Soldat* in an informal on-stage version, nine of us sitting around on upturned beer crates wearing our oldest clothes to reconstruct the sort of immediate postwar performance for which Stravinsky had written this strange work. Robert Helpmann was the Devil, Moira Shearer the Princess, with the title role played by Terence Longdon and Anthony Nicholls as the Narrator. It was an all-star cast, and I can still recall the way in which Hans, in old clothes like the rest of us, used to distinguish himself by carefully unfolding a scarlet silk handkerchief and placing it with great affection upon his own upturned beer crate. It wasn't in the script, but it seemed most natural for him to do so. 1955 was a great season, with Vittorio Gui conducting Verdi's *Falstaff* (it was Geraint Evans' second season in the title, and sensational). He also conducted Rossini's *Comte Ory* and Gluck's *Alceste*, while John Pritchard gave us Wolf-Ferrari's *Susanna's Secret* and Strauss' *Ariadne auf Naxos*, and Paul Sacher handled with great expertise Stravinsky's *Rake's Progress*. All this was quite exotic, and remarkably exciting – but we had to relax sometime, and it was a most welcome break to settle down to the lovely and familiar music of Mozart's *Figaro*, again with Geraint Evans, and the excellent Michel Roux as the Count, and simply enjoy the music-making of our friend Hans Schmidt-Isserstedt. It is among the pleasantest of all Mozart memories for many of us.

Leopold Stokowski (1887–1977) was a conductor I am always glad I met, because when I was quite a small boy he brought me one of my earliest musical thrills. By that time he was, at the age of 50, very much in his prime (conductors are like that!). The particular thrill I remember was hearing an old black-label HMV record of him conducting his Philadelphia Orchestra in Bach's Toccata and Fugue in D Minor, with Stokowski's own orchestration and a fabulous sound. That sound never left me, and when he first came to conduct the RPO in 1948 (by which time he was even more in his prime at the age of seventy-one) I hoped he might bring us that arrangement. He did not, but instead insisted upon reseating the orchestra in his own strange fashion, with the winds where the cellos should be, and then altering much of the scoring of Tchaikovsky's Fifth Symphony. He need not have gone to all that trouble, because he was the possessor of the remarkable gift of getting his own characteristic sound from any orchestra by standing in front of it. Stokowski was in many ways a strange man. He was London-born, of Polish parents, but even at an advanced age he still spoke very broken English, and there are many who think he regarded this as a most useful artistic asset. His most famous utterances, both of which have become legendary in musical circles, were his constant and invariable admonition to one or other of the back-desk fiddlers who may have been less than attentive: 'You, sirr – vatch the conductor!' and his childlike query addressed to the agent who was taking him to the Royal Festival Hall past the Houses of Parliament: 'Please, vat you call big clock?'

It is not true that his real name was Stokes, as some people have suggested, though he may have used that name in his youth for the sake of convenience in a land where anything south of Dover was outlandish at the time. He was an organist, and had the post of choirmaster at St James's Church in Piccadilly until 1905 when he decided that the USA had more to offer. It certainly had. It is said that while he was in Philadelphia he was by far the highest-paid conductor of his day, and his film appearances and personal relationship with Greta Garbo made him the best-known as well. He was capable of combining great sincerity with his showmanship, and created, among other important orchestras, the All-American Youth Orchestra.

I think all orchestral players enjoyed working with him, because the aura of greatness hung about him, and his performances were never less than brilliant. His last appearances in London (in 1977 on his ninetieth birthday and the following day) were memorable occasions. None of us thought he would make it, because at two of the rehearsals during that week he had to be carried out in a state of collapse due to extreme exhaustion; but he came back bright and early the following day in each case, having apparently been revived by acupuncture. The concert was being recorded for an album, and in case of any mishap it could be cross-cut with the performance to be given the next day. One such disaster occurred in Debussy's *L'Après Midi d'un Faune* with a bubble of water in a clarinet pad. Stokowski showed no sign of having heard it; but the next night he sprang suddenly to life at that very bar, watching and listening intently until he was sure the mistake was well covered, after which he relaxed. (It is a pity that the engineers did not seem to be so wide awake, because that bubble is clearly audible on the finished record – or was there another reason? Stokowski was always very much in charge of all editing sessions! Perhaps he just liked it.)

If Toscanini was the last of the Great Bandmasters and Beecham the last of the Conducting Wizards, Stokowski was the final candidate for the title of Supreme Showman – and that does nothing to detract from his stature as a remarkable master of music. Perhaps he is as good an example as any with which to end this brief survey of conductors in my own time who have left a deep impression. There are others who have made their personal mark, and I apologise for the omission of their names and characteristics (if in fact any of them care one way or the other). It would be invidious to make a list of these, as even then there would certainly be vital omissions. Stokowski was in some ways the essence of them all – for he was 'all conductor'. One could imagine him as nothing else. Sargent could have been a diplomat or a civil servant, Beecham would have been a great lawyer or even politician, and there have been nicknames applied to many a maestro with some justice – 'the Neuter Computer', 'the Screaming Skull', 'the Hangman', 'Flash Harry', 'Sir Jaws' and even 'the Dentist of Buchenwald' and 'the Goldfish'; but Stokowski was always just 'Stokie', and never hinted at any subsidiary occupation.

How, then, does the orchestral player best approach these shining individuals successfully, if he wishes to continue to grace their presence as the years roll on? Perhaps the best answer to that is 'as naturally as possible', because there is a job to be done, and if both parties have a decent respect for each other (and I am happy to say this is most often the case) the job is liable to be done both more swiftly and more easily. I would, however, beg the orchestral aspirant to be soft-spoken and sparing of words at rehearsal. My own voice, not small by nature and greatly fortified by all those years as a physical training instructor, has been known to give the wrong impression when asking the simplest question such as 'How many beats at Letter D, maestro?' I am sorry for this. My other piece of advice, if you want to stay on the right side of the conducting fraternity, must be 'never write a book about them'. Even so, I hope to keep on nodding-terms with quite a few of them. They are a most interesting species, as are all musicians.

14

Coda: Sempre Risoluto, Ma Con Dolore
('Keep On Trying But Expect the Worst')

Sometimes it can be a good thing, after looking at all sides of a subject, be it a musical theme or a slice of life, to return to its first aspect. By doing this one can find in it something which may not have been obvious before, but is now surprisingly significant. What about that first impact of the strange ritual of concert attendance with all its excitement and complexity? Has it become easier to understand with the revelation of all its details, or does it remain mysterious in its inner functions and true meaning – as mysterious as it was before? I rather think this could be the case, because in spite of all the familiar and friendly trappings, the humour and the drama, the joys and frustrations, an orchestral concert still seems a strange and wondrous happening which is not easy to explain away. Many have tried to do so. Indeed there was a very strong lobby of opinion among the musical intelligentsia in the 1950s and 1960s which tried to convince us all that the symphony orchestra was as dead as the Dodo in our century, being a relic of the eighteenth and nineteenth which had somehow become stranded in the twentieth. There was never any suggestion that concerts should be declared obsolete, but merely that the medium of expression should be radically altered to the musical language of the present day. That language itself seemed to be the key to the whole situation. Melody had been tried, found good, and more or less exhausted. Polyphony (which is simply a number of melodies all played together in quite a jolly way as Bach, Handel and their friends originally ordained) had been taken to its logical limits, and in the end almost any series of notes played at one time could be considered to be a chord. There was nothing left but a sort of ordered chaos, a fragmented style of composition with an extreme complexity of rhythm which was cerebrally rather than physically orientated, and a compression of utterance which insisted that music should be not only shorter in duration, but smaller in stature. The symphony orchestra was too big.

Soon it seemed to many highbrow musicians that only certain instruments were *de rigueur*, even though a reasonably full body of strings was retained, purely as a sort of atmospheric factor. There were tootles on the woodwind, stabbings on the brass, but the future was with the percussion, whose function it became to carry the main burden of the work's message. Thus the balance of the orchestra became less than symphonic and more like large-scale chamber music. If this could then become a dramatic happening, with people moving around or even sitting in cages, so much the better; and if new uninstrumental sounds could be introduced in addition, this was also very advantageous. A combination of both drama and novelty must be the ultimate, and this was almost certainly achieved in one work of the late 1960s which had the breaking of eggs as its focal point of philosophical interest. Even the world of recording had its moments of this sort, like the surprise I once had in recording a modern quartet for voice, flute, clarinet and 'prepared' piano. The composer stopped the recording because he could not hear the footfalls of the two woodwinds as they stamped their way across the studio to the piano. We had tiptoed our way across, but it seems that he wanted footfalls as part of the score!

This 'New Sound' had a very strong lobby, and one which had a lot of support from the BBC in particular, perhaps one of the few organizations able to afford the lack of audience it attracted. Now, for that very reason, this image seems to have faded a little, and although there are still excursions in most countries into these new channels, they are less frequent and less eccentric. There are probably several other reasons for this change of emphasis. One of these may well be a reaction in exactly the opposite direction among those whose taste in music sets the trend. The New Establishment (though they certainly resent the title, they are none the less nothing if not that) have decided in the past few years that the best view of music is not, after all, forward. It is back to the Baroque, with the emphatically expressed view that Victorian, Georgian and even our present later Elizabethan treatment of this music has been misguided and provided only an opaque and rusty view of something bright, clear and virile. Much has been revealed in the renewal of old values by the painstaking mastery of old instruments or the creation of faithful copies which can be played much more expressively than some of those which have been worn out for centuries. There are many extremely skilled performers now who really are trying to play old music as they believe the composers of the more distant past would have wanted it, and in their work we have an interest which has to some extent taken the sting out of the 'squeaky-gate' image of the music of the present. Much could, and certainly is, being written about this fascinating topic, but we cannot discuss it here. Certainly the way in which it is now being presented is very much more persuasive that it was when the movement first started to gain momentum. Antique wind instruments have been mastered in a remarkable way, and are producing sounds much more acceptable and with infinitely superior intonation than they did a few years ago. The sound of gut strings played with upward-curving bows instead of the reversed arch of the modern bow is very different and possibly has more 'edge', and this is especially so when played *senza vibrato*; but there are now many players who can prevent the ugly 'bulge' in the middle of any note longer than a quaver which used to mar the performances of a few years ago. The interest in this ancient music is certainly no passing fancy, and many people think that it can and will exist side by side with the symphony orchestra *and* the modern chamber music group.

So, what is the future of the orchestra? Having existed for so long, has it a future as full and rich as it has had, even in my own lifetime? Probably not, at any rate in exactly the type of music it has been employed to play. Almost certainly the symphony orchestra of the future will need to take into its repertoire not only the two other aspects of music-making mentioned above, the ancient and modern, but several others. These may be musical forms of the future so far undreamed of, with the emergence of pre-recorded sounds perfectly reproduced and laced into the texture by musicians of great skill who are also sound technicians. They may be aspects of historic jazz or *avant-garde* 'entertainment music' of great inventive freedom, in which the performer may well become a composer in his own right, and the fusion of every sort of music may well be the factor which will create orchestras bearing little relation to the classical symphony orchestra of the past and present, but will none the less be able to present the music of Purcell, Vivaldi, Mozart, Beethoven, Brahms, Stravinsky and Schoenberg as well as a host of other composers whose works are in a very different category. The orchestra of the future *must* do this, because the writing is on the wall if it fails to do so. What it must *not* do is to keep on solidly doing what it has been doing as a matter of social ritual, because there are signs that even now, at least in the studio, it can be replaced by the invidious and all-too-common silicon chip.

I was reminded of this development in 1986 when, after an absence of some months, I played in a studio I used to visit quite often to record background music for one TV series or another with a variety of composer-conductors. The music in each case was different, but the orchestra almost invariable – about forty-five strong, the size of the average small symphony orchestra, possibly overweighted in winds and underpowered in strings, but correctly balanced by careful use of microphone technique. This time it was different, even though the composer was familiar; there were only four string players, three woodwinds, a percussionist in his little private glass cubicle, keeping in touch only through a head-set, and two gentlemen, also wearing headphones, tucked into a corner and playing what looked and sounded like the silent dummy keyboard sometimes used in a well-known BBC TV quiz show. Obviously this was chamber music, a small sound in a small studio, and it would certainly seem that the show it was serving had changed from an epic to an intimate domestic drama. The session went smoothly, and there seemed to be no difficulty in getting the little orchestra to provide excellent ensemble – indeed this was made infallible by the provision of the dreaded 'click-track' through headphones to all concerned, and if one could bear the distortion of sound always caused by shutting off the ears from the instrument, there was no excuse for playing anything else but dead on the beat. It was thumped at you, and later removed from the recording you were making. Somehow, the music sounded less than distinguished, even incomplete. But in background scores such as this, which merely underline the action, this is understandable. Soon it was coffee-and-meter-feeding time, and it was then that revelation came. Upon passing the open door of the control cubicle it was impossible not to hear the playback of the music we had just recorded. It was just recognizable because of the odd landmark here and there, but now the string section had become a hundred strong by overlaid tape sequence, and the woodwind were surrounded by a golden halo of resonance which only a Royal Albert Hall could be expected to provide. But that was not all. There were eight horns, superb in attack and chording, matched in sound and style, and six gleaming trumpets sitting on the very top of the whole orchestration, secure and supreme. More surprising still, there was now a wordless chorus of a thousand voices, equal to any to be found in Huddersfield, Luton or London, to give an impression of floating over the clouds which were part of the title-montage we had just completed. It was all very impressive, and all just a little depressing – because of course those 1,014 excellent musicians had just been supplied by the two quiet gentlemen in the corner at their 'dummy' keyboards. Later, if you picked up the right pair of headphones, you could hear them setting-up on their synthesizers the new orchestral colours they were going to record – cor anglais, flute, clarinet, tenor saxophone or trombone – and they were able, by computerized controls, to give more than just the sound of the instrument, as an organ has always been more or less able to do. The new synthesizer can reproduce the 'tootle' of the clarinet, the 'waffle' of the flute, the *cor de chasse* attack of the horn section, and even something of the lazy *legato* of the trombone. Somehow the strings are not completely convincing – yet. They certainly will be.

Can it be, then, that the symphony concert of the future may be performed by six of these remarkable machines, with an audience hearing them through head-sets and a master controller taking the maestro's applause for a thoroughly good mixture? I think not, fortunately, because that would be missing the whole point of a concert, with people listening together to an orchestra which is at any rate trying to *play* together. That, of course, is where we came in. The intangible magic remains, and it is as inexplicable as ever it was. A symphony concert is greater than the sum of its parts – much greater. It is a meeting of minds, a celebration of achievement, not merely the appreciation of the sounds the composer had in his mind when he wrote his symphony. It must not be too slick or too facile either, and there must always be the unpredictability which comes from a multi-shared endeavour. It is a *happening*, and with any computerized touch it ceases to be that.

What, then, of the people who will be needed for the orchestras of the future? As we have seen, they must be much more all-embracing in their repertoire than musicians of the past. I think they are so already, having spent quite a lot of time teaching some of them, and it is no surprise that they should be, given that every generation obviously starts where the previous one left off, and that models from which to learn are all around on tape, disc or film (to say nothing of some very honest teaching such as did not exist forty years ago). One can say that versatility will have to be the main feature of future orchestras, or otherwise the straightforward symphony concert which is only part of the pattern in Britain today will become the sole activity, and the rest will be taken over by the sort of inhuman agencies I have described. Concerts will need to be more numerous, and of many different types, if orchestras are to survive, because the more commercial aspects of their activity is certain to shrink. Perhaps the world is waiting for something new in music to arrive. Perhaps it *will* come. It is certainly necessary unless the sort of generosity to be found in some countries is generated here, and that seems quite unlikely in a nation which has never regarded music or arts in general as necessities of life.

Meanwhile, what of the host of young people who have felt compelled to pin their hopes and spend every ounce of their energy on a future in music? In 1987 a trip to London can be an enlightening experience of their talent and determination. Recently, about to emerge from the depths of the Central Line of the Underground at Chancery Lane, I was startled to hear the beautifully produced sound of a horn accompanied by a not-so-well modulated orchestra in a quite unexpected work. The horn was 'live', with the player standing at the bottom of the escalator and facing the downward section. The accompaniment was on tape, and was a 'Music Minus One' recording. It was not, as it happens, a horn concerto, but the Rodrigo Guitar Concerto which is now a bestseller, and played by this horn student with a technique and style that was almost arrogant, as this music demands. Twenty years ago this playing would have been sensational. Now it was merely good – as it is expected to be. I was pleased to see that people were duly impressed and even slightly cheered by this encounter. A day spent on the tube nowadays can be educative as well as stimulating with these bright young people as the very mobile focuses of interest. There is a definite pecking-order involved. An hour later, descending the same escalator, I was delighted to hear a young virtuoso of the flute dashing off the *Badinerie* from Bach's B Minor Suite for flute and strings, accompanied by what looked like the same rent-an-orchestra machine. She was equally excellent. Still later, passing a draughty precinct in Croydon, the ear was delighted by a very intense young clarinetist half-way through the finale of one of Crusell's concertos – and so the list goes on endlessly. There is no doubt as to the ability of these young musicians – and we have all been told what incredible earnings accrue from this alfresco music-making. Whether this is true or not, it wasn't really what they originally intended to do, and I am sure we all hope that they will not be compelled to continue its progress for long, however much we enjoy their quite valuable contribution to the awakening day.

Their orchestral world, if they enter it, will certainly be different from mine, and this inevitably invites the question, 'Would you do it again?' Fifteen years ago I had no hesitation at all in my reply to this. I said then that, even without the usual proviso 'knowing what I know now', my answer was 'Yes, by God'. Having taken this detailed survey of things as they stand today, I feel that I am not by any means so certain. Could it be that we had, in those postwar days of expansion and the sustained period of improvement which followed, the best of it? Or is hindsight possibly casting a halo around past deeds which may be a false illusion? Maybe there have been moments when past achievements may have seemed greater than the final result, and to illustrate this I feel I must quote my old friend the bass clarinetist Wilf Hambleton for one last time.

He was recalling a visit he had paid to Petticoat Lane the day before, and he'd found something to amuse him there in addition to all the Cockney wit of the 'barkers' who sell their highly-coloured and perhaps shoddy wares in that most famous of London's narrow and noisy open-air markets. 'It was raining,' said Wilfred, 'cold and miserable, and not even the barkers could raise any real enthusiasm. I looked around for anything interesting, but all the clothes were tucked away, and even the china-ware was in short supply. On the last stall but one I found a pile of old records without any sleeves or covers, and not in any way sorted into categories. Among some of the Beatles and a few by Ambrose and his orchestra I found one we did together with Philharmonia in Karajan's day. You probably remember it – Tchaikovsky Five. He made a tremendous fuss, and wouldn't record the slow movement at all because Dennis Brain wasn't there that day. We finally got it done, but it cost blood, and several of the orchestra said "Never again" – they were right as it happened, because Karajan left pretty soon afterwards. Well, there it was, five years later, wet, unprotected and for sale at sixpence per time like all the rest. I watched for a bit. The Beatles' records went first, and then Ambrose. Several people looked at Karajan's but nobody put down that sixpence. I finally asked the barker about the Tchaikovsky, and he said, "Tell you wot, mite, yer can 'av it fer fourpence. I don't want ter tike it home!" Sometimes I think I get a strong sense of non-achievement!'

Wilfred was of course absolutely right. Music is for *now*. To look back on it may be to invest it with virtues it never possessed, and to give it an importance it may have presumed to have, without real justification. At the same time it is only fair to remember that the only *real* records now in existence were those made in those far-off days. They were records of *performances*, not merely the compound resultant of a group of skilled sound engineers juggling with a thirty-six-track multi-tape package which they can assemble in any shape and with any balance they desire, to make the record they think *they* like. What is even worse is that with the latest computerized electronics it is even possible for them to select the tempo as well – to make it faster is no longer to make it sharper in pitch, as science in the past would have dictated. So the last bastion of the performing artist has been stormed. Music is what is made, not what the performer makes it. I can get great amusement out of hearing one of my fifteen-year-old records. It is of a trio by Mendelssohn for clarinet, basset horn and piano, and a delightful work. I wish I could have heard its first performance, given by the great Heinrich Baermann (the clarinetist for whom Weber wrote his excellent clarinet works), his son Karl (who was the greatest teacher of clarinet and basset horn of his day) and a young man called Mendelssohn who had just written it. My own record sounds quite good, but there is just something about the matched styles of the clarinet and basset horn which is unsatisfactory. The two players do not sound like father and son; they sound like the same person, as they are – Brymer in both cases, and allowed to do this by the genius of one Bob Auger, a superb engineer. It is, as I said, an amusing record – and even musically attractive and worthy. It was also done without anything added or taken away from the sound, and no computerized tempo adjustment; but of course it's phoney, because two players always should, and always will, sound like two, unless someone makes sure they don't. Modern recordings are much more phoney, because they fail in many cases to reflect the mental image which is in the performer's mind as he plays – or so it seems to me, listening to some of the results of performances I have known and taken part in. Many performers would, I believe, be happier to return to honest recordings, because while we all wish to sound as good as we possibly can, I feel sure most of us want to sound like ourselves, and not like some imagined super-being such as is now normally presented as the acceptable minimum of achievement. Some of my most treasured possessions are those old recordings of Fritz Kreisler, with blemishes in every one of them, and the occasional 'swoop' which is no longer fashionable – but with the most tender violin-playing ever heard on this earth in all but a very few. Kreisler is still alive on all of them. I do not feel the same about some of his modern counterparts, at least so far as their records present them. *They*, unlike Kreisler, *are* still alive, but I do not meet them on their wonderful compact discs.

All this is a digression. The question was supposed to be, 'Would I do it all again?' Once more I have to say that I have reservations. Things are changing so quickly now that a passing thought is too slow for them. Until the middle of 1986 I should have been tentatively on the 'Yes' side of the answer. As I said earlier, in spite of the poverty of the British scene, it has always been one which had a high morale and presented a united front to those who have constantly tried to disunite it. There is now some evidence that this is changing, which is probably inevitable now that orchestral management is Big Business, where takeovers and other sharp practices are all part of the game. This surely could be the end of the whole structure, the break-up of the community, and a move which must make one doubt the wisdom of entering such a profession. I think that now, given a choice, my answer would be 'No – unless things could be as they were, to give me at least a fighting chance'; and a fighting chance is what one needs. It always was. As the celebrated clarinetist Frederick Thurston used to say, 'My first chat with every new class at the Royal College is always centred around the fact that my advice to those about to enter the profession is the traditional one given to those about to marry – Don't! It makes no difference. They always do.' I have a feeling they always will.

It is probably something to do with the fact that musicians actually like making the noises they do and are willing to put up with quite a lot just to be allowed to continue so doing. And that 'quite a lot' can be much greater than some people think. Two tours of the USSR in the 1960s, one with the RPO and the other with the BBC Symphony Orchestra, illustrate this quite forcibly. Almost every possible disaster which can happen to any touring company came to us on each of these. Both were in January and February – not the best of months for a Napoleonic trip to those parts – and contained such delights as being delayed in a siding in the snow for fifteen hours without food, drink or adequate plumbing, trips over mountains in buses with an inch of ice *inside* the windows, missed concerts, and an orchestra of 105 having to share one changing room (in turns) for the only wash possible in thirty-six hours. There was also the time our manager Paul Huband managed to get us all breakfast on a night train, and it was put on the tables at 6.45 am in a frozen dining car and uneatable by 6.48 am. The final disaster came just before the last concert in Leningrad. By that time we so wanted to see the lights of home that nobody complained when we found we were being done out of payment due for the TV relay of the concert; but another announcement was made which proved to be the last straw, and seemed even worse than the moment our bus had been stalled on a level crossing outside Moscow by a drunken driver, and had to be pushed off the line by all hands in the face of what we were certain was an approaching train. The announcement was to the effect that they had suddenly discovered that the runway in Leningrad was not sufficiently long to permit the take-off of our quite large plane the next morning. We would therefore spend a day in getting to Moscow by train, spend another night there, and take off at 17.00 hours on the second day, to be home by midnight – just thirty-six hours late. They were sorry, but in case of any request for an earlier departure, the answer was a simple 'Niet, tovarich!' To this the amiable Paul Huband added the information that if anyone had a serious reason for being in London earlier, the BBC would consider this and, if approved, a scheduled flight could be arranged for those involved. This was a loop-hole indeed, and an obvious inspiration for those with inventive minds and glib tongues. Some of us suddenly had urgent pregnancies to attend. Others got out diaries to show chamber concerts or concertos in remote parts of the realm. The National Philharmonic, that *ad hoc* collection of specialists from every orchestra, suddenly found itself recording a Verdi opera with Joan Sutherland and Richard Bonynge. There was one percussionist, however, who had no such qualms, and felt no need to invent any. He was Jack Lees, the toppler of tam-tams at the final Dorati concert, and he really did want to get home more than somewhat. Asked why he had to do so, his reply was succinct. 'Because if I don't go,' he said, 'I'm going to punch you right in the bloody nose!' He went.

Perhaps more orchestral players should start to adopt this attitude. I wonder if perhaps they do not suffer too much too silently. The trouble may be that because they move *en masse* and are constantly to be seen with suitcases and other sorts of clutter they give the impression of a mob. They are not, and never could be. Unless they were very special people they could never ascend to the heights of artistic achievement they do. Since leaving their everyday life I have had quite a few opportunities of rejoining them in the midst of some quite hectic activities, and seeing them in this objective light has been a revelation – of incredible talent, of amazing energy and industry, of patience; and above all of a deep and abiding love of music which they hide under a flippant attitude which sometimes can be mistaken for cynicism. Just occasionally I wonder if perhaps changes are afoot which could well mean that the youngest among them may never be as lucky as I have been in the sheer continuity of enjoyment I have experienced. I hope they may. I am always glad I met my orchestral friends. I hope they go on, playing together.

Index